S0-CFA-530

Changing Realities:
Social Trends Among Ukrainian Canadians

CHANGING REALITIES:
Social Trends Among Ukrainian Canadians

Edited by
W. Roman Petryshyn

The Canadian Institute of Ukrainian Studies
Edmonton 1980

THE ALBERTA LIBRARY IN UKRAINIAN-CANADIAN STUDIES

A series of original works and reprints relating to Ukrainians in Canada, issued under the editorial supervision of the Canadian Institute of Ukrainian Studies, University of Alberta, Edmonton.

Editorial Board:
Bohdan Bociurkiw, Carleton University (Social Sciences)
George S. N. Luckyj, University of Toronto (Humanities)
Manoly R. Lupul, University of Alberta (Ukrainians in Canada)
Ivan L. Rudnytsky, University of Alberta (History)

Canadian Shared Cataloguing in Publication Data

Petryshyn, Walter Roman, 1946–
Main entry under title: Ukrainian Canadians.
ISBN 0–920862–06–3

1. Ukrainians in Canada. 2. Ukrainians in Canada—Social conditions.
3. Canada—Population.

FC106.U5

Cover design: Larisa Sembaliuk

Cover photographs (left to right): Service for V. Moroz, Legislative Grounds, Edmonton, Alberta, 1974 (Roman Petriw); Threshing Crew (Provincial Archives of Manitoba); Vancouver's Annual Ukrainian Festival Concert, 1979 (Roman Petriw); Women Gathering Cabbage, East Kildonan, Manitoba, 1916 (Provincial Archives of Manitoba); Edmonton's Dnipro Ensemble at Expo '74, Spokane, Washington, 1974 (Roman Petriw); "Tin Can" Cathedral, Winnipeg, Manitoba, c. 1905 (Provincial Archives of Manitoba); Vera Drobot at Elk Island National Park, Alberta, 1972 (Roman Petriw); Prosvita, Transcona, Manitoba, 1917 (Provincial Archives of Manitoba).

Printed by Hignell Printing Limited, Winnipeg, Manitoba.
Distributed by the University of Toronto Press.

CONTENTS

PREFACE

Since its creation in July 1976 the Canadian Institute of Ukrainian Studies has sponsored annual academic conferences to examine the Ukrainian experience in Canada. This volume consists of selected papers from the second conference entitled "Social Trends Among Ukrainian Canadians," held at the University of Ottawa, 15–16 September 1978. The national conference, sponsored jointly by the Institute, the Multiculturalism Directorate of the Secretary of State and the Ukrainian Canadian University Students' Union (SUSK), was attended by over one hundred participants.

The Institute's conference series is interdisciplinary in nature and is open to the public. Conference organizers believe an interdisciplinary approach is necessary for successful scholarly analyses of the Ukrainian-Canadian experience, while public participation helps to ensure that research reports are relevant. To this end, travel grants were made available for regional representatives of the Ukrainian Canadian University Students' Union to attend both the conference and the SUSK workshop on "Social Development Projects in the Ukrainian-Canadian Community: An Assessment," which followed.

The central focus for discussion of social trends at the conference was the recently completed "Statistical Compendium on the Ukrainians in Canada, 1891–1976" (hereafter the Compendium). This manuscript was compiled by an Ottawa-based research team and edited by Drs. William Darcovich and Paul Yuzyk. The research team included Boris Myhal and Drs. Ivan Tesla, Zenon Yankowsky and John Woychyshyn. The Compedium is a comprehensive source of historical census data on Ukrainian Canadians. Its appearance provided the opportunity for the Institute to assemble over one dozen academics, who identified and interpreted social trends with the help of statistics made available by the Compendium. It has therefore shown itself to be an important and useful source of information for researchers in both Ukrainian-Canadian and Canadian ethnic studies.

Although statistical trends were the focus of the conference discussions, many conference speakers prefaced their remarks by identifying the limitation of statistics in social analysis. Data created through a structured census question have at least two serious limitations. First, no single question can be devised to gauge all attitudes and behaviour. For example, since the census question defines ethnicity through patrilineage, it cannot provide data on ethnic self-identity. Second, a degree of error is inevitable in designing and conducting surveys, especially with relatively small populations. For these and other reasons, statistical analyses must be evaluated critically, despite their usefulness in presenting quantified data longitudinally.

Work in organizing this second conference was facilitated by the resourceful and reliable co-operation of Mr. Ivan Jaworsky and Ms. Assya Berezowsky of the Canadian Institute of Ukrainian Studies, who handled all arrangements. I also wish to thank Drs. William Darcovich and Paul Yuzyk for allowing the Compendium manuscript to act as a basis for conference research papers and Dr. Manoly Lupul for his advice on organizing the conference and preparing its proceedings for publication. The editorial work of Mr. George Melnyk is also gratefully acknowledged.

WRP

CHANGING REALITIES: INTRODUCTION

W. Roman Petryshyn

Ethnic relations are a phenomena integral to Canada's economic, political, legal, status and cultural systems. The patterns of ethnic relations in Canada have been shaped by the historical development of Canadian society. Consequently, Canada's patterns of ethnic interaction exhibit a strong regional character. The uniculturalism of Atlantic Canada and the biculturalism of New Brunswick stand in contrast to the varieties of multiculturalism in Ontario, Quebec and the Prairies, which in turn differ from the multilingualism and multiculturalism of northern Canada.[1]

The ethnic pluralism of the Canadian population has been one of the factors contributing to the formation of local identities that have mitigated against the emergence of a unicultural, centralist Canadian nationalism. Historically, central Canada has used foreign capital to create a dependent, staples producing industrial economy that has given Ontarians a dominant position in the financial, political and cultural hierarchies that collectively make up Canadian society. Geographic realities such as the availability of resources, proximity to American markets and the location of energy and transportation facilities have favoured the economic growth of central Canada's metropolitan areas in comparison to that of the peripheral regions. The result is a set of unevenly stratified regional economies in Canada among which conflicts, exacerbated by ethnic, linguistic, religious and cultural differences, are inevitable.

Within this pyramid of regional and economic stratification, the Anglo-Celtic values of the ruling classes of industrial central Canada have dominated the nation and its self-image for over a century. Recently, however, the stability of these economic and political hierarchies and their accompanying cultural norms have been challenged by an autonomist political current in the wealthy province of Alberta, and more fundamentally, by the national independence movement in Quebec.

The pivotal structure of Canadian Confederation—the alliance between Ontario and Quebec that created centralist tariff, transportation and banking policies to the detriment of other regions—is disintegrating. Following the emergence of new resources in the western provinces, a parallel growth in the United States and the availability of improved transportation, the axis of the Canadian economy has been shifting west in recent years. A relative slow-down of development in eastern and central Canada has caused a scarcity of opportunity; in Quebec this has made the internal cultural divisions between the anglophones and francophones politically salient. Quebec's nationalists are arguing that their economy must be led by a sovereign government, that an independent Quebec must reclaim powers of taxation and policy control co-opted by the federal government and that an interventionist economic strategy is needed to modernize Quebec society and ensure the survival of French language and culture.

Thus centralist control of tariff, taxation, transfer payments and fiscal policies have all come under attack. Should the traditional alliance between Quebec and Ontario falter (replaced perhaps by new regional co-operation between Quebec and Alberta) Ontario and Canada would be weakened.

Economic reorganization, highlighted by Quebec's national movement, has contributed to a destabilization of Canada's traditional economic, political and ethnocultural relations. One unforeseen consequence of this has been to give other minority groups, whose ethnocultural concerns had been largely excluded from the political process, the opportunity to re-evaluate publicly their position in Canadian society. As a result, new ethnic demands have been expressed, especially in the social and political areas, during various phases of the national conflict between Anglo-Canadians and the Quebecois.

Any study of a particular ethnic group today must therefore be placed within the context of conflicts among the stratified, plural structures making up Canadian society. Analysis of any one minority group—whether native, racial, immigrant or ethnocultural—must be situated within the context of conflicts among regions represented by provincial governments and between Canada's Anglo-Canadian society and the emerging Quebecois nation. It is within this framework that students of Canadian ethnicity have recently observed ethnic strategies as diverse as isolationism, separatism, multiculturalism, binationalism and tri-nationalism (Native, Quebecois and Anglo-Canadian) acted out on Canada's political stage.

Ukrainian Canadians are one of the minorities whose public response has been strongest in the debate resulting from Canada's changing patterns of ethnic relations. An examination of social trends among Ukrainian Canadians may help to explain the underlying factors behind the response and help to show the Ukrainians' potential for continued survival and development as a Canadian ethnic minority. Regionally, Ukrainian Canadians are located primarily in central Canada and the Prairies; socially, they are located primarily in a lower-middle position on the economic and prestige hierarchies which mark Canadian society; numerically, they are one of Canada's middle-range minorities, representing 2.7 per cent of the population in 1976.[2]

Given this situation, it is not surprising that politically their aspirations for ethnocultural rights have been limited to demands for reform of government policies supporting ethnic groups.[3] In the debates on Canada's intergroup relations, Ukrainian Canadians have expressed strong support for multiculturalism rather than other ethnocultural strategies, such as nationalism, which has been adopted by the Quebecois and Dene, or isolationalism, used by the Hutterites. In contrast to the Quebecois and the Dene, Ukrainian Canadians are not capable of emerging as a Canadian nation or isolating themselves as an ethnic enclave. Ukrainians are an ethnocultural minority without a millenarian philosophy. They do not control or occupy any substantial territory nor do they have a demographic or economic base that would enable them to isolate themselves from or transform the present structure of Canadian society. Apart from immigrant community leaders, the political power base within the Ukrainian community stems from the influence its leadership garners from being an integral part of Canadian class relationships. Ukrainian Canadians occupy no distinct enclaves within the urban economy and are thus fully integrated. With few exceptions, the Ukrainian language is not used as a language of employment by most ethnic Ukrainians. In the social realm, Ukrainian Canadians are experiencing increasing assimilation of many of those common traditional experiences and institutions that in the past gave Ukrainians a clear sense of peoplehood in Canada.

While not potentially a nation, neither are Ukrainian Canadians merely a statistical category. A considerable historical, literary, artistic, religious and social literature documents Ukrainian Canadians as a highly organized community with internal competing leaderships in many sectors of life. These groups have consciously expressed the sentiments and aspirations of Ukrainians throughout Canada in an historically cohesive and systematic manner. In view of the size and compactness of the Ukrainian community in Canada, its extensive community infrastructure, its cultural vitality and its articulated beliefs, there is every reason to believe that it will continue to be a dynamic minority for some generations to come.

Ukrainian Canadians, then, are an ethnocultural minority with a social potential less than that of an emerging nation, yet considerably more than that of a mere ethnic census category that has no internal cohesion and is unconcerned about its common fate. Regionally and socially, Ukrainian Canadians find themselves in a situation which leads them to express clearly their concern for group survival, community development and multiculturalism.

The historical and interdisciplinary statistics presented in this volume can be best understood if read against this background. Studies in this compilation show that Ukrainian Canadians are an increasingly urban, Canadian-born population who are slowly entering upper-middle class positions, while still excluded from elite positions in Canadian society and overrepresented in agricultural occupations. With a decline in rurality, the appearance of subsequent Canadian-born generations and the absence of large-scale immigration, Ukrainian Canadians are increasingly intermarrying, leaving traditional religions and using English instead of their own language. What in the past was a fairly homogenous rural culture is today diversifying and approximating Anglo-Canadian, urban cultural norms. Many of today's social trends among Ukrainian Canadians (birth rates, literacy, migration, urbanization, gender inequality and political allegiances) are more a reflection of general Canadian processes than of autonomous Ukrainian social currents. William Darcovich demonstrates that Ukrainians have become similar to the Canadian average in endogamy, urbanization and birthplace. Leo Driedger shows how three-quarters of all Ukrainians, like Canadians generally, are urbanized, and how, with the emergence of subsequent generations, identity factors are increasingly more like those of Anglo-Canadian society. Wsevolod Isajiw and Oleh Wolowyna confirm that the major trends in Ukrainian income and occupational structures resemble Canada's male working population as a whole. Convergence to the Canadian mean is also the case for marital status and fertility patterns, according to Jean Wolowyna, and for Ukrainian-Canadian female participation in the labour force, according to Marusia Petryshyn.

Despite this overall picture of a structurally assimilating, white, middle- and working-class minority, Ukrainian Canadians as individuals and as a group continue to exhibit a strong distinctive identity. This is evident in Warren Kalbach's and Madeline Richard's evidence on religious affiliation, Darcovich's data on overrepresentation in traditional agricultural occupations, Driedger's observation that the majority of Ukrainian Canadians remain residents of the Prairies. Olga Kuplowska's data on how the Ukrainian language is maintained for non-instrumental purposes and in Ivan Myhul's and Michael Isaacs' evidence that Quebec's Ukrainians have a situation-specific ethnic social pattern as a consequence of that province's unique ethnocultural and political environment.

Today the major dilemma facing Ukrainian Canadians is the

apparent need to become culturally and socially similar to Anglo-Canadians in order to gain benefits of income, education and prestige not previously available. The elimination of visible external social differences between Ukrainians and other Canadians has relieved some of the earlier constraints of identity affecting Ukrainian Canadians. However, this has also made Ukrainian-Canadian cultural life more voluntary, more atomized and less certain of survival and development. Being Ukrainian Canadian today is increasingly more a function of individual socialization into Ukrainian culture than a product of inter-group relations. At the heart of the Ukrainian-Canadian dilemma is an antagonism between accepting the standardized, but assimilating, benefits and values of a profit-oriented, technological, Anglo-Canadian society and holding on to a co-operative, minority-group lifestyle on which the Ukrainian ethnic community in Canada has built a distinctive historical identity. Maintaining this community has exacted its penalties from participants. While the community satisfies many human needs, it often has its values and work deprecated by society at large.

The analyses in this volume are not the first discussion of social processes among Ukrainian Canadians. The Ukrainian-Canadian experience has been extensively discussed in the fields of history, literature, bibliography and sociology. Historical writings, for example, have evolved to the point that a "sociology of knowledge" approach has already been used to survey extant materials. Frances Swyripa has shown that English-language historical writings on Ukrainian Canadians have moved from the period of superficial stereotyping through a period of self-laudation to the emergence of analytical scholarly research.[4] Literary writings on Ukrainian Canadians parallel this development and a similar process is also evident in bibliographic works.

Sociological methods, however, reveal the evolution of these social processes most clearly. Fortunately, sociological studies have always been present in Ukrainian-Canadian studies so that today there is a substantial literature in this area. The first important sociological study of Ukrainians in Canada was J.S. Woodsworth's unpublished study, "Ukrainian Rural Communities," done for the Bureau of Social Research in 1917.[5] This research was extended with periodic analyses by W. G. Smith, R. England and C. H. Young in the 1930s, and supplemented later by some three dozen university dissertations dealing specifically with the sociology of Ukrainian Canadians.[6] In addition, descriptive demographic studies by N. J. Hunchak, W. Darcovich, I. Tesla and C. W. Hobart et al. have been published.[7]

In the past decade a movement comparable to that observed by

Swyripa for historical writings has also taken place in the social sciences. As the Ukrainian-Canadian community has matured, its intellectual analyses have improved. Sociological writings about Ukrainian Canadians are growing increasingly more sophisticated and analytical. For Ukrainians, this has coincided with a heightened community concern in Canada for political dissenters in the Ukrainian S.S.R., debates over Canada's national unity and identity and the development of government multicultural policies.[8] These developing social and political conflicts have stimulated a need for contemporary sociological analyses and have resulted in works such as the Royal Commission on Bilingualism and Biculturalism's *The Cultural Contribution of the Other Ethnic Groups,* W. W. Isajiw's *Ukrainians in American and Canadian Society* and M. R. Lupul's *Ukrainian Canadians, Multiculturalism and Separatism: An Assessment.*[9]

Ethnic studies today have become a critical element within Canadian studies generally.[10] In turn, Ukrainian-Canadian scholarship has become recognized as an integral part of ethnic studies. This collection of papers extends this field of research. Focusing specifically on Ukrainian Canadians, this book offers a fresh perspective on the sociological processes among Ukrainian Canadians. But the descriptive statistics and analyses in this book are not meant simply as an exercise in pure knowledge. For those who live as Ukrainian Canadians, the processes described are personal and familiar, and the collection has a role to play in the debate on how best to use independent community resources and state institutions to maximize the survival and development of Ukrainian-Canadian identity. Increasingly, Ukrainian Canadians are compelled to ask more precise and honest questions about the most effective way to develop as an ethnocultural minority. Though limited solely to demographic analyses, this volume will play its part in this debate by allowing Ukrainian Canadians to appraise more critically their potential strengths and demonstrated weaknesses.

Much more remains to be done, however. As yet, little research has been done on the subjective and qualitative dimensions of Ukrainian-Canadian ethnicity. Future studies will have to discuss the emotional and experiential aspects of Ukrainian-Canadian identity. Such studies will undoubtedly deepen the insights available from quantitative studies alone. Several of the articles in this volume suggest the direction future research might take. John Kralt's discussion shows how ethnic identity is circumstantial and malleable. He challenges those who believe that Ukrainian-Canadian identity comes in only one everlasting form and leads one to ask what varieties of ethnicity are open for Ukrainians to develop in the future. Further, since Kalbach, Richard and Wolowyna show that Canada's political economy penalizes those who maintain ethnocultural differences, future researchers might ask why Canadian society favours individualized economic attainment over community survival. In future, should Ukrainian Canadians and other minorities rely on the achievements of individuals or on collective struggle for group recognition and representation? Isajiw's observations lead one to ask whether multicultural education is desirable considering that it might penalize Ukrainian children within the class structure in Canada where disavowal of ethnic background is required to attain elite economic positions. With March, Myhul and Issacs showing that "Ukrainian Canadian power" (though limited) is real, future research must ask how much additional autonomous power can be developed for self-preservation and cultural pluralism solely through social and political mobilization in the absence of economic wealth. These are just some of the questions which flow from the studies included in this volume.

In large measure the value of a sociological work can be judged by how fruitful its studies are for generating questions relevant to providing directions for future action. Many such questions emerge. Is multiculturalism really a viable option for Ukrainian Canadians? When minorities create more relevant Ukrainian-Canadian culture for an urban population, can they ensure that it will keep a distinctive Ukrainian character? Should those working for a viable Ukrainian community and identity conduct their actions on the basis of their own private resources or is it more useful to carry general issues to the public? Does the "Canadian dream" promise minorities equal success on the basis of merit, or will class and ethnic stratification in Canada continue to dominate minorities and prevent equal mobility?

These are the dilemmas of ethnic activists today and in the future. Their resolution, as Charles Keely indicates, will be other than a linear historical process. It will be the result of the abilities of those with ethnic consciousness to mount a process of a creative and forceful interaction between themselves as Ukrainians and the social dynamic within the political economy of Canadian society as a whole.

NOTES

1. Leo Driedger, ed., *The Canadian Ethnic Mosaic: A Quest for Identity* (Toronto: McClelland and Stewart, 1978), 10. Relationships of ethnicity to languages and religions in Canada's regions are reviewed in Harry H. Hiller, *Canadian Society: A Sociological Analysis* (Scarborough: Prentice-Hall of Canada, 1976), 21–6.
2. W. Roman Petryshyn, "The Ukrainian Canadians in Social Transition," in *Ukrainian Canadians, Multiculturalism and Separatism: An Assessment*, ed. Manoly R. Lupul (Edmonton: University of Alberta Press, 1978), 95.

3. Bohdan Bociurkiw, "The Federal Policy of Multiculturalism and the Ukrainian-Canadian Community," in ibid., 98-128.

4. Frances Swyripa, *Ukrainian Canadians: A Survey of their Portrayal in English-Language Works* (Edmonton: University of Alberta Press, 1978).

5. J. S. Woodsworth, "Ukrainian Rural Communities," Report of an Investigation by the Bureau of Social Research, Governments of Manitoba, Saskatchewan and Alberta (Winnipeg: 1917). See also the relatively unknown manuscript written in the 1920s by Paul Crath (Pavlo Krat) et al., "Survey of Various Communities in Manitoba, Saskatchewan and Alberta Made Under the Direction of the Board of Social Service Methodist and Presbyterian Churches" [Winnipeg: n.d.]. Available in the fugitive file, Canadian Institute of Ukrainian Studies and in the United Church of Canada Archives, Toronto.

6. W. G. Smith, *Building the Nation: The Churches' Relation to the Immigrant* (Toronto: Ryerson Press, 1922); Robert England, *The Central European Immigrant in Canada* (Toronto: Macmillan, 1929); Robert England, *The Colonization of Western Canada: A Study of Contemporary Land Settlement (1896-1934)* (London: P. S. King and Son, 1936); Charles H. Young, *The Ukrainian Canadians: A Study in Assimilation*, ed. Helen R. Y. Reid (Toronto: Thomas Nelson and Sons, 1931). Stephen W. Mamchur, "The Economic and Social Adjustment of Slavic Immigrants in Canada: With Special Reference to the Ukrainians in Montreal" (M.A. thesis), McGill University, 1934); C. M. Bayley, "The Social Structure of the Italian and Ukrainian Communities in Montreal, 1935-1937" (M.A. thesis, McGill University, 1939).

For an annotated bibliography of more recent sociology dissertations and those from other disciplines in Ukrainian-Canadian studies, see Frances Swyripa, "Theses and Dissertations on Ukrainian Canadians: An Annotated Bibliography" *Journal of Ukrainian Graduate Studies* 4 (Spring 1978): 91-110. Sociological theses examining Ukrainian Canadians have been written by Jessie Marion Deverell and Alphonse-Marie Côté in the 1940s; Caroline Rose Harasym, Mathew James Foster, Ronald Donald Fromson, Michael Francis Hopkinson, Andrew Koshelanyk, Benjamin Kubrakovich, Geoffrey A. Lester, J.-M. Lewyckyj, Andrew Johnson Milnor, Ernest Harvey Reid, Alexander Royick, Marlene Stefanow, Hugo L. P. Stibbe and W. Vossan in the 1960s; Alan Betts Anderson, Roderic Paul Beaujot, Margaret Alice Binns, David Garth Bryans, Judith Nancy Byers, Lydia Emanuel, Yarema Gregory Kelebay, Mona S. King, Marlene Marie Mackie, Nancy L. Penny, Wes Pue, Alec Saruk and Marlene Stefanow in the 1970s.

7. William Darcovich, *Ukrainians in Canada: The Struggle to Retain Their Identity* (Ottawa: Ukrainian Self-Reliance Association [Ottawa Branch], 1967); C. W. Hobart, W. E. Kalbach, J. T. Borhek, and A. P. Jacoby, "Persistence and Change: A Study of Ukrainians in Alberta" (Toronto: Ukrainian Canadian Research Foundation, 1978); N. J. Hunchak, *Canadians of Ukrainian Origin: Population* (Winnipeg: Ukrainian Canadian Committee, 1945); I. Tesla, *Ukrainian Population of Canada: Settlement and Demographic Characteristics* (Toronto: The Shevchenko Scientific Society of Canada, 1968); I. Tesla and P. Yuzyk, *Ukrainians in Canada—Their Development and Achievements* (Munich: Ukrainian Technical-Economic Institute, 1968); I. Tesla, "The Ukrainian Canadian in 1971," in *The Jubilee Collection of the Ukrainian Free Academy of Sciences in Canada*, eds., A. Baran, O. W. Gerus and J. Rozumnyj (Winnipeg: UVAN, 1976), 481-521.

8. The federal and various provincial governments' recognition of multiculturalism has stimulated a great deal of academic research and publishing on Canadian ethnic minorities. The Inter-University Committee on Canadian Slavs, which published the proceedings of three academic conferences, became the Canadian Ethnic Studies Association in 1971. Since then it has had four academic conferences and has regularly published its journal, *Canadian Ethnic Studies*. A variety of other agencies have also contributed recently to ethnic studies: the Canadian Plains Research Centre, University of Regina; the Canadian Institute of Ukrainian Studies, University of Alberta; the Ontario Institute for Studies in Education, University of Toronto; and the federal government's Canadian Ethnic Studies Advisory Committee.

9. Royal Commission on Bilingualism and Biculturalism, *Report of the Royal Commission on Bilingualism and Biculturalism, Book IV: The Cultural Contribution of the Other Ethnic Groups* (Ottawa: Queen's Printer for Canada, 1970); Wsevolod W. Isajiw, ed., *Ukrainians in American and Canadian Society* (Jersey City: M. P. Kots Publishing, 1976); Manoly R. Lupul, ed., *Ukrainian Canadians, Multiculturalism and Separatism: An Assessment* (Edmonton: University of Alberta Press, 1978).
10. Cornelius J. Jaenen, "Introduction: Ethnic Studies: An Integral Part of Canadian Studies," in *Identities: The Impact of Ethnicity on Canadian Society*, ed., Wsevolod Isajiw (Toronto: Peter Martin Associates, 1977), xi.

PART I
Ethnicity and the Census

THE "STATISTICAL COMPENDIUM": AN OVERVIEW OF TRENDS

William Darcovich

This essay consists of two parts: the first describes the "Statistical Compendium on the Ukrainians in Canada, 1891–1976," with its objectives and limitations, and the second part analyses its data on important social trends among Ukrainians in Canada.*

PART ONE: THE ESSENCE OF THE COMPENDIUM

A compendium is a work summarizing the important features of a field of knowledge or subject matter. The working group which compiled the Compendium viewed it as a comprehensive statistical work presenting systematically in one volume relevant data on Ukrainians in Canada.** The Compendium is comprehensive because, with few exceptions, it includes statistics for all fields in which data are available on Ukrainians, a total of twenty subject areas with the available historical data for each.

To make the Compendium systematic, the working group has provided data which is comparable both in detail between different sections and over the length of each series. Considerable effort has been made to maximize this consistency by maintaining uniform classifica-

---

* William Darcovich and Paul Yuzyk, eds., "Statistical Compendium on the Ukrainians in Canada, 1891–1976," (Unpublished typescript, Ottawa, 1977). Hereafter Compendium.

** Besides the author of this paper, other members of the group were Paul Yuzyk, Ivan Tesla, Boris Myhal, Zenon Yankowsky and John Woychyshyn.

tions between sections, by filling data gaps, by extending the series beyond the period for which the figures were originally published and by making the series more comparable over time. The Compendium also uses a standard format for the presentation of data. Series on Ukrainians are juxtaposed with their counterpart series for "all origins," a synonym for the total population. This provides the Ukrainian series with a convenient standard of reference and base of comparison. There is some departure from this standard format in a few sections where data are also included on selected non-Ukrainian origins to aid interethnic comparisons.

The Purpose of the Compendium

The idea to compile a Compendium originated with the preparation of *Historical Statistics for Canada*, a systematic collection of historical data on many aspects of Canadian life which appeared in 1965.[1] The question then arose of a similar volume dealing specifically with Ukrainians, an ethnocultural group with four generations of life in Canada.

The need for a basic reference source of factual and objective information on Ukrainians became evident to those who later were to form the working group. Over the years, much published data in the census and other sources had accumulated and it was evident that these data were not being utilized fully due to inaccessibility, unorganized form, uncertainty of meaning and a general lack of awareness about their existence. Moreover, the working group felt that Ukrainians had reached that stage of maturity in Canada which allowed them to undertake and accept a more objective and critical examination of themselves. The working group also wished to inform other ethnic groups about Ukrainians.[2]

With the support of the Ottawa and Toronto chapters of the Shevchenko Scientific Society, a working group was established to produce a compendium and financing for the project was obtained from the Canada Council.

The Clientele

The Compendium is intended for a wide clientele. In present form, its data may be used by students, teachers, journalists, politicians and the public at large to deduce historical trends, to provide population distributions and to make some interethnic comparisons. The data are also intended to serve as an analytical reference point and statistical tool for scholars and researchers, enabling them to do more quantitative work and test hypotheses in ethnology, demography, sociology, history, political science and other fields. Moreover, the Compendium should help researchers become more efficient and effective in their work by providing ready access to basic data. By reducing time spent searching for and assembling data, the researcher will be freed for such higher priority tasks as mustering other relevant data; formulating, articulating and testing hypotheses; and drawing conclusions on some of the issues which face Ukrainians in Canada.

The data in each section are preceded by a text which describes the nature of the series and evaluates its data gaps, weaknesses and strengths. The text is meant to help clients interpret and understand the data better in order to use them more effectively.

Place of Analysis

It was not the intention of the working group to provide an analysis of the data. Inevitably, some analysis did creep into the text of some sections to provide better insight into the nature of the data, to clarify some aspects of their use, to derive or adjust series, to justify corrections to series and to compare series between different sections. In the course of this work, the group examined several hypotheses. It did not attempt to go beyond that point.

Sources of the Data

Published and unpublished material from government agencies are the main sources of data. At Statistics Canada, the censuses of population and agriculture and administrative data on vital, morbidity and crime statistics, obtained with the co-operation of provincial governments, are the major sources. Federal departments concerned with immigration provided immigration statistics. The *Reports of the Chief Electoral Officer* and the *Canadian Parliamentary Guide* provided data on candidates running for office and on the results of voting in federal and provincial elections. The Audit Bureau of Circulation of Canadian Advertising provided statistics on the ethnic press.

Improvements to the Series

One of the earliest commitments undertaken by the group was to attempt to fill various data gaps by recourse to unpublished material from worksheets, microfilms and other archival material in census, immigration, vital and other statistics. By providing missing data for 1931 and 1941 for the Ukrainian (Greek) Catholic denomination, major improvements were made to religious statistics. As well, many gaps were filled in the published series on occupations of Ukrainians for 1931, thereby providing a continuous occupation series from 1921 to 1971.

Similarly, major improvements were made to immigràtion statistics by adding figures on Galicians and Bukovynians to the series previously designated Ukrainians, and by putting all immigration statistics on a calendar year basis.

The total Ukrainian population reported in the censuses from 1901 to 1971 was considered to have been underestimated and was therefore adjusted upward. It was also extended back to 1896 using both the corrected immigration series and the data on births and deaths in the Compendium. The concept of "British subject" in citizenship statistics was redefined in line with the concept of citizenship used in the 1947 Citizenship Act and the relevant statistics reaggregated to provide series for the British-born. Some education statistics were recompiled for the population "five years of age and over," providing a more uniform treatment of the literacy series in all years and a more meaningful definition of persons in the categories "not attending school" and "without schooling."

Existing ethnic classifications were augmented by using proxies for ethnicity and by creating "new" ethnic classification series. The Greek Catholic and Greek Orthodox denominations were used as proxies in the marriage series to represent the Ukrainian ethnicity of brides and bridegrooms. Place of birth was used as a proxy to determine the ethnicity of Ukrainian farm operators before 1941, thereby extending the series to 1921 and 1936 censuses. A special ethnic classification was developed to determine Ukrainian candidates running for political office in federal and provincial elections.

Data Limitation

In spite of its efforts to provide a complete and comprehensive volume, the working group realizes that the Compendium cannot be "all things to all men." Researchers doing detailed analyses will still need to go back to original publications or to copies of unpublished material used in the Compendium (deposited with the Public Archives of Canada) either to obtain finer breakdowns or to obtain data on ethnic origins which are not provided. The Compendium increases researchers' opportunities to support their analyses with alternative sources of data.

The Compendium does not include all the subjects for which statistics are available. Data are not provided on the political participation of Ukrainian candidates at the local or municipal level, the financial position and membership of Ukrainian-run co-operatives, and the military service of Ukrainians in both world wars. Such data were or could have been made available, but the magnitude of the undertaking made it prohibitive. Furthermore, the Compendium does not include special tabulations on Ukrainians requested by individual researchers from the 1961 and 1971 censuses, data on microfilm and summary tapes in the 1971 census, data from the 1976 census and the results of special studies or surveys.

Ethnic classifications in both census and administrative statistics allowed leakage of Ukrainians to Austrian, Polish, Russian, Romanian and other origins. On balance, this produced statistics which did not include all Ukrainians and hence were biased downward. In 1901 the underestimation was in the vicinity of 75 to 80 per cent, but by 1971, due to improvements in ethnic data enumeration, it had been reduced to 15 to 20 per cent.[3] Except for the data corrections already noted, the same degree of error is considered to prevail in all census and administrative series for Ukrainians. The underestimation of Ukrainians should be viewed from the perspective that all ethnic statistics, especially those for Ukrainians, are some of the most difficult to classify and may be subject to considerable error. In historical comparisons, errors in the level of the series may be minimized by using percentages and per-person averages rather than the data themselves.[4]

Summary

The Compendium is a reference work intended for a wide clientele which puts the vast majority of available statistics about Ukrainians in Canada into one volume. In it, data are presented systematically, important gaps are filled and limitations are drawn to the attention of users.

In the spirit of multiculturalism, the working group hopes that the Compendium increases the knowledge Ukrainians have about themselves; that it contributes to a greater awareness of Ukrainians by other ethnic groups; and, most importantly, that it will increase rapport and tolerance among all ethnic groups.

PART TWO: TRENDS AMONG CANADIAN UKRAINIANS

Despite some incomparabilities among series, the Compendium is particularly suited to showing historical trends. The following subjects were chosen: population, the Canadian-born, rural and urban status, agriculture, mother tongue, religious affiliation and intermarriage, professional and technical occupations and political participation.

Population

How many Ukrainians are there in Canada and how have their numbers changed over time? According to Table 1, the number of

8

Ukrainians has grown because of immigration and natural increase from approximately 6,000 in 1901 (a decade after they started arriving) to 581,000 in 1971 (eight decades later). In 1971 they were in seventh position after the English, French, Scots, Irish, Germans and Italians.

TABLE 1
Total Ukrainian Population, Canada, 1896 to 1971

	Census Numbers		Corrected Numbers	
	As Reported (x 1000)	Percentage of Total	As Calculated (x 1000)	Percentage of Total
1896	—	—	1	—
1901	6	0.1	26	0.5
1911	75	1.0	128	1.8[a]
1921	107	1.2	220	2.5
1931	225	2.2	333	3.2
1941	306	2.7	402	3.5
1951	395	2.8[a]	500	3.6
1961	473	2.6	622	3.4
1971	581	2.7	711	3.3

Note: [a]Peak years

In 1971 Ukrainians comprised 2.7 per cent of the total population. This was a decline from the high of 2.8 per cent in 1951, the census year which felt the brunt of the postwar immigration, but an increase over the 2.6 per cent of 1961. Ukrainians appear to have reached a period of numerical decline in relation to the total population. With Ukrainian immigration virtually non-existent and birth rates declining rapidly, one can postulate that, although their numbers will continue to increase in the future, the proportion of Ukrainians relative to the total population will probably decline.

At this point it is useful to examine the corrected estimate for total Ukrainians in Canada.[5] The absolute level is higher than the census figures in all years. For example, the corrected figures estimate 711,000 Ukrainians in 1971, 130,000 more than the census. As in the census series, 1951 remains the peak year in the corrected series with relative numbers declining to 1971. While recognizing that the corrected estimate, made under certain assumptions, has its weaknesses, the conclusion of a decline in the relative importance of the Ukrainian population in Canada is corroborated.

The Canadian-born

A related trend, shown in Table 2, is the proportion of Ukrainians who are Canadian-born. In 1971 Ukrainians were the fourth most autochthonous group in Canada, after the French, Indian, Eskimo and British. This 1971 position reflects the passage of eighty years since the beginning of Ukrainian entry to Canada, the duration and spacing between three waves of immigration and its virtual cessation since the late 1950s. Because the flow of immigration is not likely to resume in our generation, Ukrainians will become increasingly Canadian-born and, in the future, should approach Native, French and British peoples in degree of nativity.

TABLE 2

Percentage Canadian-born by Selected Ethnic Origins in Canada, 1931 to 1971

Ethnic Origin	1931	1971
French	97.4	98.2
Indian, Eskimo	99.3	98.1
British	74.9	87.6
Ukrainian	57.0	81.7
Scandinavian	43.6	78.0
All Origins	78.6	86.6

The increased nativity should have important applications for future activities. Twice in Canadian history (in the late 1920s and around 1950), Ukrainian cultural activities have been revitalized by an inflow of new immigrants. A third rejuvenation, however, cannot presently be foreseen. By cutting the umbilical cord that has tied many to the Old Country, the stage is being set for the development of new relationships with Ukraine and for fresh approaches to Ukrainian ethnic survival based entirely on developing one's own resources in Canada. Another possibility is that the stage is being set for accelerated assimilation into the anglophone sea.

Rural and Urban Status

Ukrainians started out in Canada as a predominantly rural people. The 1901 census classified 96.5 per cent of them as rural (Table 3), while the figure for the total population was only 62.5 per cent. In subsequent censuses, Ukrainians became less rural, because (1) the second and third immigrations contained fewer agricultural settlers and (2) Ukrainians became subject to the same urbanizing forces as the total population. By 1971, the rural proportion of the Ukrainian population had fallen to 25.0 per cent, only slightly above the 23.8 per cent figure for all origins.

TABLE 3
Percentage Rural Status of the Population, Canada, 1901 to 1971

	Ukrainian	All Origins
1901	96.5	62.5
1911	85.0	54.6
1921	80.1	50.4
1931	70.5	46.3
1941	66.0	45.7
1951	49.7	38.4
1961	34.8	30.4
1971	25.0	23.8

Table 3 indicates that the urbanizing process has gone a long way and has cut deeply into the former rural lifestyle. Today one must look for the wellsprings of Ukrainian activity in Canada, not on the farms in the Prairie provinces, but in the large centres of Ukrainian settlement across Canada: Winnipeg, Edmonton, Toronto, Vancouver and Montreal, and such intermediate-sized settlement centres as Saskatoon, Calgary, Hamilton and Thunder Bay. Larger towns such as Yorkton, Dauphin and Vegreville have also developed important cultural activities of their own.

Agriculture

Table 4 indicates that by 1971 only 11.3 per cent of the Ukrainian labour force was occupied in agriculture, a decline of almost one-half from 1961, and only one-sixth the figure fifty years earlier. From this it might appear that the Ukrainians have shed their "sheepskin coat" image. On the contrary, farming was still twice as prevalent among the Ukrainians in 1971 as for all other origins.

Other trappings of the earlier image also remain. Data from the 1971 census suggest that, because of their original settlement on poorer land in the aspen grove belt of the Prairie provinces. Ukrainians still have smaller farms, lower capitalization and mechanization and lower incomes than the average Canadian farmer.[6]

TABLE 4
Percentage Labour Force Employed in Agriculture, Canada,
1921 to 1971

	Ukrainians	All Origins
1921	67.2	32.8
1931	55.1	28.7
1941	48.2	25.6
1951	36.1	15.6
1961	20.9	9.9
1971	11.3	5.6

The economic forces that have caused the decline in farm numbers should continue to operate and could very well reduce the number of Ukrainian farmers to the 5 per cent level in the forseeable future. This would be approximately 12,000 to 15,000 farm operators distributed across the three Prairie provinces. Can such small numbers form a sufficient "critical mass" to contribute meaningfully to the cultural strength of the urban areas, or will the Ukrainian farm population survive ethnically only because of cultural feedback from the urban centers?

Mother Tongue, Religious Affiliation and Intermarriage
The rural (especially farm) population and its organized community life have been regarded as strongholds of Ukrainian traditions and bulwarks against assimilation. With the decline of the farm population, this cultural protection has been withdrawn, with important effects on retention of the Ukrainian language, religious affiliation and marriage within the group.
Over 90 per cent of the Ukrainian population in 1921 reported knowledge of the Ukrainian mother tongue. By 1971, this had fallen to 48.9 per cent. The decline in actual knowledge of the language is likely greater than indicated because the census requirement for knowledge of the mother tongue became weaker with successive censuses. For example, in 1921 the requirement for knowledge of the mother tongue was that it be the language of customary speech; since 1941 the requirement has been only that the language be understood, with the level of understanding left unspecified. Consequently, there is no measure for those who understand the language progressively less well over time.

TABLE 5
Knowledge of the Ukrainian and English Languages
Among Ukrainian Canadians, 1921 to 1971

	Knowledge of Ukrainian by Ukrainians			Knowledge of English by Ukrainians
	Total	Urban	Rural	
1921[a]	91.7	—	—	73.8
1931	93.1	88.9	94.9	77.9
1941	92.1	—	—	93.0
1951	79.6	72.0	87.4	93.1
1961	64.4	59.3	73.9	97.2
1971	48.9	45.9	57.8	97.8

Note: [a]Population 10 years of age and over

In 1971, 22.8 per cent of the Ukrainian population gave Ukrainian as the language most often spoken at home. This is less than half the 48.9 per cent shown as having knowledge of the mother tongue. Since the 1921 definition of mother tongue is close to the 1971 definition of language spoken at home, one could say that Ukrainian language use has declined from over 90 per cent in 1921 to about 23 per cent in 1971.

At the same time as knowledge of Ukrainian was decreasing, knowledge of English by Ukrainians was increasing. This should soon reach its saturation point. In this regard, Ukrainians are well integrated into the anglophone part of Canadian society.

Affiliation of Ukrainians with their traditional denominations, the Greek Catholic and Greek Orthodox churches, is shown in Table 6. In the four decades from 1931 to 1971, Ukrainians formed the majority in

TABLE 6
Percentage of Ukrainian Population Religiously Affiliated with
Traditional Ukrainian Denominations, Canada, 1931 to 1971

	Total	Urban	Rural
1931	82.6	75.3	85.6
1941	79.0	—	—
1951	69.8	61.6	78.1
1961	58.5	52.8	69.1
1971	52.2	49.7	59.7

these two denominations. However, this majority has been declining. In 1971 only 52.2 per cent of the Ukrainians were adherents, compared to 82.6 per cent in 1931. Conversely, the proportion of Ukrainians in non-traditional denominations has been growing and may attain a majority position if the trend continues. This movement of affiliation from the former to the latter denominations represents a form of assimilation in which the traditional faith is abandoned but Ukrainian ethnicity is still retained.

The trend in endogamous marriages from 1921 to 1971 is shown in Table 7. From 87.4 per cent in 1921, endogamous marriages for Ukrainians in Canada declined steadily to about 39 per cent in 1971. The data in Table 7 are proxies for Ukrainian ethnicity based on endoga-mous marriage rates for the Greek Catholic and, in part, the Greek Orthodox denominations. Changes in the rate of endogamy in Table 7 are large, continuous and consistent with the level of and changes in other data on endogamy, such as that for couples already married and ethnic origin of parents in birth statistics. They are also consistent with the declines in rurality, Ukrainian language knowledge and church affiliation given in earlier tables. Therefore, marriage data are part of a package of inter-related series subject to the same influences and displaying the same trends.[7]

TABLE 7

Percentage of Endogamous Marriages Among Ukrainians in Canada, 1921 to 1971

1921	87.4
1931	81.5
1941	65.9
1951	59.2
1961	53.5
1971	38.7

Tables 5 and 6 indicate that language and religious assimilation was greater in the urban sector than the rural. While one could conclude from this that the rural sector was more protective of Ukrainian language and religion, this was not entirely so. The rural sector also experienced a downward trend in language knowledge and Ukrainian religious affiliation. Rural-urban migration encroached on the rural sector, thinning out its population and making it more vulnerable to outside forces. Even without this encroachment cultural life in the rural sector would not have remained frozen. Longer residence in Canada together with a greater knowledge of the English language would have subjected all Ukrainian culture to outside influences.

Unfortunately, the marriage data in Table 7 cannot be subdivided into urban and rural components to indicate marriage levels and trends in the rural sector.

Professional and Technical Occupations

From 1921 to 1971 (Table 8) the rate of increase of professional and technical occupations among Ukrainians was more rapid than the national average, suggesting that Ukrainians increasingly acquired the motivation, training and financial means to join these groups. Despite this progress, professional and technical occupations were still some 20 per cent less represented among Ukrainians in 1971 than among all other origins, indicating that Ukrainians have some way to go before this gap can be closed.

These occupations are the sources from which much of the Ukrainian elite and future leadership tends to be drawn. Their increase augurs well for the future. These leaders may be the indigenous resource which will rejuvenate Ukrainian cultural life and give it a new orientation in Canada. Formerly, this function was performed by successive waves of Ukrainian immigrants.

TABLE 8

Percentage of Labour Force in Professional and
Technical Occupations, Canada, 1921 to 1971

	Ukrainians	All Origins
1921	1.0	5.4
1931	1.4	6.1
1941	2.1	6.7
1951	3.4	7.1
1961	6.6	9.7
1971	10.4	12.7

A further development, not shown in Table 8 but discernable from the Compendium data, is the increase in diversity and complexity of professional occupations. In 1921 the Ukrainian professional occupational spectrum was very simple. Teachers were the major group, with some religious personnel and a smattering of other occupations. By 1971, the spectrum had broadened considerably as a significant number of Ukrainians penetrated over fifty different occupations.[8] Consequently, Ukrainians are approaching the pattern of professional occupations prevailing for the entire population. This is providing a diversified base from which the Ukrainian elite can be drawn.

Political Participation

The participation of Ukrainian candidates in Canadian politics, which started federally in 1904 and provincially in 1912, is summarized in Table 9. In the early years there were few electoral successes as most Ukrainian candidates were not taken seriously by the electorate. Over the years, however, the status of Ukrainians increased and the number of constituencies where they are considered serious challengers has grown. Appointments to higher federal and provincial political offices have come with greater success at the polls.

TABLE 9
Numbers of Ukrainians Participating in Elections and Appointments to Higher Political Office, Canada and the Provinces, 1904 to 1977

	Federal	Provincial	Total
	Electoral Results		
Total Candidates[a]	286	643	929
Female Candidates	11	17	28
Constituencies Contested	226	455	681
Successful Candidates	62	189	251
Successful Women Candidates	—	5	5
Different Candidates (Total)[b]	23	82	105
Different Candidates (Women)	—	3	3
	Appointments to Higher Office		
Cabinet Ministers	2[c]	17	19
Senators	4	—	4
Lieutenant Governors	1	—	1

Notes: [a]Last elections included: the 1974 federal election; provincially, the 1973 election for Manitoba, and the 1975 elections for Ontario, Saskatchewan, Alberta and British Columbia.
[b]Some candidates are elected more than once. This total shows the number of different candidates elected at least once or more. For example, in federal elections, twenty-three different candidates were elected sixty-two different times. On average each successful candidate was elected 2.7 times.
[c]Second minister appointed in 1977.

After the Second World War, the Ukrainian political power base spread from rural to urban areas, and from the Prairie provinces to Ontario, British Columbia and the City of Montreal. Progress was rapid after 1957. Up to 1957, for example, eight of eleven successful federal candidates were rural; after 1957 twenty-eight of fifty-one successful candidates were urban. In 1974 only three of the eight candidates elected federally represented rural ridings.

These shifts are in line with the decline in rurality indicated previously and the increasing electoral strength of the urban Ukrainian population. Urban inroads into provincial elections in the Prairie provinces were slower than those in the federal field. While the number of urban MLAs has increased in all three provinces, it was only in the 1971 and 1975 elections that the urban members were the majority in Alberta. This occurred in the 1973 election in Manitoba and in the 1975 election in Saskatchewan.

The electoral strength of metropolitan Winnipeg has differed from metropolitan centres such as Edmonton and Toronto. Edmonton East has elected a Ukrainian candidate to the House of Commons continually since 1953 and Toronto federal ridings have elected three members since 1953, with serious contenders in four others. In comparison, the City of Winnipeg has not sent any Ukrainian members to the House of Commons. The only exception are those parts of Winnipeg included in federal rural ridings which are adjacent to the city, such as Springfield.

On the other hand, Winnipeg has been stronger in electing provincial members than either Edmonton or Toronto. Since the start of the Second World War, Winnipeg has provided twenty Ukrainian electoral victories. In a comparable period, Edmonton elected eighteen and Toronto eight.

Another trend has been party polarization. Many of the early candidates ran as independents or under the banner of splinter parties. But success at the polls tended to elude them and Ukrainians began shifting toward established parties. Until 1957 Ukrainian candidates had been successful eleven times in federal elections, with two each for the Liberal, Conservative, Social Credit, CCF and UFA parties and one for a splinter party. It could be said there was no polarization. The situation changed after 1957. Of fifty-one federal election successes, forty-one were for the Progressive Conservatives, six for the Liberals, and two each for the Social Credit and NDP parties. This polarization toward the Progressive Conservatives has lasted for more than fifteen years of Liberal rule in Ottawa and does not appear to be a short-term phenomenon.

All three Prairie provinces have had changes in party polarization for

Ukrainians. In Manitoba the change was from the Liberals (Progressives) to the New Democratic Party; the 1977 change to the Progressive Conservatives did not affect the Ukrainians as their elected members continued to come from the New Democratic Party. In Saskatchewan the change was from the Liberals to the New Democratic Party and in Alberta from the Social Credit to the Progressive Conservatives.

Summary

The trends chosen for this paper show strong and consistent, even dramatic, changes in the eighty-year history of Ukrainians in Canada. Canada's rapid urbanization after the Second World War, the decline of the farm and rural sectors and the virtual absence of Ukrainian immigration in the last twenty years has increased assimilation. There have been pronounced declines in the knowledge of the Ukrainian language, in affiliation with traditional Ukrainian church denominations and in the rate of marriage within the group.

On the other hand, there has been an increasing Ukrainian participation in the professions and in Canada's political process. This has resulted in important developments in the policy of multiculturalism, a subject outside the framework of the Compendium's statistics.

NOTES

1. M. C. Urquhart and K. A. H. Buckley, eds., *Historical Statistics of Canada* (Toronto: Cambridge University Press, 1965).
2. John W. Berry, Rudolf Kalin, Donald M. Taylor, L. Lamarche and J. Christian, *Multiculturalism and Ethnic Attitudes in Canada* (Ottawa: Supply and Services Canada, 1977), 93.
3. William Darcovich and Paul Yuzyk, eds., "Statistical Compendium on the Ukrainians in Canada, 1891–1976" (Unpublished typescript, Ottawa, 1977), 755.
4. For example, if there is 50 per cent underestimation of both the total and male populations, the ratio of males in the total population will still be correct.

   50 Per cent
   Underestimated   Corrected Levels

   $$\frac{47}{78} = \frac{86}{156} = 55.1 \text{ per cent of males in total population}$$

   For this reason, Tables 2 to 8 in my paper rely on percentages to show trends.
5. Darcovich and Yuzyk, 755.
6. Ibid., Series 41.93–128, 433–7.
7. William Darcovich, *Ukrainians in Canada: The Struggle to Retain Their Identity* (Ottawa: Ukrainian Self-Reliance Association [Ottawa Branch], 1967), 19–26.
8. Darcovich and Yuzyk, Series 40.179–180, 401.

ETHNIC ORIGIN
IN THE CANADIAN CENSUS, 1871–1981*

John M. Kralt

The last decennial census (1971) identified approximately 300,000 Canadians as being of either Native Indian or Inuit ancestry. The remaining twenty-one and one-quarter million persons were either immigrants or the descendants of immigrants. Although immigration to Canada before 1760 was dominated by people from France and after 1760 by those from the British Isles, large numbers of immigrants have come from all parts of the globe. How these immigrants and their descendants have interacted with each other has influenced Canadian society and history for the past 350 years.

Governments and the population as a whole have been interested in these different groups and their descendants. With the exception of 1891, every decennial census since 1871 has contained a question dealing with the origins of Canadians, i.e., where did the respondent's ancestor come from before arrival in Canada? Historically, the intent of the question has been to provide estimates of the size of each origin or "stock group" and to show how socio-economic activities of the various origins differ.

This essay first examines the census concepts of racial and ethnic origin used between 1871 and 1971 and the problems encountered with them, and secondly, discusses the rationale for the concept and question being proposed for the 1981 census.

---

* Opinions expressed in this article are those of the author and not necessarily those of Statistics Canada.

CENSUS CONCEPTS FROM 1871 to 1971

Although bureaucracy is noted for the mountains of paper which it produces, documentation about ethnic origin is extremely sketchy. I have been able to find only two references to the concept of ethnicity for each census between 1871 and 1911: one in *The Enumerators Manual* and the other in the introduction to the volumes of tabulations produced for each census. Memoranda and other related documents appear to be an extinct species. Beginning in 1921, census monographs and general reviews have provided detailed sources of information, but it is the definitions or instructions given to the enumerators between 1871 and 1971 that provide the best continuous indication of the various concepts used. These appear in Appendix A.

From the limited documentation available for 1871, it is clear that the intention of the question on origin was to create a sharp distinction between "origin" and "citizenship or nationality."

The subject matter of Table III (Origins of the People) is a new feature in our census statistics. None of the former censuses of the various Provinces had it, except in so far as the French origin was concerned, in the former Province of Canada. What is given in previous returns under the head *origin*, was simply the enumeration of people by their *place of birth*. But a moment's reflection shows at once that these two subjects of information are as different as they are important. The two tables of *origins* and *birth places* of the people taken in connection with the others, afford invaluable means of statistical comparisons and deductions.[1]

It is apparent that there was some concern over the accuracy of these "racial origin" data, since the report continues:

In taking down the information from the people, the enumerators had, of course, to record the answers given to them. Whenever no definite answer was obtained, the column was then filled with the word or sign *not given*, and this as a fact has occurred most particularly in families of mixed origin. It is in this way that only two *half breeds* have been reported. True again it is that the word half breed is now generally made specifically to mean persons of mixed Indian blood of the West, of whom there are very few settled within the four Provinces. However, the proportion of *not given* in this table, as well as in all others, is comparatively very small, so much so, that it would be insufficient, inasmuch as the figures apply to all origins, to make any notable difference in the ratio of the important elements of the population.[2]

It would appear that users of these 1871 data were relatively happy with the concept because the enumeration instructions did not change for the 1881 census.

For some reason, the racial origin question was virtually eliminated in 1891. The only item which remained in the census was a count of the persons of French ancestry. As indicated by the "Introduction" below the tables, this procedure was not very successful.

In table III, the columns headed "French Canadian" and "others" require some explanation. An attempt was made by means of these columns to ascertain the number of French Canadians and French Acadians in the several provinces of the Dominion. It was intended that the French Acadians should be enumerated in the columns marked French Canadians and instructions were given accordingly. Each person who was asked the other questions in the Census schedules, was also asked if he or she was a French Canadian (or Canadian French), or a French Acadian (or Acadian French) and the answers given were noted in these columns by the enumerators.

It has been claimed, however, with much appearance of reason, that the columns headed "French Canadians" does not show the number of persons of French *origin* in Canada; that in the case of Acadians in the Maritime Provinces and the Half-Breeds of Manitoba and the North-west Territories, the question was misunderstood and that in the Province of Ontario owing to various causes, many persons of French Canadian origin have not been so enumerated.

This fact is here noted so that persons, using the results published, may not be misled by supposing that the number of persons of French Canadian *origin* has been ascertained with precision or that the actual increases or decreases are such as a comparison with former Census returns might seem to show.

The answers given to the enumerators have been correctly compiled and placed before the public.[3]

One can assume that the lack of success with this 1891 question was in part responsible for the reintroduction of a racial origin question in 1901. In that year, the planners recognized that mixed origins were a problem which could not be ignored as had been done in 1891. Thus persons with mixed Native Indian and European parentage were classified as having such ancestry. The controlling factor for persons having other combinations of origins was the paternal ancestor.

Labelling persons of mixed Native Indian and other origins does not appear to have been successful, because the 1911 procedure used instead the maternal ancestor as the controlling factor, while persons of other mixtures were again asked to use the paternal ancestor. In 1921 this procedure was again used with an additional instruction prohibiting the use of "Canadian" and "American" as origins. These two responses were used to distinguish formally "nationality and citizenship" from "racial origin."

In 1929 the monograph, *Origin, Birthplace, Nationality and Language of the Canadian People (A Census Study Based on the Census of 1921 and Supplementary Data)*, was published.[4] In its introduction it identified relatively clearly the concept of "racial origin" used to that time.

> In a strictly biological sense, the term "race" signifies a subgroup of the human species related by ties of physical kinship. Scientists have attempted to divide and subdivide the human species into groups on the basis of biological traits, such as shape of the head, stature, colour of skin, etc., and to such groups and to such only, would the biologist apply the term "race."[5]

However, the term "racial origin" was seen as being "less precise" than the "scientific" use of the term "race."

> The term "origin," therefore, as used by the census usually has a combined biological, cultural and geographical significance. It suggests whence our people come and the implied biological strain and cultural background. Following popular usage, the terms, "English stock," "French stock," "Italian stock," etc., are employed to describe the sum total of the biological and cultural characteristics which distinguish such groups from others. Such usage is familiar to the public in general, and only when our "origin" classifications follow such lines, can they be collected by a census, be understood by the people or have any significance from the practical standpoint of the development of a Canadian nation.[6]

Equally interesting are the ethnocentric prejudices of the analysts of that day.

The significant fact in the present connection is this. The combined biological and cultural effect on Canada of the infiltration of a group of English is clearly different from that produced by a similar number of, say, Ukrainians coming to the country. This is partly due to the different biological strains and partly to different cultural environment in the home country. It would be futile from a practical point of view to attempt to separate the biological and the cultural influence. It is known, for example, that biologically the Orientals are not assimilable in Canada, even if culturally assimilation were possible. On the other hand, neither Mennonites nor Doukhobors are easily assimilated culturally, though biologically an infusion could be effected. But the relative importance of the biological and cultural factors is not subject to quantitative measurement. Both, however, are combined under the term "origin."[7]

The reasons for the use of paternal ancestor for persons with mixed origins are also outlined in some detail.

The male line is used in the census for tracing "origin" derivation. In this connection the population falls into two main catagories: (1) the less assimilable peoples who have maintained their original purity, and (2) those who have intermarried freely for several generations. In the case of those falling within the first category, the procedure of the census is obviously satisfactory. It might be objected in the case of those falling within the second category, however, that there are many individuals whose origins are so intermixed through intermarriages that their designation as of the origin indicated by their fathers' patronymic is largely meaningless. This may be accepted as true in so far as the individual is concerned. It remains true, however, that by the law of large numbers in the mass, the adoption of the practice followed in the census will yield approximately accurate measurements of the different infusions of blood that have gone to make up the total.[8]

The monograph also identified very clearly the reasons for collecting these data.

The above becomes clear when we consider in greater detail the purposes for which "origin" data are collected. Apart from purely scientific studies such data have two types of use. First, they have an important bearing on the study of immigration, for they show with what measure of success the newer peoples are mixing with the basic stocks of the country and adapting themselves to Canadian institutions. In the second place, such data have considerable historical interest in recording not only the continuous infusion of foreign blood and foreign cultures from abroad, but the combined effect of natural increase and immigration on the "origin" structure of the population.[9]

The monograph by Professor Hurd, based on the 1931 and 1941 censuses, shows no significant difference in the purpose for the data.[10] Racial origin data were designed to measure the extent to which desirable racial groups were present in Canada. This desirability was based on the extent of assimilation to "the basic origins of the country...to Canadian institutions...[and] the combined effect...on the origin structure of the population."[11] This phrasing can be translated to mean the extent to which non-British immigrants had adapted themselves to British customs and institutions.

Changes to the 1931 instructions resulted from problems encountered in the enumeration of origins for central and eastern Europe in 1921. This stemmed from the break-up of the Austro-Hungarian Empire after the First World War and the abrupt termination of the Russian Empire in 1917. Although the format of the 1941 instructions was revised, the instructions *per se* were not altered radically from those of 1931.

The 1951 question was similar in intent to the racial origin question of earlier censuses. However, 1951 was the first time that the word "racial" was dropped and the term "origin" defined for the enumerator.

The origin of a person in the 1951 Census was established by asking the language (i.e., native tongue) spoken by the person's paternal ancestor, or the person himself in the case of an immigrant, at the time of first arrival on this continent. . . . In the event a person's origin could not be established by using the language criterion, they (the enumerators) were to ask a further question such as: "Is your origin in the male line English, Scottish, Ukrainian. . . ."[12]

The changes listed below were also introduced at this time, and were used more or less to 1971.

a. If the person insisted on "Canadian" or "American," this answer was accepted.
b. If the person insisted that he or she did not know their origins, this was accepted.

c. Native peoples on reserves were labelled as Native Indians, while those off the reserves had their origin determined through the father (a 180 degree turn from previous censuses).[13]

The use of language as the main criterion for determining origin was dropped in 1961. Instead, this specific question appeared for the first time on the forms used by enumerators: "To what ethnic or cultural group did you or your ancestor (on the male side) belong on coming to this continent?" All references to "race" were deleted from the questionnaire and the instructions. Another innovation was the division of Native Indians into two groups—Band (Treaty) and Non-Band (Non-Treaty).

The 1971 questionnaire used the same question as had been used in 1961. However, the context of this question was completely different. Instead of relying on trained enumerators to obtain census data, the vast bulk of the 1971 questionnaires were filled in by householders themselves. The 1971 question used language as a guide for determining ethnic origin when applicable and again split Native Indians into Band (Treaty) and Non-Band (Non-Treaty) groups.

THE 1981 VERSION OF THE CENSUS QUESTION*

Problems With the 1971 Concept of and Data on Ethnicity
Reaction to the 1971 ethnic question suggested the need for a careful review of its utility and scope. Major criticisms were made about the relevance of the paternal ancestor as a measure of ethnicity, as well as a number of oddities within the data. This led to a re-evaluation of the need for ethnic data and the meaning of ethnic origin. The remainder of this paper outlines several of the problems encountered with the 1971 data, the results of two tests of the questions planned for 1981 and the reasons for recommending the retention of the historical concept of ethnicity rather than shifting to some form of ethnic self-identification.

Changes in Ethnic Groups
Although analysts prior to 1951 indicated that few problems were

---

* It should be clearly understood that this discussion of the 1981 version of the question reflects current thinking within Statistics Canada's census and household surveys field. The question used in 1981 is not necessarily going to be the question presented here, nor is it certain there will be a question on ethnicity. The final wording and the inclusion or exclusion of the question are subject to the approval of the federal cabinet, which may or may not accept the question proposed by Statistics Canada.

encountered by enumerators in collecting "ethnic origin" or "racial origin" data, the ethnic origin concept remains among the most ambiguous of the traditional census concepts.[14] Even if the roots of two individuals are from the same general geographic area and they use the same language, their date of arrival in Canada has a tremendous impact on the relevance of ethnic origin for these two persons.

It may be assumed that there are two distinct ethnic subgroups for every ethnic group in Canada, which have been labelled elsewhere as "Old Ethnic" and "New Ethnic."[15] "Old Ethnic" groups developed as a result of their quest for some sense of self-identification in their new country. These immigrants either tended or were pushed by external forces to seek out association with others who spoke similar languages or dialects. In so doing, however, their identification with a specific locality and dialect was enlarged to include either the country from which they had come or its language. For example, identification with a small hamlet in East Prussia changed to a sense of German nationalism. For pre-First World War immigrants, this represented the first step in the process of Americanization or Canadianization.[16]

For post-Second World War immigrants (New Ethnics), ethnic identification resulted from different forces. In Europe both urbanism and immigration to North America brought peasants from hamlets to the cities and threw thousands from all these small regions together. Old regional allegiances, although still present, were forced into the background and were gradually replaced by identification with the larger nation-state.[17] As the First World War approached, the increased emphasis on nationalism rather than regionalism was clearly shown by the severe agitation for the independence of linguistic groups within the old European empires.[18] The result was the ultimate break-up of the old empires into countries whose basis was largely a common ethnicity based on language.[19]

Canadian census data grouped together both those persons whose ethnic group identification was the result of growth in ethnic consciousness in Canada and others whose ethnic group identification was developed prior to immigration to Canada. These two types of ethnic group identification should be distinguished. Since the data collected in 1971 suggest that there are indeed two subgroups within each ethnic group, with significant socio-economic differences between them, the usefulness of a single census question which does not differentiate between the two subgroups is open to question. Unfortunately, it is doubtful whether such a distinction could be drawn from the data to be collected through the proposed 1981 census questions.

Decline in Ethnic Group Numbers

It can be shown theoretically that, barring large-scale emigration, the absolute size of an ethnic group should not decline. Nevertheless, between 1961 and 1971 several groups have declined in absolute number. Why this has occurred is a matter of conjecture, but undoubtedly it was partly the result of (a) the change-over to self-enumeration, (b) overreporting of English ethnicity (the first answer category in the question) and (c) a poorly defined awareness of individual "ethnic roots."

The Paternal Ancestor

Since the completion of my study, *Ethnic Origins of Canadians*, I have undertaken further investigation into the relevance of the paternal ancestor criterion. It would seem that the best indicator of a match between an individual respondent and his or her paternal ancestry would be the ethnic origin of a child matched with the ethnic origin of the child's father. It is assumed that this instruction would be followed most easily for a child living with its father. Using Statistics Canada's STATPAK retrieval system, a tabulation was run in which children's ethnic origins were compared to the ethnic origin of each child's father, as shown in Table 1.

This table shows that reporting was not very accurate for two successive generations. The important question is this: if the criterion of paternal ancestory is not followed for one of every ten children who live with their father, how relevant is it for persons whose paternal ancestry is eight or ten generations removed?

Band and Non-Band Indians

A major reason for having the ethnic origin question is to provide a count of Native peoples. When 1971 census counts were compared to the Indian Register maintained by the Department of Indian and Northern Affairs, there appears to have been a 10 per cent undernumeration of Band Indians. Undernumeration in the Non-Band group was even greater. The census counted approximately 64,000 persons, while unofficial estimates ranged from 250,000 to 750,000. This, plus a general dissatisfaction with the Band/Non-Band terminology, suggested the need for a review of the ethnic origin question in this area.

Questionnaire Design

The influence of questionnaire design on the data is extremely difficult to measure and assess. Some indication of the impact of the positioning and presence of codes in the questionnaire is shown in Table

TABLE 1

Families Showing Ethnicity of Father by Ethnicity of Child (Same/Different), Canada, 1971

Ethnicity of father	Total	No Children	Ethnicity of Children[a]			
			All Same	All Different	Some Same, Some Different	Any Different 6 = 4 + 5
	1	2	3	4	5	
Total	4,605,485	1,369,775	2,875,610	247,755	112,355	360,110
British	2,059,865	691,070	1,198,490	117,020	53,285	170,305
French	1,217,875	301,540	875,200	25,605	15,535	41,140
German	315,575	93,505	178,650	30,025	13,395	43,420
Italian	177,425	34,735	128,880	9,430	4,380	13,810
Ukrainian	137,240	45,145	78,190	10,160	3,745	13,905
Jewish	73,585	26,725	45,195	1,335	335	1,670
Dutch	96,095	22,925	61,490	7,410	4,265	11,675
Scandinavian	92,795	30,950	48,195	9,535	4,110	13,645
Polish	75,115	23,820	41,685	7,280	2,330	9,610
Greek	29,745	6,510	21,495	1,150	590	1,740
Portuguese	22,475	4,320	16,760	840	550	1,390
Chinese	23,410	5,665	16,575	700	475	1,175
Japanese	8,470	2,265	5,680	285	230	515
Indo-Pakistani	11,535	2,870	8,005	335	325	660
Indian and Eskimo	40,680	6,495	28,805	2,900	2,480	5,380
Other	223,600	71,240	122,305	23,730	6,325	30,055

Note: [a]360,110 families had one or more children with an ethnic origin different from the father; the actual number of children represented by these families is 722,370.

TABLE 2
Comparison of Ethnic Group Increase With the Increase of the
Total Population and Position of Group in the Question, 1961 and 1971

Ethnic Group	Position of Group in the Question		Percentage change 1961-1971 less 18.3 per cent[a]
	1961	1971	
English	5	1	+ 30.6
French	8	2	- 6.8
German	9	3	+ 7.2
Irish	13	4	- 28.1
Italian	14	5	+ 44.0
Jewish	15	6	+ 53.0
Native Indian	22	7 + 8	+ 23.4
Netherlands	18	9	- 19.2
Norwegian	19	10	+ 2.3
Polish	20	11	- 20.5
Scottish	24	12	- 27.9
Ukrainian	27	13	+ 4.4
Austrian	1		- 78.8
Belgian	2		- 35.0
Czech	3		+ 1.4
Danish	4		- 29.7
Estonian	6		- 16.9
Finnish	7		- 18.7
Greek	10		+102.1
Hungarian	11		- 13.8
Icelandic	12		- 27.2
Lithuanian	16		- 29.5
Negro	17		- 11.1
Romanian	21		- 55.8
Russian	23		- 64.2
Slovak	25		- 21.1
Swedish	26		- 34.6
Welsh	28		- 66.6
Yugoslav	29		- 34.7

Source: Table prepared by N. Collishaw, Demographic Sector, Census Field.
Note: [a]18.3 per cent was the percentage increase in the Canadian population as a whole from 1961 to 1971.

2, which compares the relative increases and decreases of the various ethnic groups to the growth of the population as a whole. Each group is also examined for its presence as an option available to the respondent in 1971 or to the enumerator in 1961.

While the correlations are not perfect, it is noteworthy that all ethnic groups (except the Czech and Greek), which were in the questionnaire in 1961 but not in 1971, decreased in comparison with the growth of the total population. Many of these groups had fewer members in 1971 than in 1961.

The Development of the Ethnic Origin Question for 1981

When discussions about the 1981 census question on ethnic origin were started, the above problems had to be addressed and the basic question of whether the ethnic origin concept was still relevant had to be answered. If the question is still significant in today's world, is its formulation and concept in the census meaningful or should it be changed? Also, what can be done to minimize the impact of questionnaire design; and how can the enumeration of Native peoples be improved?

Count of Native Peoples

From the outset of the planning process, one major concern was improving the enumeration of Native peoples. The terms "Band" and "Non-Band" were to be re-evaluated and "Métis" was to be included. Undoubtedly, the exclusion of this latter term in 1971 was one of the reasons for the undercount of non-status Indians. To improve enumeration, representatives of both federal departments dealing with Native peoples and Native associations were consulted. The terms below were selected as most likely to be the best understood. The caption "Native Peoples" was used to avoid confusion with Asian Indians and to draw attention to the fact that Native peoples were to check the appropriate box in this section.

Native Peoples
11 ☐ Inuit
12 ☐ Status or registered Indian
13 ☐ Non-status Indian
14 ☐ Métis

Self-Identification Versus Roots

By adopting these terms for the Native peoples, the historical ethnic origin concept of "roots" was chosen instead of a question on "ethnic self-identity." Paternal ancestry was also eliminated because the "Métis" designation is not theoretically possible using only the paternal ancestor. If paternal ancestry was accepted, such a person would be either Native Indian or European.

This decision was made in spite of the fact that a number of census data users—academics, governments and ethnic organizations—had suggested dropping the "roots" concept in favour of some form of "ethnic self-identification." At a census workshop in September 1977, there was considerable support for this latter form of ethnicity. Aside from the problem of constructing a less prosaic question than simply "What is your ethnic self-identification?" there were other problems in making this concept operational.

a. What constitutes ethnic self-identification is not clear. Even if it is known that a person identifies closely with ethnic group X, what the respondent means by this self-identification is unknown.

b. The probability of multiple responses, increased in the "roots" concept by eliminating the paternal ancestor question, will not necessarily diminish with self-identification. In fact, it can be argued that multiple responses will be encouraged, e.g., a person's "ethnic self-identification" will be both Canadian and German.

c. "Self-identification" has been suggested as being more useful than the "roots" concept for assessing multiculturalism. But in order to determine the real strength of multiculturalism and the relevance of ethnic origin, it would seem necessary to identify all potential members of an ethnic group, both those for whom their "roots" do have relevance and those for whom they do not. In assessing multicultural programmes and ethnic group requests, it seems equally important to know how many potential members of the group exist as well as how many presently identify with it.

d. Applying the "roots" concept to the census, makes "Canadian" and "American" unacceptable responses, while they are legitimate and likely in the context of a self-enumerated questionnaire using self-identification. However, these two responses would make the interpretation of any data on self-identification very difficult. If only 20 per cent of the population responded "Canadian," the data collected on ethnicity would be relatively useless.

e. Even if ethnic self-identification is possible for adults, the problem of interpreting results for children remains. Asking for ethnic self-identification from young children who have not yet developed their own sense of self-identity creates a whole new set of problems.

In summary, the concept of "ethnic self-identification" would be useful as a supplement to the "roots" concept. However, the self-identification concept cannot stand on its own as a census question.

The Order of Ethnic Groups

To minimize the impact of questionnaire design on the groups enumerated, especially British, it was decided to place "English, Irish, and Scottish" in sequence. It was felt that in 1971 persons who should have answered "Irish" or "Scottish" answered "English," because this was the first code on the list which seemed to apply. "Irish" and "Scottish" being separated from "English" by a number of other entries. The eight largest groups in the 1971 Census were listed in size from largest to smallest. Since putting "French" in sequence by size would have required splitting the British groups, it was placed first. The ethnic origins appearing on the questionnaire are:

1 ☐ French
2 ☐ English
3 ☐ Irish
4 ☐ Scottish
5 ☐ German
6 ☐ Italian
7 ☐ Ukrainian
8 ☐ Dutch (Netherlands)
9 ☐ Polish
10 ☐ Jewish
   ☐ ....
        Other (specify)

The Testing Programme

Two versions of the ethnic origin question have been tested. In February 1977 a test was carried out in Toronto, Vancouver, Trois-Rivières and Montreal. Questionnaires consisting of a series of proposed census questions on language, citizenship, nativity and ethnic origin were delivered to households in the sample for completion by the householder. One to three weeks later, an interviewer picked up the completed questionnaires and filled in an interview schedule designed to measure the accuracy of responses.

The relatively simple formulation "What is your ethnic origin?" was used, with an instruction to check one box only. Reports by census staff on the comments of enumerators and an analysis of householder comments on the questionnaires showed this formulation to be of limited value. The conclusion drawn from these reports was that more specific instructions were required so respondents would have a clearer understanding of what information was required.

In March 1978 a complete census questionnaire was tested. Unlike the earlier test, which was limited to urban centres, this one was drawn at a national level. The questionnaire was mailed out for return by mail. The question used in this test was:

27. To which ethnic or cultural group did you or your ancestors belong on first coming to this continent?

1 ☐ French   Native Peoples
2 ☐ English   11 ☐ Inuit
3 ☐ Irish   12 ☐ Status or registered Indian
4 ☐ Scottish   13 ☐ Non-status Indian
5 ☐ German   14 ☐ Métis
6 ☐ Italian
7 ☐ Ukrainian
8 ☐ Dutch (Netherlands)
9 ☐ Polish
10 ☐ Jewish
     ☐ ....
          Other (specify)

This additional instruction was included in a separate booklet:

27. Ethnic or cultural group refers to the "roots" of the population, and should not be confused with citizenship or nationality. Canadians belong to many ethnic or cultural groups—English, French, Irish, Scottish, Ukrainian, Native Indian, Chinese, Japanese, Lebanese, Dutch, etc.

If applicable in your case, a guide to ethnic origin may be the language which you or your ancestors used on first coming to this continent, e.g., Dutch, Japanese. Note, however, that in cases where a language is used by more than one ethnic group, you should report the specific ethnic group, e.g., Austrian rather than German.

Although "non-response" was higher than anticipated, results of this test were satisfactory from the point of view of data quality. Table 3 shows the percentage distribution of single and multiple responses by language of questionnaires.

TABLE 3
Percentage Response Rates for Ethnic Origin, 1978 Census Test

	Total	Single Responses	Multiple Responses (<3)	Multiple Responses (≥3)	No Response
All Questionnaires	100	82.0	10.8	0.8	6.4
English Questionnaires	100	78.7	14.1	1.1	6.2
French Questionnaires	100	91.4	1.6	0.0	6.9

Tables 4 and 5 show that the incidence of multiple response on French questionnaires is so small that it can be ignored. They suggest that the bulk of the multiple responses on English questionnaires are the result of a conscious effort on the part of the respondent to provide his or her main ethnic origins. Only 1.1 per cent gave more than three origins. As well, it appears that the percentage giving multiple responses increases with person number. This suggests that respondents are reporting multiple ethnic origins for their children if the parents are of different ethnic origins. This is shown by the fact that the multiple response rates (less or

TABLE 4
Distribution of Single and Multiple Responses to the Ethnic Origin Question by Person Number and by Language of the Questionnaire, 1978 Census Test

	Total	Single Responses	Multiple Responses (≤3)	Multiple Responses (>3)	No Response
All questionnaires					
Total	27,489	22,547	2,963	228	1,751
Person					
1	8,898	7,549	771	39	539
2	7,503	6,375	653	26	449
3	5,035	3,896	736	73	330
4	3,507	2,732	494	56	225
5	1,610	1,256	216	21	117
6	638	499	69	12	58
7	154	124	15	1	14
8	80	65	5	—	10
9	33	25	4	—	4
10	17	14	—	—	3
11	12	10	—	—	2
12	2	2	—	—	—

English questionnaires

Total	20,240	15,919	2,846	227	1,248
Person					
1	6,784	5,620	741	39	384
2	5,587	4,626	620	25	316
3	3,616	2,583	707	73	253
4	2,494	1,795	478	56	165
5	1,144	833	210	21	80
6	440	325	67	12	36
7	90	68	14	1	7
8	47	36	5	—	6
9	21	16	4	—	1
10	9	9	—	—	—
11	6	6	—	—	—
12	2	2	—	—	—

French questionnaires

Total	7,249	6,628	117	1	503
Person					
1	2,114	1,929	30	—	155
2	1,916	1,749	33	1	133
3	1,419	1,313	29	—	77
4	1,013	937	16	—	60
5	466	423	6	—	37
6	198	174	2	—	22
7	64	56	1	—	7
8	33	29	—	—	4
9	12	9	—	—	3
10	8	5	—	—	3
11	6	4	—	—	2
12	—	—	—	—	—

equal to three) for one and two persons are relatively similar (10.9 and 11.1 per cent respectively on English questionnaires). The multiple response rates for three, four, five, six and seven persons are also relatively homogeneous but roughly twice as high (19.6, 19.2, 18.4, 15.2, 15.6 per cent). A similar pattern is shown for those who have reported more than three ethnic origins.

These data also offer an explanation for the high incidence of non-matches between the ethnic origins of fathers and children in 1971. The 1971 data-capture procedure retained only one response, even if

TABLE 5
Percentage Distribution of Single and Multiple Responses
to the Ethnic Origin Question by Person Number and by Language
of the Questionnaire, 1978 Census Test

	Total	Single Responses	Multiple Responses (≤ 3)	Multiple Responses (>3)	No Response
All questionnaires					
Total	100.0	82.0	10.8	0.8	6.4
Person					
1	100.0	84.8	8.7	0.4	6.1
2	100.0	85.0	8.7	0.3	6.0
3	100.0	77.4	14.6	1.4	6.6
4	100.0	77.9	14.1	1.6	6.4
5	100.0	78.0	13.4	1.3	7.3
6	100.0	78.2	10.8	1.9	9.1
7	100.0	80.5	9.7	0.6	9.1
8	100.0	81.3	6.3	—	12.5
9	100.0	75.8	12.1	—	12.1
10	100.0	82.4	—	—	17.6
11	100.0	83.3	—	—	16.7
12	100.0	100.0	—	—	—
English questionnaires					
Total	100.0	78.7	14.1	1.1	6.2
Person					
1	100.0	82.8	10.9	0.6	5.7
2	100.0	82.8	11.1	0.4	5.7
3	100.0	71.4	19.6	2.0	7.0
4	100.0	72.0	19.2	2.2	6.6
5	100.0	72.8	18.4	1.8	7.0
6	100.0	73.9	15.2	2.7	8.2
7	100.0	75.6	15.6	1.1	7.8
8	100.0	76.6	10.6	—	12.8
9	100.0	76.2	19.0	—	4.8
10	100.0	100.0	—	—	—
11	100.0	100.0	—	—	—
12	100.0	100.0	—	—	—

French questionnaires

Total		100.0	91.4	1.6	0.0	6.9
Person					
1	100.0	91.2	1.4	—	7.3
2	100.0	91.3	1.7	0.1	6.9
3	100.0	92.5	2.0	—	5.4
4	100.0	92.5	1.6	—	5.9
5	100.0	90.8	1.3	—	7.9
6	100.0	87.9	1.0	—	11.1
7	100.0	87.5	1.6	—	10.9
8	100.0	87.9	—	—	12.1
9	100.0	75.0	—	—	25.0
10	100.0	62.5	—	—	37.5
11	100.0	66.7	—	—	33.3
12	—	—	—	—	—

more responses were provided. If it is assumed that similar patterns of reporting were present in 1971 as in 1978, then the high non-match rate can be viewed as the result of an inadequate data-capture procedure. The following algorithm presents this hypothesis more clearly:

IF: a group of fathers report ethnicity A for themselves;
and IF: for 20 per cent of the total of these fathers' children, ethnicity A and B are reported;
and IF: the reading device assigns 50 per cent of these children to ethnic group A and 50 per cent to ethnic group B;
THEN: (1) 10 per cent of the total children match their fathers' ethnic origin;
THEN: (2) 10 per cent of the children do not match their fathers' ethnic origin.

A manual examination of 2,977 records with multiple responses produced the results shown in Table 6. Unfortunately, the language of the questionnaire was not controlled. It is evident that the vast bulk of multiple responses involved the British ethnic groups alone (37.2 per cent), the British ethnic groups and the French ethnic group (17.6 per cent) and the British and other ethnic groups (15.9 per cent). The high incidence of multiple responses on English questionnaires is due in part to the division of the British ethnic groups into three segments. The bulk of these groups answered English questionnaires; the French ethnic group, which mostly answered French questionnaires, was limited to

TABLE 6
Distribution of Multiple Entries for Specific Ethnic Origins, 1978 Census Test

	Frequency	Percentage
Total	2,977[a]	100.0
British Groups Only	1,107	37.2
English and Irish	247	8.3
English and Scottish	426	14.3
Irish and Scottish	257	8.6
English, Irish, Scottish	177	5.9
British and French	524	17.6
French and English	223	7.5
French and Irish	107	3.6
French and Scottish	70	2.4
French, English, Irish	31	1.0
French, English, Scottish	21	0.7
French, Irish, Scottish	28	0.9
French, English, Irish, Scottish	44	1.5
British and Other	474	15.9
English and German	114	3.8
English and Italian	32	1.1
English and Ukrainian	38	1.3
English and Dutch	32	1.1
Irish and German	68	2.3
Irish and Dutch	21	0.7
Scottish and German	75	2.5
Scottish and Ukrainian	25	0.8
Scottish and Dutch	23	0.8
English, Scottish, German	23	0.8
English, Irish, Scottish, German	23	0.8
French and Other	71	2.4
French and German	49	1.6
French and Italian	22	0.7
Other Multiples	801	26.9

Note: [a]Excludes 228 persons for whom the questionnaires were unobtainable in the course of the examination of documents.

only one segment choice. The absence of multiple responses on French questionnaires is also due in part to the comparatively recent arrival in Quebec of other ethnic groups.

Processing of Ethnic Origin in 1981

The data-capture methodology presently envisaged for 1981 is a manual key entry operation. An operator will key entries from a terminal to a computer file. Using this procedure, it is virtually impossible to instruct the operator to key in only one entry, except by providing a blanket instruction, e.g., to key the first entry encountered. This would have an extremely adverse effect on data quality. Likely, the decision will be to enter all responses as provided by respondents. Multiple responses will be dealt with at a later stage of processing. Although this issue has not yet been resolved, the following arguments have been advanced in favour of retaining all multiple entries:

a. Many Métis or non-status Indians are likely to indicate both Métis and European ancestry. In order to provide an accurate count of Métis and other Native peoples, which is the major purpose of the question, it is necessary to accept multiple entries.

b. The traditional criterion (paternal ancestor) used to select one origin is irrelevant and sexist, with the same weakness applicable to maternal ancestry. Yet, such an alternate criterion as "ethnic self-identification" does not offer a viable solution because considerable ethnic exogamy has been reported in each census. To insist on one origin is increasingly less relevant for many Canadians.

c. The testing programme and discussions within and outside of Statistics Canada show that persons who have more than one origin prefer to report multiple origins, or else they write in "Canadian," thereby defeating the purpose of the question.

d. The retention of multiple responses allows for the identification of at least a part of the population whose socio-economic activities have been influenced by a number of heritages.

e. If multiple responses are retained in 1981, the ethnic origin question would provide very broad groups of multiple responses. Those wishing to examine specific combinations of ethnic origins would be able to do so by special request.

A second aspect of processing, not yet resolved, is the assignment of an ethnic origin or origins when the respondent has not provided an answer. This assignment was made in 1971 by computer and in 1961 by a clerical procedure. Nevertheless, there was a "Not Stated" category in 1961.

A third aspect of processing under review is the coding manual used to assign codes to written entries. The 1971 manual was inadequate in a number of areas, especially in regard to Asian and African origins. Revision of the manual will remove some of these inadequacies.

Comparability 1961–1981

The disruption of historical comparability because of the removal of the paternal ancestor criterion from the 1981 question and the proposed retention of multiple responses appears to be a concern. While this concern is well-founded, a brief examination of past and proposed processing procedures shows that data is not easily comparable, even had the same question been used in all three censuses.

In 1961 data was collected by an enumerator or interviewer. This individual had some training and was not likely to provide multiple responses. For example, the interviewer could use available information, such as the surname, to assist in answering the original question. Similarly, 1961 interviewers did at times assign ethnic origin to children from information obtained about the ethnic origin of the children's father. It has been proposed that in 1981 the respondent provide his or her own information. Evidence suggests that multiple entries will be provided to this question, regardless of instructions to the contrary.

The transfer of data from questionnaires to computer in 1971 was completely different than in 1961. In 1961 a mark-sense reader was used. Documentation of the procedure used if multiple responses were encountered is not available. In 1971 questionnaires were microfilmed and an optical scanning device (FOSDIC) was used to transfer the data to the computer. If more than one entry was encountered, the darkest mask was accepted as the "correct entry" and retained for further processing.

In 1961 non-responses were assigned clerically using available information from other household members or from "assignment charts." Only the largest ethnic groups were shown in the assignment charts. Smaller groups had no chance of being recorded if there was no information available on the questionnaire. In 1971 the assignment of non-responses was done by computer. All ethnic groups had a chance of being selected.

The combined impact of changes from (a) enumeration to self-enumeration, (b) mark-sense cards to FOSDIC and (c) clerical to computer assignment of non-responses have had a great impact on data comparability between censuses, even without changes in concept and wording of the question.

CONCLUSION

The present plan is to retain the historical concept of "roots" for ethnic origin rather than change to some form of "ethnic self-identification." The major change from 1971 is the removal of paternal ancestry as the criterion for selecting one origin if the person has more than one.

The census question has changed over time and thus strict comparability between censuses is impossible. Even though the question was not changed between 1961 and 1971, changes in enumeration and processing techniques make historical comparability problematic. Data from 1971 suggest that the criterion of paternal ancestor was irrelevant in many cases, and its maintenance would simply be the retention of a fictional standard. The limited analysis possible from the March 1978 test suggest that respondents do provide "true" answers to the question proposed for 1981 and that the resulting data is of relatively "good quality."

APPENDIX A
Ethnic or Racial Origin as Defined in Enumerator's Manuals Between 1871 and 1971

1871   COLUMN 13. Origin is to be scrupulously entered, as given by the person questioned; in the manner shown in the specimen schedule, by the words English, Irish, Scotch, African, Indian, German, French and so forth.

1881   COLUMN 13. Origin is to be scrupulously entered, as given by the person questioned; in the manner shown in the specimen schedule by the words English, Irish, Scotch, African, Indian, German, French and so forth.

1891   Racial origin not asked.

1901   53. Among whites the racial or tribal origin is traced through the father, as in English, Scotch, Irish, Welsh, French, German, Italian, Scandinavian, etc. Care must be taken, however, not to apply the terms "American" or "Canadian" in a racial sense, as there are no races of men so called. "Japanese," "Chinese" and "Negro" are proper racial terms; but in the case of Indians the names of their tribes should be given, as "Chippewa," "Cree," etc. Persons of mixed white and red blood—commonly known as "breeds"— will be described by addition of the initial letters "f.b." for French breed, "e.b." for English breed, "s.b." for Scotch breed and "i.b." for Irish breed. For example: "Cree f.b." denotes that the person is racially a mixture of Cree and French; and "Chippewa s.b." denotes that the person is

Chippewa and Scotch. Other mixtures of Indians besides the four above specified are rare, and may be described by the letters "o.b." for other breed. If several races are combined with the red, such as English and Scotch, Irish and French, or any others, they should also be described by the initials "o.b." A person whose father is English, but whose mother is Scotch, Irish, French or any other race, will be ranked as English, and so with any others—the line of descent being traced through the father in the white races.

1911   100. RACIAL OR TRIBAL ORIGIN. The racial or tribal origin, column 14, is usually traced through the father, as in English, Scotch, Irish, Welsh, French, German, Italian, Danish, Swedish, Norwegian, Bohemian, Ruthenian, Bukovinian, Galician, Bulgarian, Chinese, Japanese, Polish, Jewish, etc. A person whose father is English but whose mother is Scotch, Irish, French or other race will be ranked as English, and so with any of the others. In the case of Indians the origin is traced through the mother, and names of their tribes should be given, as "Chippewa," "Cree," etc. The children begotten of marriages between white and black or yellow races will be classed as Negro or Mongolian (Chinese or Japanese), as the case may be.

1921   94. COLUMN 21.—RACIAL OR TRIBAL ORIGIN. The racial or tribal origin is usually traced through the father, as in English, Scotch, Irish, Welsh, French, German, Italian, Danish, Swedish, Norwegian, Bohemian, Ruthenian, Bukovinian, Galician, Bulgarian, Chinese, Japanese, Polish, Jewish, etc. A person whose father is English but whose mother is Scotch, Irish, French or other race will be ranked as English, and so with any of the others. In the case of Indians the origin is traced through the mother, and names of their tribes should be given, as "Chippewa," "Cree," etc. The children begotten of marriages between white and black or yellow races will be classed as Negro or Mongolian (Chinese or Japanese), as the case may be. The words *"Canadian" or "American" must not be used for this purpose, as they express "Nationality" or "Citizenship" but not a "Race or people."*

1931   122. COLUMN 21: RACIAL ORIGIN. The purpose of the information sought in this column is to measure as accurately as possible the racial origins of the population of Canada, i.e., the original sources from which the present population has been derived.

In the case of distinct stocks, involving differences in colour (i.e., the black, red, yellow or brown races) the answer will be Negro, Indian, Japanese, Chinese, Hindu, Malayan, etc., as the case may be.

In the case of persons deriving from European stocks, the proper answer will in many cases be indicated by the country or portion of the country from which the family of the person originally came, for example, English, Scotch, Irish, Welsh, French, but certain stocks may be found in more than one European country. In such cases the country of birth or the country from which they came to Canada may not indicate their racial origin. For example the Ukrainians (Ruthenians) may have immigrated to Canada from Poland, Russia, Austria, Hungary but they should not be classed as Poles, Russians, Austrians, Hungarians, but as Ukrainians. Similarly many immigrants from Russia are of German origin. The enumerator should make specific inquiry and should not assume that the country of birth discloses origin. A German born in France is not French by origin although he may be a citizen of France.

1931   123. ORIGIN IS TO BE TRACED THROUGH THE FATHER. A person whose father is English and whose mother is French will be recorded as of English origin, while a person whose father is French and whose mother is English will be recorded as of French origin, and similarly with other combinations. In the case of the aboriginal Indian population of Canada, the origin is to be traced through the mother, and the names of their tribes should be given as Chippewa, Cree, Blackfoot, etc. The children begotten of marriages between white and black or yellow races will be recorded as Negro, Chinese, Japanese, Indian, etc., as the case may be. The object of this question is to obtain a knowledge of the various constituent elements that have combined from the earliest times to make up the present population of Canada.

1941   100. COLUMN 25—RACIAL ORIGIN.

     1. *What is racial origin?* The word "race" signifies— "descendants of a common ancestor."

         a. It is imperative to understand that a person's racial origin, and nationality very often are different, for instance the Canadian nationality comprises many different racial origins, e.g., English, French, Irish, Scottish, Welsh, Italian, German, etc.

b. The name of a country from which a person came to Canada gives no indication of that person's racial origin, e.g., a person may have come to Canada from Austria, but may be Polish, or German, or Italian, etc. A striking example are the Ukrainains (Ruthenians). They have no Ukrainian (Ruthenian) nationality, but have come to this country from the nations of Poland, Russia, Austria, Hungary, and other nations of Europe through which they are dispersed. No matter what country they come from, their racial origin is "Ukrainian".

c. The word CANADIAN does not denote a racial origin, but a nationality; the same applies to the word AMERI-CAN.

d. It is therefore necessary for the Enumerator to ascertain a person's racial origin separately from his country of birth, or nationality.

2. WHAT DETERMINES RACIAL ORIGIN? As a general rule a person's racial origin is to be traced through his father, e.g., if a person's father is English and his mother French the racial origin shall be entered as English, while a person whose father is French and whose mother is English shall be entered as French, and similarly for other combinations.

a. CANADIAN ABORIGINES. For the Canadian aborigines, the entry will be Indian or Eskimo as the case may be. For a person of White and Indian blood, the entry shall be "Half-Breed".

b. COLOURED STOCKS. For persons belonging to stock involving difference in colour (i.e., the black, yellow, and brown races) the entry shall be Negro, Japanese, Chinese, Hindu, Malayan, etc., respectively, thus indicating the branch within the distinct ethnic stock, to which such persons belong.

c. MIXED BLOOD. The children begotten of marriages between white and black or white and Chinese, etc., shall be entered in the Column as Negro, Chinese, etc., as the case may be.

1951   17. ORIGIN

It is important to distinguish carefully between "citizenship" or "nationality" on the one hand, and "origin" on the other. Origin refers to the cultural group, sometimes erroneously called "racial" group, from which the person is descended;

citizenship (nationality) refers to the country to which the person owes allegiance. Canadian citizens are of many origins—English, Irish, Scottish, Jewish, Ukrainian, etc.

For Census purposes a person's origin is traced through his father. For example, if a person's father is German and his mother Norwegian, the origin will be entered as "German."

You will first attempt to establish a person's origin by asking the language spoken by the person (if he is an immigrant), or by his paternal ancestor *when he first came to this continent*. For example, if the person replies that his paternal ancestor spoke French when he came to this continent, you will record the origin as "French". However, if the respondent should reply "English" or "Gaelic" to this question, you must make further inquiries to determine whether the origin is English, Irish, Scottish, or Welsh.

If the respondent does not understand your first question, or you cannot establish the person's origin from the answer you receive, you will ask "Is your origin in the male line English, Scottish, Ukrainian, Jewish, Norwegian, North American Indian, Negro, etc.?"

Ordinarily, persons born and bred in Canada or the United States will report some European origin, such as English, French, or Spanish. However, if a person *insists* that his origin is Canadian or American, you are to accept that answer and write it in the space provided.

Do not confuse Question 12 (Language first spoken in childhood) with this question. Above all, do not assume that the answer given to Question 12 establishes the answer to the question on origin.

For persons of mixed white and Indian parentage, the origin recorded will be as follows:

a. For those living on Indian reserves, the origin will be recorded as "Native Indian."

b. For those not on reserves the origin will be determined through the line of the father, that is, by following the usual procedure.

If a person states that, because of mixed ancestry, he really does not know what to reply to the question on origin, you will mark the oval "Unknown."

10. To what ethnic or cultural group did you or your ancestor (on the male side) belong on coming to this continent?

Austrian	Belgian	Czech	Danish	English	Estonian	Finnish	Native Indian
French	German	Greek	Hungarian	Icelandic	Irish	Italian	Band member
Jewish	Lithuanian	Negro	Netherlands	Norwegian	Polish	Roumanian	Non-Band
Russian	Scottish	Slovak	Swedish	Ukrainian	Welsh	Yugoslavic	

If not listed, write here:

Mark ONE SPACE only.

It is important to distinguish carefully between "citizenship" or "nationality" on the one hand and "ethnic" or "cultural" group on the other. "Ethnic" or "cultural" group refers to the group from which the person is descended; citizenship (nationality) refers to the country to which the person owes allegiance. Canadian citizens belong to many ethnic or cultural groups—English, French, Irish, Jewish, Scottish, Ukrainian, etc.

For Census purposes a person's ethnic or cultural group is traced through his father. For example, if a person's father is German and his mother Norwegian, the entry will be "German."

If the respondent does not understand the question as worded on the questionnaire, you will ask the language spoken by him on arrival if he is an immigrant, or by his ancestor on the male side on first coming to this continent. For example, if the person replies that his ancestor on the male side spoke French when he came to this continent, you will record "French."

However, if the respondent should reply "English" or "Gaelic" to this question, you must make further inquiries to determine whether the person is English, Irish, Scottish or Welsh.

If the respondent does not understand the question as worded on the questionnaire or you cannot establish the ethnic or cultural group through the language of the ancestors, you will ask "Is your ethnic or cultural group on the male side English, French, Jewish, Negro, North American Indian, Norwegian, Scottish, Ukrainian, etc.?"

PROCEDURE FOR PERSONS REPORTING BRITISH ISLES:

If a person reports "British Isles" but does not know if he is English, Irish, Scottish, or Welsh, enter "British Isles" in the write-in space.

PROCEDURE FOR PERSONS REPORTING NATIVE INDIAN:

1. If a person reports "Native Indian" ask an additional question: "Is your name on any Indian Band membership list in Canada?" If the answer is "Yes," mark the space for "Band member." If "No" mark "Non-band."

Note that "Treaty Indians" should be marked "Band member."

2. If the person is of mixed white and Indian parentage:
   a. Consider those living on Indian reserves as "Indian" and determine Band status as outlined above.
   b. For those not on reserves, determine the ethnic or cultural group through the line of the father.

PROCEDURE FOR PERSONS REPORTING "CANADIAN," "U.S.A." or "UNKNOWN":

Since this question refers to the time when the person or his ancestors came to this continent, the answer should refer to the ethnic groups or cultures of the old world. However, if, in spite of this explanation, the person insists that his ethnic or cultural group is "Canadian" or "U.S.A.," enter his reply in the write-in space.

If the person states that he really does not know what to reply to this question, enter "Unknown."

1971   QUESTION 15—ETHNIC OR CULTURAL GROUP
From Questionnaire

15. To what ethnic or cultural group did you or your ancestor (on the male side) belong on coming to this continent?

English	Native Indian	Polish
French	—Band	Scottish

German	Native Indian	Ukrainian
Irish	—Non-band	
Italian	Netherlands	
Jewish	Norwegian	_____

Other, write here

From Instruction Booklet

15. Ethnic or cultural group refers to descent (through the father's side) and should not be confused with citizenship. Canadians belong to many ethnic or cultural groups—English, French, Irish, Scottish, German, Ukrainian, Jewish, Native Indian, Negro, Chinese, Lebanese, etc.

Use as guide if applicable in your case:
1. The language you spoke on first coming to this continent, if you were born outside of Canada.
2. If born in Canada, the language spoken by your ancestor on the male side when he came here.

From Content Manual

Additional Information
1. It is important to distinguish carefully between "citizenship" or "nationality" on the one hand, and "ethnic" or "cultural" groups, on the other. "Ethnic" or "cultural" group refers to the group from which the person is descended; citizenship (nationality) refers to the country to which the person owes allegiance.
2. For census purposes, a person's ethnic or cultural group is traced through his father. For example, if a person's father is German and his mother Norwegian, the entry will be "German."
3. If the ethnic origin of an adopted child is not known, ethnic origin of the adoptive father may be reported.
4. Procedure for persons reporting British or British Isles: If a person is of "British Isles" but does not know if he is English, Irish, Scottish, or Welsh, he should enter "British Isles" in the "Other" space.
5. Procedure for persons reporting "Canadian," "U.S.A." or "Unknown":
Since this question refers to the time when the person or

his ancestors came to this continent, the answer should refer to the ethnic groups or cultures of the Old World except for Native Indians and Eskimos. However, if, in spite of this explanation, the person insists that his ethnic or cultural group is "Canadian" or "U.S.A.," he should mark the circle for "Other" and write "Canadian" or "U.S.A." in the space provided. If the person states that he really does not know what to reply to this question, he should write in "Unknown" in the space provided for "Other."

Why We Ask This Question

(i) The main purpose of this question is to provide an indication of the cultural or ethnic composition of Canada's people, for example, those of British Isles descent, those of French descent, and those whose forebearers came from the many other cultural groups.

(ii) Statistics from this question are used extensively by many groups of people, such as sociologists (for studies of living standards or degrees of cultural intermingling), government officials (for studies related to the Indian or Eskimo population), embassy officials (for information related to ethnic groups associated with their particular country), politicians (for factual data on the ethnic composition of their ridings), advertisers and market researchers (for the promotion of certain types of products), and ethnic societies (for statistical data related to their particular ethnic group).

(iii) Although a number of ethnic or cultural groups can be identified by the question on language, the one-to-one relationship is only partial, since many new immigrants soon acquire English or French as their working language. Furthermore, certain important groups, such as Negroes, Jews, Irish and Scottish cannot be identified on the basis of language, hence the need for data on ethnic or cultural groups.

NOTES

1. *Census of Canada 1870-71*, 5 vols. (Ottawa: 1873), 1:xxii.
2. Ibid., xxiv.
3. *Census of Canada 1890-91*, 4 vols. (Ottawa: Queen's Printer, 1893), 1:xviii.

4. Dominion Bureau of Statistics, *Origin, Birthplace, Nationality and Language of the Canadian People (A Census Study Based On the Census of 1921 and Supplementary Data)* (Ottawa: King's Printer, 1929).
5. Ibid., 12.
6. Ibid., 13.
7. Ibid., 12-14.
8. Ibid., 14.
9. Ibid.
10. Burton W. Hurd, *Ethnic Origin and Nativity of the Canadian People*, 1941 Census Monograph, Dominion Bureau of Statistics (restricted) (Ottawa: Queen's Printer, n.d.).
11. Ibid., 31.
12. Dominion Bureau of Statistics, *Ninth Census of Canada 1951*, 11 vols. (Ottawa: Queen's Printer, 1956), 10:132-3.
13. Ibid., 133.
14. Norman B. Ryder, *The Racial Origin Classification in Canadian Statistics*, Dominion Bureau of Statistics, Reprint No. 282 (Ottawa: Queen's Printer, n.d.), 3; Hurd, 29.
15. John Kralt, *Ethnic Origins of Canadians*, 1971 Census of Canada, Profile Studies (Ottawa: Queen's Printer, 1977), 23.
16. Will Herberg, *Protestant-Catholic-Jew: An Essay on American Religious Sociology* (New York: Doubleday and Co., Anchor Books, 1955), 14.
17. Joseph Bensman and Bernard Rosenberg, *Mass, Class, and Bureaucracy: The Evolution of Contemporary Society* (Englewood Cliffs, N.J.: Prentice-Hall, 1963), 171.
18. Gordon A. Craig, *Europe Since 1815* (New York: Holt, Rinehart and Winston Inc., 1961), 397-404.
19. Ibid., 528.

PART II
Economic Status

TRENDS IN THE SOCIO-ECONOMIC STATUS OF UKRAINIANS IN CANADA, 1921-1971

Oleh Wolowyna

This paper traces the evolution of the socio-economic characteristics of Ukrainians in Canada from the early 1900s to 1971. It is purely descriptive and is intended as a base for more analytical studies in the future. It is based on statistics presented in the "Statistical Compendium on the Ukrainians in Canada, 1891-1976,"[1] and a few analyses using 1971 Census Public Use Sample Tapes. Given the broad scope of this paper, only selected indicators of socio-economic trends have been selected for presentation.

The main objective is to estimate time trends in education, income and occupation for Ukrainians in Canada and to compare them to respective trends for the total Canadian population. Time series will be presented for the period 1921-1971, though in some instances, the series will be shorter or will have gaps through lack of data. The presentation of time series is followed by a more detailed analysis for 1971 using Public Use Sample Tapes.

There are serious problems with data quality and comparability from one census to another. Problems with the ethnicity and racial origin question in the Canadian census have been adequately discussed by Ryder.[2] Definition changes from one census to another, as well as changes in self-identification among large sectors of Ukrainians in Canada, have produced important shifts in population size from one census to the next. For example, the increase among Ukrainians between 1921 and 1931 was 11 per cent, from 106,721 to 225,113. During the same decade the number of Austrians decreased from 107,671 to 48,635. It is clear that many Ukrainians from areas belonging to the Austro-Hungarian Empire changed their ethnic self-identification between 1921 and 1931.[3] The impact on socio-economic trends among Ukrainians in Canada of these and other shifts is difficult to evaluate.

Definitions of schooling, labour force, income, etc. have undergone important changes in Canadian censuses. Details of these changes and their implications are discussed in the Compendium and numerous Statistics Canada (or Dominion Bureau of Statistics) publications. Here only major problems about specific tables shall be discussed. Because of comparability problems, compromises and assumptions have had to be made in order to generate time series. In some instances, these have affected our estimates. In those cases we have opted for presenting differences only between Ukrainians and all origins. This decision is based on the assumption that, although some of the absolute figures may be inaccurate, the biases on trends of differences will be tolerable.

In some instances, similar cross-tabulations were not available for all census years. Important factors such as sex, nativity, rural and urban residence could not be controlled, resulting in gaps in time series. The results should be viewed with all these qualifications in mind, though, in spite of these problems, the trends presented are in all likelihood correct, even if some of the absolute figures may be in error.

TRENDS IN SOCIO-ECONOMIC INDICATORS

Status of Entry

The low socio-economic status of Ukrainian immigrants to Canada before the Second World War is a well-known fact. The few statistics presented here will illustrate the situation in more detail and provide a base of comparison for trends to be presented below. Among Ukrainian immigrants arriving before 1911, 79 per cent were agricultural workers at the time of their arrival, while among immigrants of all origins only 35 per cent were engaged in agriculture. Only 12 per cent of these Ukrainians were blue collar workers, while the percentage for immigrants of all origins was 33. The occupational distribution among successive waves of Ukrainian immigrants underwent significant changes. Agricultural occupations among Ukrainian immigrants arriving between 1926 and 1936 dropped to about 60 per cent, while the percentage in blue collar occupations increased to 25, thereby approaching the 37 per cent among immigrants of all origins.

The educational level of Ukrainians in 1921 and 1931 is illustrated in Table 1. About 30 per cent of Ukrainians were illiterate in 1921, compared to 5 per cent of all Canadians. Similar percentages in Ontario and the Prairie provinces, while in Quebec only 1½ Ukrainians were illiterate.[4] The rapid educational upgrading ians in Canada can be seen by comparing 1921 and 1931 cens and foreign-born and Canadian-born Ukrainians within each census. In 1921 about 40 per cent of foreign-born Ukrainians were illiterate, while the percentage for Canadian-born Ukrainians was only 7.6. In Ontario Canadian-born Ukrainians had proportionately slightly fewer illiterates than all Canadians. In Quebec the percentage of illiterate Ukrainians was much lower than in other provinces; among Canadian-born Ukrainians the percentage of illiterates was much lower than among all residents of Quebec. Comparing 1921 and 1931 figures, we observe a substantial decrease in illiteracy among foreign-born Ukrainians and a very strong decrease among Canadian-born Ukrainians.[5]

Male-female comparisons indicate that Ukrainian females were educationally disadvantaged. For both census years, Ukrainian females had a substantially higher rate of illiteracy than males, while overall Canadian females had a lower per cent of illiterates than males in most cases.

In summary, early Ukrainian immigrants were preponderately in agricultural occupations and had a very high level of illiteracy. In successive immigrant waves, the percentage in agricultural occupations decreased, while the proportions in blue collar and other occupations increased. Children of Ukrainian immigrants showed a drastic decrease in illiteracy; in the case of Quebec, their position was more favourable than that of the total population. Ukrainian females had consistently higher levels of illiteracy than Ukrainian males.

Education

Two indicators are used to measure time trends in levels of education —the per cent illiterate and the mean number of years of schooling attained. The per cent illiterate is the only more or less consistent indicator available for all census years. There are some problems with changes in the definition of illiteracy and with the base population, which changed in 1941 from ten years of age and over to five years of age and over. By presenting differences between the percentage illiterate among all Canadians and Ukrainians, these problems are minimized. Table 2 presents data from 1921 to 1961. The general trend among Ukrainians is one of convergence toward the level of illiteracy in the total population of Canada. By 1961 foreign-born Ukrainians still had higher levels of illiteracy than all Canadians, while Canadian-born Ukrainians had about equal, if not lower levels of illiteracy.

TABLE 1

Percentage Illiterate for Population 10 Years of Age and Over, by Ethnic Origin, Sex and Nativity, for Canada and Selected Regions, 1921 and 1931

	Canada				Prairie Provinces			
	1921		1931		1921		1931	
	Ukrainians	All Origins	Ukrainians	All Origins	Ukrainians	All Origins	Ukrainians	All Origins
Total Population	30.4	5.0	13.9	3.7	30.8	6.1	14.5	4.0
Male	24.5	5.6	10.9	4.3	24.7	5.3	11.2	3.6
Female	38.1	4.3	17.8	3.2	38.4	7.0	18.6	4.5
Canadian-born	7.6	4.7	1.8	3.5	7.8	4.3	1.9	2.5
Male	6.6	5.6	1.4	4.3	6.7	4.0	1.5	2.5
Female	8.8	3.7	2.2	2.6	8.9	4.6	2.3	2.6
Foreign-born	39.5	5.9	23.7	4.4	41.0	7.6	26.0	5.8
Male	30.8	5.8	17.3	4.2	31.9	6.4	18.9	4.8
Female	51.6	6.0	33.5	4.7	53.2	9.5	36.2	7.2

	Ontario				Quebec			
	1921		1931		1921		1931	
	Ukrainians	All Origins	Ukrainians	All Origins	Ukrainians	All Origins	Ukrainians	All Origins
Total Population	29.7	3.0	10.4	2.3	15.5	6.2	12.3	4.8
Male	25.7	3.6	9.1	2.7	11.8	7.9	10.7	6.2
Female	37.6	2.3	12.4	1.9	21.1	4.5	15.3	3.3
Canadian-born	2.4	2.5	1.0	1.9	3.7	6.4	2.2	4.9
Male	1.6	3.2	1.0	2.4	0.0	8.2	2.4	6.5
Female	3.2	1.9	1.0	1.4	6.9	4.5	2.1	3.2
Foreign-born	31.9	4.1	14.3	3.2	16.5	4.9	15.3	3.8
Male	27.1	4.4	11.6	3.4	12.5	4.7	12.6	3.7
Female	41.7	3.7	19.5	0.3	22.6	5.1	21.4	3.9

Source: W. Darcovich and P. Yuzyk, eds., "Statistical Compendium on the Ukrainians in Canada, 1891–1976," (Unpublished typescript, Ottawa, 1977), Series 32.1–12, 273–6. Hereafter Darcovich and Yuzyk, "Statistical Compendium."

TABLE 2
Illiteracy Differentials for Population 10 (or 5) Years of Age and Over,
Between All Origins and Ukrainian Origin Populations by Nativity,
for Canada and Selected Regions, 1921 to 1961

	1921	1931	1941	1951	1961
Canada					
Total population	-25.4^a	−10.2	−8.8	−6.9	− 2.8
Canadian-born	− 2.9	+ 1.7	—	—	− 0.1
Foreign-born	−33.5	−19.3	—	—	−10.8
Prairie Provinces					
Total population	−24.7	−10.5	−8.4	−7.7	− 3.1
Canadian-born	− 3.5	+ 6.0	—	—	+ 0.4
Foreign-born	−33.4	−20.2	—	—	−16.4
Ontario					
Total population	−26.7	− 8.1	−6.7	−5.0	− 1.4
Canadian-born	+ 0.1	+ 0.9	—	—	− 0.1
Foreign-born	−27.8	−11.1	—	—	− 3.5
Quebec					
Total population	− 9.3	− 7.5	−5.5	−1.0	− 0.9
Canadian-born	+ 2.7	+ 2.7	—	—	− 1.3
Foreign-born	−11.6	−11.5	—	—	− 3.3
British Columbia					
Total population	− 5.6	− 3.3	−3.7	−3.1	− 1.7
Canadian-born	+ 5.3	+ 3.1	—	—	− 0.2
Foreign-born	− 7.3	− 7.0	—	—	− 7.9

Source: Darcovich and Yuzyk, "Statistical Compendium," Series 32.1–12, 273–6; 32.107–120, 290–2; 32.93–106, 286–9; 32.160–173, 304–8; and 32.121–136, 293–6.
Note: ^{a} An illiteracy differential is percentage illiterate for total population minus percentage illiterate for ethnic Ukrainians.
For 1921 and 1931, population 10 years of age and over.
For 1941 and 1961, population 5 years of age and over.

Mean number of years of schooling attained for the years 1941 to 1971 are presented in Table 3. Differences between all origins and Ukrainian populations are presented in order to minimize possible biases due to comparability problems from one census to another. While starting with a difference of 2.3 years in 1941, Ukrainians had lowered the difference to 0.8 years by 1971. This difference is slightly lower in Ontario but higher in the Prairie provinces.

58

TABLE 3
Difference Between Mean Years of Schooling Attained,
Between All Origins and Ukrainian Origin Populations by Sex,
for Canada and Selected Regions, 1941 to 1971

	1941	1951	1961	1971
Canada				
Total population	2.3^a	2.2	1.0	0.8
Males	2.2	2.1	0.9	0.7
Females	2.3	2.7	1.1	0.9
Ontario				
Total population	2.3	2.1	0.9	0.7
Males	2.8	2.1	0.8	0.7
Females	2.2	2.1	1.0	0.9
Prairie Provinces				
Total population	2.0	2.7	1.0	1.2
Males	2.0	3.0	0.8	1.0
Females	2.0	2.5	1.2	1.3

Source: Darcovich and Yuzyk, "Statistical Compendium," Series 32.107–120, 290–2;
32.93–106, 286–9; 32.137–152, 297–300; and 32.121–136, 293–9.
Note: ^{a}Mean number of years of schooling for total Canadian population minus the
mean number of years of schooling for ethnic Ukrainians.

The evolution of male-female educational differences is also significant. Table 4 presents data for the percentage illiterate by sex. Although
Ukrainian females show a converging trend similar to Ukrainian males,
in 1961 Ukrainian males (Canada and selected regions) were relatively
better off than Ukrainian females in comparison to the total Canadian
population. This is confirmed in Table 3. In 1971 Ukrainian females,
in relation to the respective means for all Canadians, had a lower mean
number of years of schooling than Ukrainian males.

Starting from a very low educational level, Ukrainians have almost
achieved parity with the total Canadian population. Their slight
disadvantage is due to the foreign-born component among them. The
lower educational level of Ukrainian females has also disappeared
among Canadian-born Ukrainains. As will be shown later, the male-
female educational differential is practically non-existent among Canadian-born Ukrainians.

Income
Census data on income for Ukrainians is available only since 1951 in
the Compendium. Because there are serious comparability problems for

TABLE 4

Illiteracy Differentials for Population 10 (or 5) Years of Age and Over,
Between All Origins and Ukrainian Origin Populations by Sex,
for Canada and Selected Regions, 1921 to 1961

Year	1921	1931	1941	1951	1961
Canada					
Total population	-25.4^a	-10.2	-8.8	-6.9	-2.8
Males	-18.9	-6.6	-7.0	-4.9	-1.7
Females	-33.8	-14.6	-11.2	-9.2	-4.0
Prairie Provinces					
Total population	-24.7	-10.5	-8.4	-7.7	-3.1
Males	-19.4	-7.6	-6.7	-5.9	-2.1
Females	-31.4	-14.1	-10.3	-9.8	-4.3
Ontario					
Total population	-26.7	-8.1	-6.7	-5.0	-1.4
Males	-22.1	-6.4	-5.7	-3.8	-0.7
Females	-35.3	-10.4	-8.0	-6.5	-2.0
Quebec					
Total population	-9.3	-7.5	-5.5	-1.0	-0.9
Males	-3.9	-4.5	-3.0	$+0.3$	0.0
Females	-16.6	-12.0	-8.7	-3.6	-2.1
British Columbia					
Total population	-5.6	-3.3	-3.7	-3.1	-1.7
Males	-3.2	-1.6	-2.9	-2.5	-1.2
Females	-10.9	-6.2	-4.6	-3.3	-1.2

Source: Darcovich and Yuzyk, "Statistical Compendium," Series 32.1–12, 273–6;
32.107–120, 290–2; 32.93–106, 286–9; 32.137–152, 297–300; and 32.121–136,
293–6.
Notes: ^{a}An illiteracy differential is percentage illiterate for total population minus percentage illiterate for ethnic Ukrainians.
For 1921 and 1931, population 10 years of age and over.
For 1941 and 1961, population 5 years of age and over.

the years 1951, 1961 and 1971, we have not presented time series for
income. The evidence seems to indicate that, although the income
differential between Ukrainians and all Canadians seems to be decreasing, Ukrainians still had a lower income in 1971. This will be qualified
below.

Some detail on income for 1961 is presented in Table 5. It should be
noted that this is income for non-farm individuals. Given the higher
percentage of Ukrainians in farm occupations and the lower income
associated with these occupations, the overall income status of Ukrainians was probably worse than that indicated in Table 5.

60

TABLE 5

Distribution of Income of Non-Farm Individuals, 15 Years of Age and Over, of All and Ukrainian Ethnic Origins, by Sex, Canada, for the Year Ended 31 May 1961

	Mean Income[a]	With No Income	Percentage in Income Category					Total Persons
			Under $1,000	$1,000–2,999	$3,000–4,999	$5,000–9,999	$10,000–and Over	
Canada								
Ukrainian Origin	2,910	26.1	18.4	22.1	23.1	9.2	1.1	242,553
All Origins	3,131	27.6	18.9	21.5	19.5	10.6	1.9	10,101,172
Males								
Ukrainian Origin	3,697	7.2	13.5	21.4	38.7	17.2	2.0	123,544
All Origins	3,999	7.4	13.2	23.3	32.3	20.1	3.6	4,977,296
Females								
Ukrainian Origin	1,599	45.7	24.5	19.7	7.0	1.4	0.2	119,009
All Origins	1,651	45.7	23.4	22.9	7.0	0.9	0.1	5,123,876

Source: Darcovich and Yuzyk, "Statistical Compendium," Series 42.7–18, 452.
Note: [a]For persons with income.

If one considers only persons with income, the mean income of Ukrainians was below the national average and the differences for females was much smaller than for males. The percentage of Ukrainians with no income was somewhat lower than for all Canadians, reflecting a higher labour participation rate. The lower mean income for Ukrainians is due to smaller proportions of the population with yearly incomes over five thousand dollars. The distributions of differences between all Canadians and Ukrainians have a very similar pattern for males and females. A more detailed income analysis for 1971 will be presented later.

Occupation

Due to the growth and diversification of the economy, the classification of occupations has experienced major changes in the various censuses. In order to mitigate intercensal differences, Zenon Yankovsky collapsed occupations into major groupings in the Compendium.[6] This classification and a similar collapsing for industries is used here.

Figure 1 presents the evolution of the occupational structure of Ukrainians between 1921 and 1971. The most dramatic change occurred in primary industries (farming, fishing, forestry and mining) with a drop from 70 per cent in 1921 to 13 per cent in 1971. All other occupational groupings grew at the expense of the primary industry sector. The category of "all other occupations," which includes transportation, communications, construction, manufacturing and unspecified, grew from 21.5 per cent in 1921 to 38.1 per cent in 1971. Service occupations increased from 3.8 to 12.5 per cent; sales from 2.7 to 9.2 per cent; clerical from 0.5 per cent to 13.1 per cent; professional and technical from 1.0 to 10.4 per cent; owners and managers from 0.5 to 3.6 per cent. The last three decades witnessed a strong reduction in the primary industry sector and a rapid expansion of ownership, managerial, professional, technical and clerical occupations.

A comparison between the occupational structure of Ukrainians and the total Canadian population for 1921 and 1971 is presented in Table 6. In 1921 the proportion of farmers among Ukrainians was about twice the proportion among all Canadians. For all the other occupational groupings the proportion among Ukrainians was smaller than the proportion for all other origins. In 1971 the situation was quite different. Farmers were still overrepresented among Ukrainians, but the distribution for all the other occupational groupings was similar to the one for all Canadians. The index of dissimilarity provides a summary measure for the comparisons in 1921 and 1971. The index of dissimilarity between the Ukrainian and Canadian occupational structure in 1921

FIGURE 1

Percentage Distribution of Major Occupational Groupings, for Ukrainian Origin, Both Sexes, Canada, 1921 to 1971

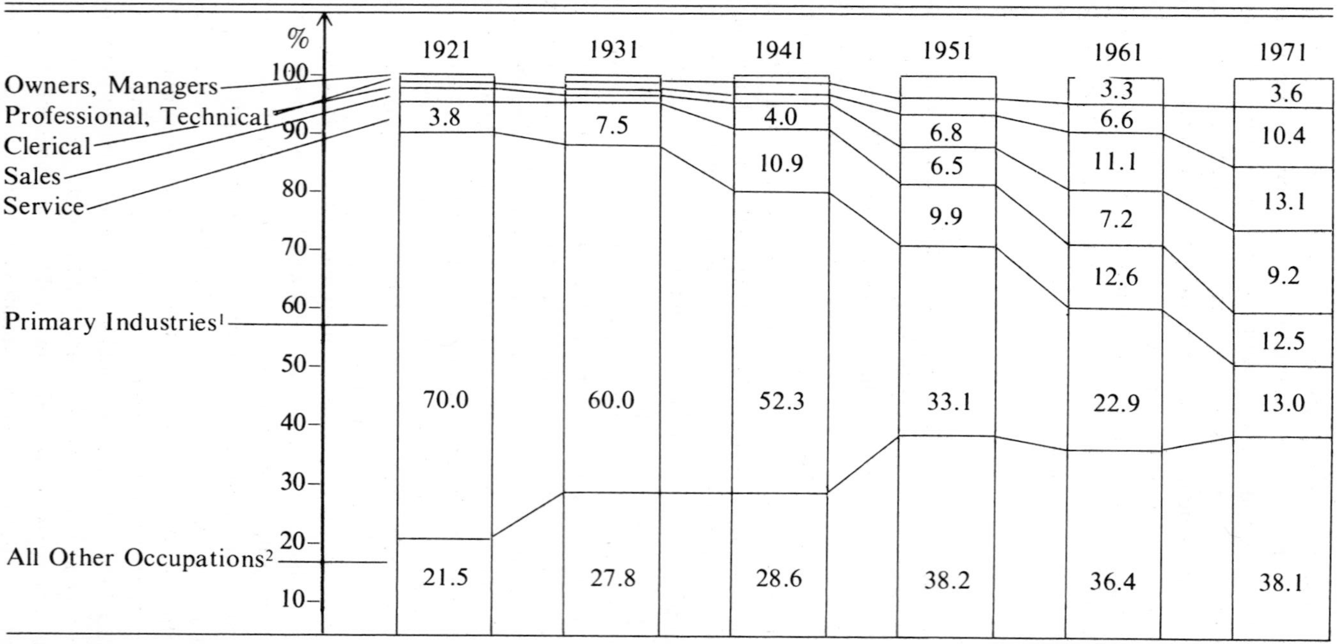

Source: Darcovich and Yuzyk, "Statistical Compendium," Series 40.31–42, 379.
Notes: [1]Includes Farming, Fishing, Forestry and Mining.
[2]Includes Transportation, Communications, Construction, Manufacturing and Unspecified.

was 33.6 per cent. This means that in order for the Ukrainians to have a similar occupational structure as all Canadians, 33.6 per cent of their labour force would have to be redistributed into other categories. As shown in the column of differences, 33.6 per cent of Ukrainian farmers would have to be redistributed to make up for the deficit in the other occupational categories.

TABLE 6

Percentage Distribution of Major Occupational Groupings, by Ethnic Origin, Both Sexes, Canada, 1921 and 1971

| Occupations | 1921 | | | 1971 | | |
	All Origins (1)	Ukrainian Origin (2)	(1)–(2)	All Origins (3)	Ukrainian Origin (4)	(3)–(4)
Owners, Managers	3.5	0.5	3.0	4.7	3.6	1.1
Professional, Technical	5.4	1.0	4.4	12.6	10.4	2.2
Clerical	8.2	0.5	7.7	14.1	13.1	1.0
Sales	9.6	2.7	6.9	10.4	9.2	1.2
Service	7.3	3.8	3.5	11.1	12.5	–1.4
Primary Industries[a]	36.4	70.0	–33.6	7.7	13.0	–5.3
All Other Occupations[b]	29.6	21.5	8.1	39.4	38.1	1.3
Total	100.0	100.0		100.0	100.0	
All Occupations (N)	3,173,169	31,745		8,626,925	265,720	

Source: Darcovich and Yuzyk, "Statistical Compendium," Series 40.31–42, 379.
Notes: [a]Includes Farming, Fishing, Forestry and Mining.
[b]Includes Transportation, Communication, Construction, Manufacturing and Unspecified.

Index of Dissimilarity:	1921	1971
	33.6%	6.7%

In 1971 the index of dissimilarity was only 6.7 per cent, indicating the need to redistribute 6.7 per cent of the Ukrainian labour force in order to achieve a similar occupational distribution to the one for all Canadians. The major excess is still in the primary industries group, followed by the

TABLE 7

Percentage Labour Force by Selected Industries and Ethnic Origin, Canada, 1931 to 1971

Occupations	1931		1941		1951		1961		1971	
	Ukrainian Origin	All Origins	Ukrainian Origin	All Origins	Ukrainian Origin	All Origins	Ukrainian Origin	All Origins	Ukrainian Origin	All Origins
Trade (Retail and Wholesale)	2.8	9.9	5.3	11.1	10.0	13.4	13.7	15.3	14.5	14.7
Finance, Insurance, Real Estate	0.2	2.4	0.3	2.1	1.2	2.7	2.5	3.5	3.4	4.2
Public Administration	0.8	2.5	0.8	2.7	2.5	5.2	5.1	7.5	6.1	7.4
All Industries (N)	77,257	3,927,230	113,921	4,195,951	164,893	5,286,153	191,680	6,471,850	263,720	8,626,925

Source: Darcovich and Yuzyk, "Statistical Compendium," Series 40.213–227, 406.

TABLE 8
Selected Professional Occupations by Ethnic Origin, Canada, 1931 to 1971

Occupations[a]	1931		1941		1951		1961		1971	
	Ukrainian Origin	All Origins	Ukrainian Origin	All Origins	Ukrainian Origin	All Origins	Ukrainian Origin	All Origins	Ukrainian Origin	All Origins
Physicians, Dentists and Veterinarians	18	15,105	74	15,513	213	20,138	517	28,283	905	36,725
Engineers and Architects	11	17,116	78	19,749	349	28,776	922	46,006	2,060	80,920
Judges, Magistrates, Lawyers and Notaries	17	8,602	38	8,398	71	9,635	208	12,922	380	17,575

Source: Darcovich and Yuzyk, "Statistical Compendium," Series 40.161–172, 394–6.
Note: [a]See note 14 at the end of the paper.

service occupation category. All the other groupings among Ukrainians have small deficits compared to the total Canadian population. The highest deficit is in the professional and technical category.

In order to obtain a better insight into the dynamics of change for higher level occupations, time series for selected occupations and industries are presented in Table 7. Proportions in trade, finance and public administration among Ukrainian and all origins populations are shown for the years 1931 to 1971. In all three industries in 1931, Ukrainians had a much smaller proportion than the total Canadian population, but by 1971 they had caught up in trade, and were slightly behind in finance and public administration.

Total numbers of health, legal and engineering professionals are presented in Table 8. From only 18 in 1931, the number of Ukrainian physicians and dentists grew to 905 in 1971. The number of Ukrainian health professionals quadrupled between 1931 and 1941, tripled between 1941 and 1951 and doubled in the last two decades, while the average growth for all Canadian health professionals was only about 30 per cent per decade. Similar increases among Ukrainians can be observed in the legal professions, while the increase among engineers has been even more spectacular.

In conclusion, between 1931 and 1971 Ukrainians in Canada underwent a drastic change in their occupational structure. The proportion in primary industries decreased from 70 per cent in 1921 to 13 per cent in 1971. This was still above the national proportion, but the distribution in the other occupational groupings in 1971 was similar to the one for all Canadians. Ukrainians have also experienced a steady growth in selected industries such as trade, finance and public administration, reaching proportions close to the national level in 1971. The growth in the medical, engineering and legal professions has been truly spectacular. The average rate of growth for engineers has been close to 200 per cent per decade, 135 per cent for medical and 110 per cent for legal professions.

SOCIO-ECONOMIC STATUS OF UKRAINIANS IN 1971

The above analysis has relied entirely on statistics from the Compendium. The 1971 Census Public Use Sample Tapes allow one to do a more extensive analysis. Although some of the results presented below are available in 1971 census publications, all reported results are based on the Sample Tapes. The One In a Hundred (1/100) Individual Province File Tape was used to produce tabulations for Ukrainians, and the One In a Thousand (1/1000) Individual Province File 1 produce tabulations for all Canadians.[7]

There may be some discrepancies with published results, since we are dealing with a 1 per cent sample for Ukrainians and a 1 in 2,000 sample for all Canadians.[8] Thus when making comparisons one should not put too much emphasis on small differences. The other source of possible discrepancies is that Prince Edward Island, the Yukon and the Northwest Territories were excluded from the Public Use Sample Tapes.[9] This has virtually no effect on the data for Ukrainians, as the number residing there is insignificant. The figures for all Canadians may be affected, but the bias is likely to be small since the populations of Prince Edward Island, the Yukon and the Northwest Territories are proportionately very small in comparison to the rest of Canada.

Education

A detailed analysis of the educational status of Ukrainians in 1971 is presented in Tables 9 and 10. In terms of mean number of years of schooling, Ukrainians are 0.7 years below the national average. A difference of similar magnitude is found for males and females. As noted above, the lower level of education among Ukrainians is due to the very low education level of the foreign-born, 6.2 years compared to 9.6 years for all foreign-born. Canadian-born Ukrainians, on the other hand, have a slightly higher mean than all Canadians. Ukrainians living in rural areas are educationally more disadvantaged than Ukrainians living in urban areas.

The low mean for Ukrainians is due to a somewhat lower proportion with post-high school education and a very high percentage with less than five years of schooling. Again these differences can be attributed entirely to foreign-born Ukrainians. Forty per cent of them have less than five years of schooling and only 7 per cent have some university, while the respective percentages for all Canadians are 9 and 13. Canadian-born Ukrainians, on the other hand, have proportionately more persons with completed high school and slightly more persons with some university.

The lower educational level of Ukrainian females compared to Ukrainian males is mainly due to differences at the university level—7 per cent for females and 12 per cent for males. But this difference disappears among Canadian-born Ukrainians. By 1971, Canadian-born Ukrainian females have achieved educational parity with Canadian-born Ukrainian males and all Canadian females.

Regional distribution of years of schooling is presented in Table 10.[10] For all regions except Quebec, Ukrainians have a lower mean education

TABLE 9

Distribution of Years of Schooling for Persons 15 Years and Over, Not Attending School Full-Time, for All and Ukrainian Ethnic Origin by Sex, Place of Residence and Nationality, Canada, 1971

	Mean Years of Schooling	Percentage in Years of Schooling							Total Persons[b]
		<5	5–8	9–11	12[a]	13–16	17+	
Canada									
All Origins	9.5	6.7	29.9	34.0	19.4	7.5	2.5	6,536
Ukrainians	8.8	15.2	27.4	30.7	17.6	7.1	2.0	3,915
Males									
All Origins	9.6	7.4	30.7	32.2	17.7	8.0	4.0	3,184
Ukrainians	8.9	14.4	29.4	29.7	15.1	8.3	3.1	1,919
Females									
All Origins	9.5	6.1	29.1	35.6	21.0	7.1	1.1	3,352
Ukrainians	8.7	15.9	25.4	31.7	20.1	6.0	0.9	1,996
Canadian-Born									
All Origins	9.5	6.1	29.6	37.1	18.0	7.1	2.1	5,136
Ukrainians	9.7	6.8	25.0	37.3	21.0	7.9	2.1	2,913
Foreign-Born									
All Origins	9.6	8.9	31.1	22.4	24.4	9.1	4.1	1,400
Ukrainians	6.2	39.7	34.4	11.5	7.8	4.9	1.7	1,002
Rural									
All Origins	8.7	9.1	39.4	32.2	14.0	4.3	1.1	1,418
Ukrainians	7.7	20.8	35.2	27.8	11.4	3.8	1.0	942
Urban									
All Origins	9.8	6.0	27.3	34.4	20.9	8.4	2.9	5,118
Ukrainians	9.1	13.4	24.9	31.6	19.6	8.2	2.3	2,973

Source: 1971 Canadian Census 1/100 and 1/1000 Public Use Sample Tapes, Individual Province File, Statistics Canada, n.d.

Notes: [a]Includes Grade 13 for Ontario.
[b]Figures for Ukrainians are based on a 1 per cent sample, and for all origins on a 0.05 per cent sample. In order to obtain 100 per cent estimates, multiply total Ukrainians by 100 and total for all origins by 2,000.

than all Canadians. The lower mean in the Prairies reflects a higher percentage with less than five years of schooling and lower percentages with some university. As compared to all Canadians, the percentage of Ukrainians with some university is slightly lower in Ontario, slightly higher in British Columbia and significantly higher in Quebec. In terms of the relative educational achievement of Ukrainians, we can rank the regions from a low level in the Prairies, followed by Ontario and British Columbia, to a high level in Quebec.

Income

Median individual income and income distribution are presented in Table 11. Ukrainians have lower income than all Canadians; the difference in the median incomes of the two populations was $440. Median incomes for Ukrainian females is much closer to the respective Canadian median than it is for Ukrainian males. In all instances the proportion of Ukrainians with no income is lower than for all Canadians, but this does not affect the medians, which were calculated only for persons with income. The lower income of Ukrainian males is due to higher proportions in low income categories and slightly lower proportions in high income categories. Median income for Ukrainian females was only $50 below the median for all females. This small differential is caused by a very similar distribution in the higher income categories for both groups. In terms of income, Ukrainian females seem to be relatively better off than Ukrainian males.

Regional variations in income distribution are presented in Table 12. Ukrainians have lower median incomes in both rural and urban areas, but the differential with all Canadians is higher in rural areas. In spite of the lower income for all Ukrainians, they have higher median incomes than all Canadians in all regions except the Prairies. This is due to the fact that 58 per cent of Ukrainians live in the Prairies, where they have very low incomes. These two factors produce an overall lower median income for Ukrainians. Income distribution by regions revealed a common pattern for all regions except the Prairies. Ukrainians have lower proportions in the highest income category of $15,000 and over, but tend to have equal or higher proportions in the income categories between $5,000 and $10,000, as compared to all Canadians.

Occupation

The seven occupational categories presented in Table 6 have been collapsed into five categories. These categories, presented in Table 13, have the following equivalences:

TABLE 10

Distribution of Years of Schooling for Persons 15 Years of Age and Over, Not Attending School Full-Time, of All and Ukrainian Ethnic Origins, by Selected Regions, Canada, 1971

Years of Schooling	Canada		Ontario		Quebec		Prairies		British Columbia	
	Ukrainian Origin	All Origins	Ukrainian Origin	All Origins	Ukrainian Origin	All Origins	Ukrainian Origin	All Origins	Ukrainian Origin	All Origins
Less Than 5 Years	15.2	6.7	12.8	5.5	8.0	15.6	6.9	17.0	4.6	11.8
5–8 Years	27.4	29.9	26.6	25.9	37.2	31.9	28.2	28.6	24.8	21.5
9–11 Years	30.7	34.0	29.6	32.7	34.7	28.4	33.9	30.9	32.9	32.4
High School Completed	17.6	19.4	20.7	24.6	11.7	5.7	20.2	16.0	28.0	22.7
1–4 University	7.1	7.5	8.1	8.3	6.3	14.2	8.9	5.9	7.0	9.4
5+ University	2.0	2.5	2.2	2.9	2.2	4.3	1.9	1.7	2.7	2.2
Total	100.0	100.0	100.0	100.0	100.0	100.0	100.0	100.0	100.0	100.0
Total Persons[a]	3,915	6,536	1,006	2,365	141	1,867	2,269	1,051	414	697
Mean	8.8	9.5	9.1	9.9	9.0	9.0	8.5	9.6	9.4	10.0

Source: 1971 Canadian Census 1/100 and 1/1000 Public Use Sample Tapes, Individual Province File, Statistics Canada, n.d.
Note: [a]See note in Table 9.

TABLE 11

Distribution of Individual Income for Persons 15 Years of Age and Over, of All and Ukrainian Ethnic Origins, by Sex, Canada, 1971

	Median [a]	With No Income	Loss	Under $2,000	Percentage in Income Category						Total Persons[b]
					$2,000–4,999	$5,000–7,999	$8,000–9,999	$10,000–14,999	$15,000–and Over		
Canada											
Ukrainian Origin	3,540	21.8	1.0	26.9	20.2	15.7	6.5	5.7	2.2		4,465
All Origins	3,979	23.8	0.2	24.1	20.7	15.7	6.5	6.3	2.7		7,516
Males											
Ukrainian Origin	5,570	8.9	1.9	20.9	18.8	23.1	11.7	10.6	4.2		2,216
All Origins	5,910	9.6	0.3	17.6	20.2	24.1	11.7	11.6	4.9		3,709
Females											
Ukrainian Origin	1,970	34.5	0.2	32.7	21.6	8.5	1.4	0.9	0.2		2,241
All Origins	2,021	37.7	0.1	30.5	21.2	7.5	1.5	1.0	0.6		3,807

Source: 1971 Canadian Census 1/100 and 1/1000 Public Use Sample Tapes, Individual Province File, Statistics Canada, n.d.
Notes: [a]For persons with income.
[b]See note in Table 9.

High white collar: owner, manager, professional and technical.
Low white collar: clerical and sales.
Blue collar: all other categories.
Service and primary industries: same as in Table 6.

TABLE 12

Median Income for Persons 15 Years of Age and Over,
of All and Ukrainian Ethnic Origins, by Rural-Urban Residence
and Selected Regions, Canada, 1971

| | Region | | | | Place of Residence | |
	Ontario	Quebec	Prairies	British Columbia	Rural	Urban
Ukrainian						
Origin	4,510	4,371	2,950	4,282	1,950	4,010
All Origins	4,251	4,000	3,500	3,976	2,680	4,230

Source: 1971 Canadian Census 1/100 and 1/1000 Public Use Sample Tapes, Individual Province File, Statistics Canada, n.d.

Such collapsing attempts to rank occupations in terms of status, where "high white collar" is the highest category and "service and primary" is the lowest. This ranking should be interpreted very loosely, since even the twenty-one major occupational groups defined by Statistics Canada are very broad and encompass a wide range of occupations. For example, the major group "occupations in medicine and health" includes occupations from surgeon to orderly. Similar examples of occupations with widely different statuses are found in all the major occupational groups.[11] The variety in our five categories is even larger, so this ranking is only suggestive.

The occupational structure of Ukrainians has been converging with the Canadian. Table 13 shows that both Ukrainian males and females have occupational distributions similar to all Canadian males and females. Among Ukrainian rural residents more than half are in primary occupations, while the proportion for all Canadians is about one-third. In urban areas Ukrainians have a surplus in service occupations and deficits in the white collar occupations, if the Canadian proportions are taken as standards.

Regional occupational distributions are presented in Table 14. In the Prairies, Ukrainians have a higher proportion in the primary and blue collar occupations and lower proportions in both white collar occupational categories. This indicates a low occupational status, if the implied ranking of the five categories is accepted. If one compares Ukrainians to

TABLE 13

Percentage Distribution of Broad Occupational Categories for All and Ukrainian Ethnic Origins,
Persons 15 Years of Age and Over, by Sex and Rural-Urban Residence, Canada, 1971.

Occupational Category[a]	Canada		Males		Females		Rural		Urban	
	Ukrainian Origin	All Origins	Ukrainian Origin	All Origins	Ukrainian Origin	All Origins	Ukrainian Origin	All Origins	Ukrainian Origin	All Origins
High White Collar	14.4	17.8	12.4	15.7	17.3	21.4	7.9	10.0	16.5	19.8
Low White Collar	25.4	28.7	15.2	19.3	40.6	44.7	9.4	16.4	30.7	31.9
Blue Collar	30.4	32.3	44.0	43.8	8.7	12.6	21.4	33.1	33.3	32.0
Service	13.6	12.7	9.2	10.2	20.3	17.1	6.2	8.8	16.1	13.8
Primary	16.0	8.6	18.4	11.1	13.1	4.3	55.1	31.8	3.5	2.5
Total	100.0	100.0	100.0	100.0	100.0	100.0	100.0	100.0	100.0	100.0
Total Persons[b]	2,800	4,451	1,677	2,807	1,123	1,644	693	922	2,107	3,529

Source: 1971 Canadian Census 1/100 and 1/1000 Public Use Sample Tapes, Individual Province File, Statistics Canada, n.d.
Notes: [a]See explanation in text.
       [b]See note in Table 9.

73

TABLE 14

Percentage Distribution of Broad Occupational Categories for All and Ukrainian Ethnic Origins, Persons 15 Years of Age and Over, by Selected Regions, Canada, 1971

Occupational Categories[a]	Canada		Ontario		Quebec		Prairies		British Columbia	
	Ukrainian Origin	All Origins	Ukrainian Origin	All Origins	Ukrainian Origin	All Origins	Ukrainian Origin	All Origins	Ukrainian Origin	All Origins
High White Collar	14.4	17.8	16.5	19.6	15.5	16.7	12.9	17.5	15.2	15.6
Low White Collar	25.4	28.7	27.2	30.7	37.1	29.4	23.8	25.2	25.9	24.9
Blue Collar	30.4	32.3	36.0	32.0	33.0	36.4	26.6	24.2	35.8	34.0
Service	13.6	12.7	14.9	11.2	12.4	12.3	12.8	13.6	15.6	18.0
Primary	16.0	8.6	5.3	6.5	2.1	5.2	24.0	19.6	7.4	7.6
Total	100.0	100.0	100.0	100.0	100.0	100.0	100.0	100.0	100.0	100.0
Total Persons[b]	2,800	4,451	786	1,735	97	1,150	1,620	766	282	450

Source: 1971 Canadian Census 1/100 and 1/1000 Public Use Sample Tapes, Individual Province File, Statistics Canada, n.d.
Notes: [a]See explanation in text.
[b]See note in Table 9.

all Canadians, the other regions can be loosely ranked from low to high relative occupational status differentials as follows: Ontario, Quebec and British Columbia. Ukrainians in British Columbia have a very similar distribution to all Canadians. The differences increase progressively for Quebec and Ontario, with the Prairies having the most dissimilar distribution.

CONCLUSION

The present analysis has documented the evolution of socio-economic characteristics among Ukrainians in Canada from a very low level in 1921 to almost parity levels with the total Canadian population by 1971. Ukrainians are still below the national levels in terms of education, income and occupation. The educational disadvantage is due to the low educational level of the foreign-born. For Canadian-born Ukrainians (male and female), the educational level is similar to the Canadian one. This is especially significant for Ukrainian females, considering the extremely low level of education they had in 1921 and 1931.

Regarding income, Ukrainians are below the national average, but Ukrainian females are relatively better off than Ukrainian males. Ukrainians still have high proportions in primary occupations and lower proportions in white collar occupations, indicating an overall lower position in occupational status compared to all Canadians.

The fact that Ukrainian females have similar income to all Canadian females, while Ukrainian males have lower income than all Canadian males seems at first sight surprising, especially if we remember that Ukrainian males and females have about equal levels of education. A close look at income distribution presented in Table 10 suggests a possible explanation. Median income for females, Ukrainian and all Canadian, was about $2,000, that is, 50 per cent of women with income made less than $2,000 in 1971. The median income for Ukrainian males was about $5,600. If there is discrimination against Ukrainians, it would be felt in higher status occupations associated with high income. This may explain the smaller proportion of Ukrainian males in the higher income categories. Practically all females had low income. Probably very few Ukrainian women have high-paying, full-time jobs or have even attempted to seek them. Thus the similar income distribution for Ukrainian and all Canadian females may be simply a function of the income level at which most females were distributed.

Little can be said about male-female differentials in terms of occupation because the crude categorization prevents us from putting emphasis on the fact that Ukrainian females seem to have proportionately fewer persons in white collar occupations than Ukrainian males, when compared to all Canadian females and males. The relative occupational status of Ukrainian women seems to be similar to the one for Ukrainian males, but more detailed occupational breakdowns would be needed for a more precise statement.

It is important to point out that this broad categorization of occupations tends to upgrade artificially the occupational status of Ukrainians. It is very likely that within each occupational category Ukrainians tend to concentrate in the lower occupations, while the distribution for all Canadians is less biased. This is supported by results from the 1973 Canadian National Mobility Study. For males in the labour force aged twenty-five to sixty-four years, the Blishen-McRoberts socio-economic occupational score was 44.57 for the whole sample. Being of Ukrainian ethnic origin implied a decrease of 2.44 points in the score, which reflects the significantly lower occupational status of Ukrainian males.[12]

Regional socio-economic differences among Ukrainians have important implications. Ukrainians residing in rural areas have relatively lower socio-economic status than Ukrainians residing in urban areas. Given the originally high concentration of Ukrainians in rural areas and the massive rural-to-urban transfer observed in recent decades, the connection between social mobility and rural-to-urban migration among Ukrainians warrants careful examination.

Depending on the indicator of socio-economic status used, the relative position of Ukrainians varies from region to region. The pattern, apart from the Prairies where Ukrainians are relatively worse off, is mixed for the other regions. In education Quebec shows no differences, while Ukrainians in British Columbia and Ontario have lower levels of education. In occupation Ukrainians have the highest relative position in Quebec, followed by British Columbia and Ontario in decreasing order. Median income differences between Ukrainians and all Canadians are negative for the Prairies and positive for the other regions. The highest positive difference is found in Quebec, followed in decreasing order by British Columbia and Ontario.

The overall socio-economic position of Ukrainians is lowest on the Prairies, slightly better in Ontario, somewhat better in British Columbia and quite good in Quebec. Their status improves across the board if only Canadian-born Ukrainians are considered, but the low status of Ukrainians on the Prairies persists.

The implications of these results for the future are important. Quebec, where the proportion of Ukrainians is small, is a special case and should be treated separately. Data from the 1971 census indicate that rural residence for Ukrainians is associated with relatively high language retention, while urban residence is associated with relatively low language retention.[13] Most rural Ukrainians live on the Prairies and have a low socio-economic status. Rural-to-urban migration seems to be associated with upward social mobility, but it also may imply increased language assimilation. As the migration from rural areas continues, the inverse relationship between upward social mobility and language assimilation may have important implications for the survival of Ukrainians as a distinct ethnic group in Canada.

NOTES

1. William Darcovich and Paul Yuzyk, eds., "Statistical Compendium on the Ukrainians in Canada, 1891–1976" (Unpublished typescript, Ottawa, 1977).
2. N. B. Ryder, "The Interpretation of Origin Statistics," *The Canadian Journal of Economics and Political Science* 21 (1955): 466–85.
3. Ibid., 471–2.
4. The per cent illiterate among Ukrainians in 1921 and 1931, especially among the foreign born, may be overestimated due to possible communication problems between census interviewers and immigrants.
5. Although differences may be somewhat smaller if the problem pointed out in footnote 4 was widespread, the general trend is clear.
6. Darcovich and Yuzyk, Series 40.31–140, 369–70.
7. There are several 1971 Census Public Use Sample Tapes available. The Individual Province Tape is composed of individual records. The geographical unit identified in each record is province of residence in 1971.
8. The 1/1000 sample tape was further sampled to produce a 1/2000 sample in order to reduce computing costs.
9. The exclusion was made for reasons of confidentiality. None of these areas met the criterion of a minimum of 250,000 inhabitants needed to avoid possible identification of particular individuals.
10. The exclusion of the Atlantic provinces from the regional analysis was the result of the small proportion of Ukrainians living there.
11. Statistics Canada, *1971 Census of Canada: Occupations: Appendix—List of Occupation Codes and Titles*, Catalogue 94–727 (Ottawa: n.d.).
12. Monica Boyd, David Featherman and Judah Matras, "Status Attainment of Immigrant and Immigrant-Origin Groups in the United States, Canada and Israel" (Paper presented at the Social and Economic Impact of Immigration session of the Annual Meeting of the Population Association of America, 15 April 1978).
13. O. Wolowyna, "Language Assimilation and Socioeconomic Status: A Comparison of Germans, Polish, Dutch and Ukrainians" (Paper presented at the Annual Meeting of the Canadian Sociology and Anthropology Association, London, Ontario, 28 May to 1 June 1978).

DIFFERENTIAL EFFECTS OF ETHNO-RELIGIOUS STRUCTURE ON LINGUISTIC TRENDS AND ECONOMIC ACHIEVEMENTS OF UKRAINIAN CANADIANS

Warren E. Kalbach and Madeline A. Richard

There are two important aspects of assimilation. Classical assimilation theory and previous research suggest that knowledge of an ethnic language will decline and that economic adjustment will improve with time and increasing generations. However, assimilation can also occur within generations. For example, immigrants can make adjustments, such as acquiring the English language and/or moving away from their traditional ethnic church, which will facilitate economic assimilation. In other words, immigrants can become less "ethnic." Second- and third-generation individuals may also choose to make a lateral move away from their ethnic ties if it seems advantageous to do so.

To what extent did both of these assimilation models hold for Ukrainian Canadians at the time of the 1971 census? This paper will examine how much linguistic and economic patterns are affected by variations in the ethno-religious orientations of Ukrainians in Canada. It is expected that those traditional ethno-religious combinations that represent Ukrainian cultural origins, i.e., Greek Catholic and Greek Orthodox Ukrainians, will show stronger retention of ethnic language and lower levels of economic adaption.

Theoretical Concerns

To facilitate the analysis of linguistic trends and economic achievements of Ukrainians in Canadian society, it is necessary to examine assimilation theory as it relates to economic adaptation and the linguistic patterns of ethnic and cultural groups.

Assimilation, as defined by the Royal Commission on Bilingualism and Biculturalism, is the giving up of cultural identity by "almost total absorption into another linguistic and cultural group."[1] An individual who is assimilated no longer uses his mother tongue although he may still know it. Michael Novak in *The Rise of the Unmeltable Ethnics* makes the Marxist observation that an individual's sense of identity is influenced by the place he assumes in the economic order. He also suggests that one must leave the ethnic group in order to be upwardly mobile because in this way one is able to view things from a more universal viewpoint.[2]

Marx suggests two thoughts relevant for Canadian society. First, if an immigrant occupies a low position in the economic order, his sense of identity is likely to be with his own ethnic group, since immigrant groups usually have lower income levels and less prestigious jobs than members of the charter groups or those of other immigrant groups who have been here for several generations. Second, an immigrant must become more like the native born if he is to become upwardly mobile, for to do so he must be able to communicate with those in the upper strata of Canadian society. It follows that linguistic assimilation, along with a possible transfer in religious affiliation, is a part of the process of removing oneself from one's ethnic group.

Andrew Greeley's idea of ethnic groups providing "mobility pyramids" offers support for these arguments. Greeley argues that these "mobility pyramids" may end up being "mobility traps." In order to avoid such happenings, individuals must shift to positions of increased influence and prestige in the host society from similar positions in their own ethnic groups. Remaining "ethnic" may impede one's mobility whereas a lateral move would tend to facilitate upward mobility.[3]

Stanley Lieberson argues that "the surrender of distinctive mother tongues is a necessary step in the assimilation of ethnic groups in contact."[4] Moreover, he states that language maintenance provides a shield against assimilation and results in a lack of ability to communicate with other groups in Canadian society. Inability to communicate, says Lieberson, is accompanied by "disadvantages in the economic, social, political and educational spheres."[5] Those of British origin dominate the industrial, commercial and financial sectors of Canadian society making English the language of "big business." Since English is also the language of technology, there is an additional incentive for individuals of other ethnic groups to become fluent in it.[6] Speakers of English seem to have the edge. Lieberson also argues that linguistic skills not only play a role in employment opportunities but also "may be a vital prerequisite for advancement and higher income."[7]

It seems clear that in order to earn higher incomes and be upwardly mobile an individual must assimilate linguistically and therefore become less ethnic. Since religion also retards assimilation, becoming less ethnic could also involve a transfer to the religious affiliation of those in positions of economic power.[8] In their studies of the elite in Canadian society, Wallace Clement and John Porter show transfer to be mainly to the Anglican or United churches. Indeed, Porter states that the United Church is "as Canadian as the maple leaf and the beaver."[9] Although these studies are mainly concerned with elites, their findings have some relevance for this analysis. They point out the denominations associated with upward mobility and economic success in Canadian society. Most "ethnics" probably do not become Anglicans or United Church members in the hope of joining the elite, but rather because they are aware of the higher status of these denominations.

Porter theorized that in a society where ethnicity is salient, emphasis on mobility will tend to submerge cultural identity, while emphasis on ethnicity endangers mobility.[10] Frank Vallee and Norman Shulman tested this statement in their work entitled, "The Viability of French Groupings Outside Quebec." They argued that collectivities have limited energies and resources which cannot be spent both on cultural maintenance and the preparation of their members for achievement in society at large.[11] General assimilation theory underlines the importance of becoming less ethnic in terms of language and religious affiliation in order to become upwardly mobile and economically successful.

Assimilation theory also addresses the generational aspect of ethnicity. Realistically, assimilation cannot be expected to occur as soon as an immigrant steps onto Canadian soil; it occurs over time and with successive generations. William Newman pointed out that members of second-generation ethnic groups often moved away from their ethnic neighbourhoods and some even changed their names or anglicized them.[12] Marcus Lee Hansen's classic study concluded that the second generation solved the problem of inhabiting two worlds simultaneously by escaping from their ethnic group ties as soon as they were free economically.[13] Hansen further argued that the third generation, now essentially free of its ethnic ties, was motivated to learn and participate in the salient ethnic activities of their group. In his famous analysis, *Protestant-Catholic-Jew*, Will Herberg worked with Hansen's thesis and concluded that among immigrant groups the third generation "regularly meant the approaching dissolution of the ethnic group which the first generation had formed and with which the second generation had perforce been identified."[14] The only exception Herberg found was the Jewish case.

There are many forces in the new land that influence the immigrant to remain ethnic or to become less ethnic. This seems particularly true for Ukrainian Canadians. Remaining ethnic seems to depend on the role of the church in the context of an ethnic community's institutional completeness; the alternative of becoming less ethnic seems dependent on the desire of individuals for a quicker route to economic success. An individual who continues to identify with his ethno-religious group and retains his mother tongue will not be as likely to exhibit as high a level of upward mobility as his counterpart who experiences both a linguistic and religious transfer to the host society.

In his research on institutional completeness, Raymond Breton found religious institutions to have the "greatest effect in keeping the immigrant's personal association within the boundaries of the ethnic community." Furthermore, he argues that the influence of these institutions is attributable to their dominant role in the community as a centre of many activities. In the church, the immigrant finds many things which are similar to his experiences in his homeland. Not only is the working language usually his mother tongue, but religious leaders frequently "provided a raison d'être for the ethnic community and a motivation for identification with it." Breton concluded that the higher the proportion of an ethnic group unable to speak either French or English, the higher was the degree of institutional completeness of that ethnic group.[15]

General assimilation literature reveals that ethnicity becomes less salient over time for most ethnic groups. It also reveals that becoming less ethnic influences an immigrant's place in the economic structure of society, and that the surrender of the ethnic mother tongue is a step toward assimilation. Individuals who retain their mother tongue and their coincidental religious affiliation would not be expected to exhibit high rates of upward mobility, while those who become less ethnic in terms of linguistic behaviour and religious affiliation would be more likely to exhibit higher levels of income. Concomitantly, the generational concept suggests that upward mobility is likely to occur to a greater extent as successive immigrant generations emerge.

The Canadian Experience

Many of the analyses reported in the literature are historical in perspective and thus set the stage for empirical investigations. One of the earliest works was published in 1947 by Gordon Davidson who traced the patterns of Ukrainian immigration to Canada. Ukrainian immigrants were predominantly rural and thus engaged in farming or farming occupations. They were associated with "the first large scale European immigration to Canada, the era of western railroad development and the general economic growth of the West."[16] Davidson portrayed these Ukrainians as people of ingenuity and tenacity who overcame the obstacles of settling in a new land and established themselves as one of the leading groups in Canadian society. This portrayal was echoed by William Darcovich and Paul Yuzyk, who also gave considerable attention to the role of the church and the problems of language for the Ukrainian communities in Canada.[17] There is no question that religion historically has played an important role in the life of Ukrainian settlers and their descendants. Usually, the church was the first public building to be constructed in the community because it also served as the centre of social and cultural activities.

Yuzyk found three general tendencies among Ukrainian Canadians in Manitoba. First, there were those who did not wish to give up the culture of their fathers and so adhered to the Ukrainian churches. Secondly, there were those Ukrainians who had assimilated and had lost the Ukrainian language. They either joined churches which were similar to the Ukrainian churches, i.e., Anglican and Roman Catholic, or became United or Presbyterian. This category was particularly characteristic of urban Ukrainians. The third group was portrayed as one which consisted of individuals who could not solve their cultural and religious conflicts and therefore did not attend any church.[18]

In the early period, Manitoban Ukrainians were opposed to English schools and English teachers because they perceived them as instruments of assimilation which would eradicate their nationality and culture. In an effort to maintain Ukrainian ethnicity on the basis of language, Ukrainian schools were built and Ukrainian nuns employed as teachers to provide instruction in the Ukrainian language and religion. Yuzyk states that the early Ukrainian immigrants settled in the rural areas of Manitoba and tenaciously held on to their cultural heritage. However, he points out that these new Canadians soon discovered that this action only perpetuated the lives of poverty from which they had hoped to escape when they left their homeland. This discovery was the catalyst for change, and the Ukrainians "acquired

English, received citizenship and learned the process of democracy."[19]

Darcovich was impressed by the two-sidedness of the identity which Ukrainians were attempting to develop and maintain in Canada. He perceived them as a group who wished to maintain their own distinct ethnic identity while at the same time being desirous of integration into Canadian society. He attributed their success to a strong and conscious effort to do so. Darcovich stated that over time English became more generally known because it was necessary for success in business or in obtaining a job in the city. However, opposition to this tendency to adopt English was strong and the problem was a matter of grave concern to "many parents, the Ukrainian churches, some lay organizations and the Ukrainian Canadian Committee." According to Darcovich, the Ukrainians seemed to have been more successful than other immigrant groups in their efforts to maintain their mother tongue even while they were learning English.[20]

David Millett has also examined the Ukrainian churches and their effect on Ukrainian Canadians. Along with other researchers, he makes the point that the church's continued use of the Ukrainian language "has provided a core around which organizations devoted to fine arts, recreation and politics have clustered." However, the second generation found that these activities of the Orthodox and the Greek Catholic churches impeded their education and employment opportunities because they kept alive old prejudices and left Ukrainian youth "ignorant of and unaccepted by Canadian society." In order to achieve upward mobility, they had to forsake their rural roots and become both urban and middle class in their orientation to society. As a consequence, the Ukrainian churches suffered as these individuals sought to minimize their cultural ties. As a result of greater use of English, changes in language habits were often accompanied by transfers to English language churches such as the Roman Catholic or United Church.

Millet found that the third generation spoke little or no Ukrainian and identified itself "as Canadian first and Ukrainian second." However, the third generation did not seem to share the anti-Ukrainian sentiments of the second generation, and it viewed the church as the "keeper of Ukrainian culture." They favoured the use of Ukrainian as a second language rather than French. The churches, therefore, have gradually introduced some English into their church services as a way of "[accommodating] the wishes and demands of the second and third generations" and strengthening their position of influence in the community.[21]

Recently, research has made greater use of census and special survey data. Of particular relevance to this paper are studies of language loss and retention, such as the work of Raj Pannu and John Young. They employed data from the 1971 census of Canada to calculate an index of language loss for five ethnic groups: German, Italian, Polish, Ukrainian and Jewish. Ukrainians were the least urbanized of the five groups, but their level of urbanization was found to be rapidly increasing. Ukrainians had the third highest level of language loss, and the difference in language loss between the native and foreign-born components was also highest for them. When urban-rural differences were taken into account for the native and foreign-born, the language loss for urban Ukrainians exceeded that of their rural counterparts.[22]

Olga Kuplowska also examined language patterns among Ukrainian Canadians using data collected for the Non-Official Languages (NOL) study.[23] She found generation to be the major correlate of knowledge of Ukrainian. Support for language retention was high among Ukrainians and strongest among those who were first generation or fluent in Ukrainian. The NOL study itself revealed only a slight relationship between income and language retention for the sample as a whole. However, when Kuplowska examined the relationship for Ukrainians alone, the data revealed that income seemed to be "an influential factor in determining the language retention rates of Ukrainians." Low income levels were associated with high retention rates and high income with low retention.[24] Jeffrey Reitz used the NOL data to determine the significance of language for the maintenance of an ethnic community. His findings reveal that retention of the mother tongue is an important and necessary factor in the maintenance of an ethnic community.[25]

The research reviewed above consists of both historical and analytical studies. The former shed light on the influence of Ukrainian churches on the lives of Ukrainian Canadians. The latter reveal patterns of linguistic assimilation for various ethnic groups through successive generations in relation to urban-rural residence and socio-economic status. The analysis which follows examines the extent to which changes in religious affiliation affect both language retention and economic achievement of Ukrainians within a generationally differentiated structure.

The Significance of Variations in Ethno-Religious Structure

Milton Gordon has discussed the factors of race, religion and national origin as components of a basic sense of ethnicity, while Harold Abramson and Andrew Greeley have demonstrated the utility and importance of examining ethno-religious factors in understanding the behaviour of immigrants and their descendants in the United States.[26]

Although considerable research on immigrant groups has been carried out in Canada, there have been too few opportunities for empirical explorations into the nature of ethno-religious behaviour in Canadian society. The 1971 census provides an opportunity to investigate the effect of the ethno-religious factor on both linguistic behaviour and the economic achievement of individuals within specific ethnic origin groups.

Not every ethnic group is as well suited as Ukrainians for this type of analysis. Ukrainians have been in Canada for a sufficient period to have produced significant numbers beyond the second generation, and their churches have played important roles in their communities from the very beginning of their settlement in Canada. To be Ukrainian is also to be Ukrainian Catholic or Ukrainian Greek Orthodox. Yet, like other predominantly agricultural groups who came to Canada, they have been exposed to and affected by forces of urbanization and industrialization in Canadian society. This analysis examines the extent to which linguistic and economic behaviour patterns have been affected by deviations from the basic ethno-religious orientations of Ukrainians in Canada, and assesses these effects in terms of their consistency with classical assimilation theory.

Data Source, Variables and Methodology

The data used in this analysis are from the Individual File of the 1971 Census of Canada Public Use Sample Tapes made available by Statistics Canada in June 1975. The Individual File represents a 1 per cent sample of individuals drawn from the Census Master File for all provinces with the exception of Prince Edward Island, the Yukon and the Northwest Territories. The latter were excluded by Statistics Canada because their small population sizes would make it difficult to preserve the confidentiality of individual information with some types of complex multi-variate analyses that might be attempted by researchers having access to the Public Use Sample Tapes.

The specific variables employed in this analysis and their definitions are as follows:[27]

1. *Ethnic Groups:* Refers to ethnic or cultural background traced through the father's side. In some cases the language spoken by the person or by his paternal ancestor on first coming to the continent was used as a guide to the determination of ethnic or cultural origin.

2. *Religion:* Refers to the specific religious body, denomination, sect or community reported in answer to the question "What is your religion?"

86

3. *Generation:* Generation status was assigned on the basis of answers to the questions concerning *birthplace* of the individual and of his (or her) parents in terms of *being born in Canada* or *outside Canada.* For example, the first generation comprises all residents who were born outside Canada. Second-generation status was assigned all residents born in Canada with one or both parents born outside Canada, while the third-plus generation consists of all residents born in Canada whose parents were also reported as having been born in Canada.

4. *Mother Tongue:* Refers to the first language a person learned that is still understood.

5. *Total Family Income:* This measure of income refers to the sum of the incomes received by all members of a family who were fifteen years of age or older from all sources during the calendar year 1970. Total family income was reported for members of families who were fifteen years of age and over.

The analysis employed here is the relatively simple one of percentage differences based on computer-produced cross-tabulations of religion and generation varying with Ukrainian mother tongue and income for persons reporting themselves to be Ukrainian in ethnic origin. Age is the only variable used as a control in the analysis. It would have been desirable to have included additional controls such as educational attainment, but this was not feasible. The relatively small size of the Public Use Sample severely restricts the number of variables that can be incorporated into any given cross-tabular analysis. The introduction of more than the most basic controls produces an instability in the data that severely limits their interpretation.

Changes in Ethno-Religious Distributions

The ethno-religious composition of immigrants arriving in Canada has tended to reflect the cultural make-up of these populations. A sense of ethnic identity develops in the new country to provide psychological support and the security of the familiar during the period of transition and adjustment. At the same time, ethnic identity often serves as an impediment to the kinds of change that would facilitate a more rapid integration and assimilation into the new society.

The distribution of first-generation Ukrainians by selected religions is shown in Table 1. It represents the minimum level of ethno-religious homogeneity for foreign-born Ukrainians. Some of those who were affiliated with the Ukrainian churches when they first came to Canada have obviously transferred to non-Ukrainian churches by the time of the

TABLE 1

Percentage Distributions of the Ukrainian Origin Population
by Selected Religions, for Generation Groups, Canada, 1971

Generation	Religion						Total	
	Ukrainian Catholic	Greek Orthodox	Roman Catholic	United Church	Anglican	Other	Per Cent	Number
First	47.9	29.3	7.8	3.9	1.1	10.1	100.0	105,500
Second	32.4	21.3	13.7	13.1	5.2	14.3	100.0	241,700
Third-plus	24.5	14.3	19.5	19.0	6.0	16.7	100.0	247,400
Total	31.9	19.8	15.0	13.9	4.8	14.5	100.0	594,600

Source: Statistics Canada, *1971 Census of Canada*, Public Use Sample, Individual File, 1975.

1971 census. Further analysis of the first generation by period of immigration would undoubtedly show that most of those belonging to non-Ukrainian churches have been in Canada for the longest period of time.

The first-generation Ukrainian population in 1971 was still predominantly Ukrainian Catholic (48 per cent) and Ukrainian Orthodox (29 per cent), accounting for slightly over three-quarters of foreign-born Ukrainians. The general erosion of their position of dominance through losses of members to other denominations within each generation as well as between generations is clearly evident. For the third generation and beyond, the Ukrainian churches' share had declined to 39 per cent. Both churches lost approximately one-half of their proportion of population between the first and third-plus generations. In contrast, the highest relative intergenerational gains are shown by Anglicans, who increased their proportional share by a factor of 5.4. The United Church showed almost the same increase with a growth factor of 4.9, while the Roman Catholic church increased its proportional share by two and one-half times.

This generational shift in the distribution of Ukrainians by religion can also be shown dramatically by examining the generational structure for each of the selected religious denominations presented in Table 2. The bulk of the Ukrainian Catholic and Ukrainian Orthodox populations are second-generation Ukrainians; over two-thirds are either first or second generation. For the major non-Ukrainian churches, over one-half of their Ukrainian members are third generation with only small representation from the foreign-born population.

The trend is very clear. There has been a considerable erosion from one generation to the next in the relative power of the two Ukrainian churches to hold their members. Movement from Ukrainian to non-Ukrainian churches suggests the extent to which the Ukrainian population is becoming less Ukrainian. Because the first generation cannot expect to be strengthened through continuing immigration, the future seems less than bright for maintaining a strong Ukrainian component in a multicultural Canadian society.

The implications for language maintenance and economic achievement of this generational shift away from the Ukrainian churches are examined in the following sections.

Mother Tongue Retention

Data in Table 3 reveal the percentages of Ukrainians with Ukrainian

TABLE 2

Percentage Distribution of the Ukrainian Origin Population by Generation Groups for Selected Religions, Canada, 1971

Generation	Ukrainian Catholic	Greek Orthodox	Roman Catholic	United Church	Anglican	Other	Total
				Religion			
First	26.6	26.2	9.2	5.0	4.2	12.3	17.7
Second	41.4	43.7	36.9	38.2	43.9	40.0	40.6
Third-plus	32.0	30.1	53.9	56.8	51.9	47.7	41.6
Total %	100.0	100.0	100.0	100.0	100.0	100.0	99.9
N	189,600	117,800	89,400	82,700	28,700	86,400	594,600

Source: Statistics Canada, *1971 Census of Canada*, Public Use Sample, Individual File, 1975.

mother tongue for selected religious denominations by generation at the time of the 1971 census. An examination of the data for all Ukrainians with Ukrainian mother tongue, regardless of religious denomination, reveals a decline in the retention of mother tongue across generations that is consistent with classical assimilation theory. Overall, Ukrainian mother tongue declined 71.5 per cent, with the greatest relative decrease of 60 per cent occurring between the second and third-plus generations. The same pattern of language loss is exhibited by each of the ethno-religious groups shown in Table 3, namely, Ukrainian Catholics, Ukrainian Greek Orthodox, Ukrainian Roman Catholics, Ukrainian United Church and Ukrainian Anglicans. The greatest loss of language occurs consistently between the second and third-plus generations. Among particular ethno-religious groupings, the greatest relative decline was 85 per cent, exhibited by Ukrainians in the United Church, followed by Ukrainian Anglicans (82 per cent) and Ukrainian Roman Catholics (75 per cent).

TABLE 3

Percentage with Ukrainian Mother Tongue
for Religious Denominations by Generation
for the Ukrainian Population, Canada, 1971

Generation	Total Ukrainian	Ukrainian Catholic	Greek Orthodox	Roman Catholic	United Church	Anglican
First	83.6	82.5	79.5	48.3	52.1	41.6
Second	58.9	77.2	73.4	40.0	39.6	33.3
Third-plus	23.8	44.0	46.6	12.0	7.9	7.4

Source: Statistics Canada, *1971 Census of Canada*, Public Use Sample, Individual File, 1975.

A comparison of data within generational categories between the five ethno-religious groups reveals that Ukrainian Anglicans exhibit the largest percentage difference in the retention of mother tongue in comparison to Ukrainian Catholics and Ukrainian Greek Orthodox. Moreover, Ukrainian Anglicans have the largest percentage difference within each generational status category, while the smallest percentage differences exist between the two Ukrainian churches.

These variations in mother tongue retention between ethno-religious groups and across generations imply that those Ukrainians who become Anglican, Roman Catholic or United Church members tend to lose the Ukrainian language they learned as a child to a greater extent than do those Ukrainians who remain with one of the Ukrainian churches. These results are not unexpected since the language of the Ukrainian churches is that of the people, while the language of the other three denominations is the language of the dominant society. By affiliating with a non-Ukrainian church, Ukrainians lose the language reinforcement for their mother tongue which occurs in Ukrainian churches. Furthermore, if the transfer reflects a purposive action to facilitate social mobility outside the Ukrainian community, it is not surprising that those who become Anglican show the greatest loss of mother tongue.

Given a possible negative correlation between generational status and average age, part of the language loss across generations may be accounted for by the presence of relatively greater numbers of young people in native-born generations. However, repeating the analysis within each of four major age categories failed to alter the basic patterns observed for all ages combined. Therefore, it can be said with some confidence that observed patterns of mother tongue retention are not an effect of age differences between ethno-religious or generational groupings.

No group appears to escape the effects of assimilative pressures from the larger society. Insofar as language behaviour is concerned, the data clearly support the classical model of increasing assimilation through successive generations. The other interesting feature in Table 3 is the degree of assimilation that occurs within each generation across ethno-religious groupings. The data clearly point to the important role that membership groups play in shaping the behaviour of their constituent members. The individual Ukrainian can clearly retard or accelerate the assimilation process through his religious affiliation.

Economic Achievement

Classical assimilation theory states that with successful adaptation, immigrants' economic status will improve with increasing length of residence and through successive generations as their children are able to take advantage of the greater educational and employment opportunities open to them. Given the peasant origins of the early Ukrainian immigrants who settled the prairies, classical assimilation theory would appear to have particular relevance. Ethno-religious groups are examined in the following analysis in order to determine which ones facilitated the process of economic adjustment to the greatest extent. Analysis of mother tongue retention has already suggested that insofar as the Ukrainian churches successfully maintained Ukrainian culture, they tended to impede rather than facilitate their members' social and economic adjustment in the larger society.

The specific measure of income employed in this analysis as an index of economic achievement is the percentage of family members fifteen years of age and older for whom total family income was reported to exceed twenty thousand dollars during the 1970 calendar year. These percentages are shown for individuals by generation and religious denomination in Table 4.

TABLE 4

Percentage Distribution of Ukrainian Census Family Members
15 Years of Age and Older, Reporting Total Family Income of $20,000+,
by Generation for Religious Groups, Canada, 1971

Generation	Total Ukrainian	Ukrainian Catholic	Greek Orthodox	Roman Catholic	United Church	Anglican
First	3.9	4.8	1.4	1.7	15.2	12.5
Second	5.5	4.7	4.7	4.0	7.6	9.9
Third-plus	4.3	2.4	8.7	3.2	6.1	4.7

Source: Statistics Canada, *1971 Census of Canada*, Public Use Sample, Individual File, 1975.

The data do not totally support assimilation theory regarding expected intergenerational changes when one considers all Ukrainians regardless of religious denomination. While a slightly larger proportion of the third-plus generation than the first generation reports total family income of twenty thousand dollars or more, the proportion for the second generation is significantly greater. The significance of this finding is enhanced by the fact that it concurs with the findings of the recent census monograph, "Immigrants in Canada, 1971," which shows that second-generation Canadians do better economically than either the first or third-plus generations.[28]

Examination of data for the five ethno-religious groups reveals that the model of generational assimilation only holds for the Orthodox Ukrainians. As successive generations emerge, Ukrainians who are Orthodox achieve greater economic success. Successive generations of Ukrainian Catholics, Ukrainian Anglicans and Ukrainian United Church members experience a decline in the proportion reporting a total family income of twenty thousand dollars or more.

Within each generation, the data reveal that Ukrainians who identify with either the United or Anglican churches do significantly better than those who belong to the traditional Ukrainian churches. This is particularly notable in the first generation and to a somewhat lesser degree for the second generation. The only exception is found in the third-plus generation. In this group Orthodox Ukrainians do better than Ukrainians of any other religion. Why this is so difficult to say without introducing additional control variables in the analysis, such as age and education, which are known to be related to economic achievement.

To determine if age was affecting the relationships evident in Table 4, the analysis was repeated for four major age groupings. However, because of the small sample size (the index of economic achievement was based on the upper end of the income distribution where the number of cases was relatively small), the analysis was somewhat inconclusive. The evidence, however spotty, does suggest that the exception noted in the third-plus generation may be due to differences in the age distributions. For the major age group, 25-44 years of age, the proportion of Ukrainian Orthodox reporting family incomes of twenty thousand and over was significantly lower than the proportion of Ukrainian Anglicans for each generational group. They did, however, still exceed the proportion of United Church Ukrainians in the third-plus generation.

Summary

Analysis of the religious composition of the Ukrainian ethnic population in Canada in 1971 by generational status shows a significant shift in the distributions of its ethno-religious groups and a significant decline in the relative size of the two principal Ukrainian churches. The proportionate shares of each generation affiliated with the Ukrainian Catholic and Orthodox denominations show almost identical rates of decline from the first to the third-plus generations, while the Anglican church shows the highest rate of increase followed closely by the United Church.

The significance of this compositional shift by generation can be seen in the concomitant changes which have occurred in the major ethno-religious groups—within and between generations—with respect to linguistic and economic behaviour. Within each of the generations, those Ukrainians who are affiliated with religions other than those represented by the two major Ukrainian churches show greater loss of Ukrainian mother tongue than is the case for Ukrainian Catholics and Ukrainian Greek Orthodox. Although they have been less than completely successful, the Ukrainian churches apparently do reinforce the ethnic factor and lessen the pressures for linguistic assimilation impinging upon their members.

Ukrainians of any generation who move away from the Ukrainian churches show greater economic achievement than those who have retained their ties. The loss of ethnic mother tongue that accompanies the shift to non-Ukrainian churches appears to facilitate upward mobility, at least in economic terms. Reinforcing the use of the ethnic mother tongue by focusing social and cultural activities around the Ukrainian church lessens the need or opportunity to acquire English and therefore tends to impede the economic assimilation of members into the larger society. The effects of the shift to United and Anglican churches are particularly striking for members of the first generation.

Classical assimilation theory does not appear to be as helpful in trying to understand observed intergenerational differences within groups. While linguistic changes between generations are shown to be entirely consistent with assimilation theory, income differences are not. The Ukrainians as a whole do show higher economic achievement for the third-plus generation than is the case for the first generation, but the second generation exhibited the highest level of economic achievement. Furthermore, the intergenerational differences for the individual ethnoreligious groups in this study show significant variations from the average. Only the Greek Orthodox Ukrainians showed the classical assimilation pattern.

The ethnic church does seem to exert a stronger positive influence than the non-ethnic church on language retention and, as a consequence of this, a negative influence on economic achievement. Regardless of age or generation, it seems that Ukrainian Canadians who move away from the ethnic church are more likely to acquire English and be upwardly mobile than their Ukrainian Catholic or Orthodox counterparts. The acquisition of English as the language of work, business and technology makes possible the lateral move necessary to escape a possible "mobility trap." The Ukrainian who becomes less ethnic is more likely to reach higher income levels than his same generation counterpart who remains totally ethnic. It would seem that the implications of a national policy designed to encourage the retention of ethnic behaviour under present conditions in Canadian society are not totally positive.

NOTES

1. Royal Commission on Bilingualism and Biculturalism, *Report of the Royal Commission on Bilingualism and Biculturalism, Book IV: The Cultural Contribution of the Other Ethnic Groups* (Ottawa: Queen's Printer, 1970), 5.
2. Michael Novak, *The Rise of the Unmeltable Ethnics: Politics and Culture in the Seventies* (New York: MacMillan Co., 1972), 35.
3. Andrew M. Greeley, *Why Can't They Be Like Us? America's White Ethnic Groups* (New York: E. P. Dutton & Co., 1970), 50.

4. Stanley Lieberson, *Language and Ethnic Relations in Canada* (New York: John Wiley & Sons, 1970), 6.
5. Ibid., 10.
6. Ibid., 22.
7. Ibid., 138.
8. Ibid., 246-7.
9. Wallace Clement, *The Canadian Corporate Elite: An Analysis of Economic Power* (Toronto: McClelland and Stewart, 1975); John Porter, *The Vertical Mosaic: An Analysis of Social Class and Power in Canada* (Toronto: University of Toronto Press, 1965), 519.
10. John Porter, "Ethnic Pluralism in Canada," in *Ethnicity: Theory and Experience*, eds., Nathan Glazer and Daniel P. Moynihan (Cambridge, Mass.: Harvard University Press, 1975), 294.
11. Frank G. Vallee and Norman Shulman, "The Viability of French Groupings Outside Quebec," in *Regionalism in the Canadian Community*, ed., Mason Wade (Toronto: University of Toronto Press, 1969), 95.
12. William M. Newman, *American Pluralism: A Study of Minority Groups and Social Theory* (New York: Harper & Row, 1973), 75.
13. Eugene I. Bender and George Kagiwada, "Hansen's Law of 'Third Generation Return' and the Study of American Religio-Ethnic Groups," *Phylon* 29, no. 4 (1968): 360-70. Bender and Kagiwada present a clear, concise review of some of the assimilation literature. Portions of this section rely on their discussion rather than on the original studies.
14. Ibid., 362.
15. Raymond Breton, "Institutional Completeness of Ethnic Communities," *American Journal of Sociology* 70 (September 1964): 193-205.
16. Gordon A. Davidson, *The Ukrainians in Canada: A Study in Canadian Immigration* (Montreal: McGill University Historical Club, 1947), 19.
17. William Darcovich, *Ukrainians in Canada: The Struggle to Retain Their Identity* (Ottawa: Ukrainian Self-Reliance Association [Ottawa Branch], 1967); Paul Yuzyk, *The Ukrainians in Manitoba: A Social History* (Toronto: University of Toronto Press, 1953); Paul Yuzyk, *Ukrainian Canadians: Their Place and Role in Canadian Life* (Toronto: Ukrainian Canadian Business and Professional Federation, 1967).
18. Yuzyk, *The Ukrainians in Manitoba*, 79.
19. Ibid., 145, 207.
20. Darcovich, *Ukrainians in Canada*, iii, 19, 20, 21.
21. David Millett, "The Orthodox Church: Ukrainian, Greek and Syrian," in *Minority Canadians 2: Immigrant Groups*, ed. Jean Leonard Elliott (Toronto: Prentice-Hall of Canada, 1971), 47-65.
22. Raj S. Pannu and John R. Young, "Patterns of Language Loss/Retention Among Selected Ethnic Groups in Canada," (Paper presented to the Canadian Sociology and Anthropology Association Annual Meetings, Fredericton, New Brunswick, June 1977), 8-14.
23. K. G. O'Bryan, J. G. Reitz and O. M. Kuplowska, *Non-Official Languages: A Study in Canadian Multiculturalism* (Ottawa: Minister of Supply and Services, Canada, 1976).
24. Olga M. Kuplowska, "Language Retention Patterns Among Ukrainian Canadians." This paper appears in this publication.
25. Jeffrey G. Reitz, "Language and Ethnic Community Survival," *Canadian Review of Sociology and Anthropology*, Special Issue (1974): 104-22.
26. Milton M. Gordon, *Assimilation in American Life: The Role of Race, Religions and National Origins* (New York: Oxford University Press, 1964), 24; Harold J. Abramson, *Ethnic Diversity in Catholic America* (New York: John Wiley & Sons, 1973); Andrew M. Greeley, *The Denominational Society: A Sociological Approach To Religion in America* (Glenview, Ill.: Scott, Foresman and Co., 1970).
27. Statistics Canada, *Dictionary of the 1971 Census Terms* (Ottawa: Ministry of Industry, Trade and Commerce, 1972).

28. Warren E. Kalbach and Anthony H. Richmond, "Immigrants in Canada 1971" 34. This monograph was prepared for the Census Analytic Programme sponsored by the Social Sciences Research Council of Canada and Statistics Canada. It is currently being prepared for publication.

PARTICIPATION OF UKRAINIANS IN BUSINESS OCCUPATIONS IN CANADA

Wsevolod W. Isajiw

The occupational structure of Ukrainians in Canada during the past four decades has converged toward that characteristic of the general Canadian labour force. However, comparisons of occupational participation from decade to decade based on the census data have presented a number of problems. Some of these are very difficult, if not impossible, to solve. Comparability of data on occupations and comparability of data on ethnic origin from decade to decade are two such problems. The categories used to classify occupations in the 1961 census were substantially different from those used in the 1971 census. Similarly, the question on ethnic origin used in previous censuses has been changed for the 1981 census and will pose serious problems for time studies in the future.

The traditional standard for evaluating the occupational composition of an ethnic group has been the occupational composition of the total labour force. The participation rate of an ethnic group's labour force in a specific occupational category or a set of such categories is compared with the participation rate of the total society's labour force in the same category or a set of such categories to ascertain how closely one approaches or supersedes the other. It is not exactly clear why this type of comparison is useful. Presumably, it provides a measure of the "adjustment" of an ethnic group to society at large. It is, however, debatable whether this is indeed a good measure of social adjustment. There is no reason to suppose that the occupational participation rates of the total labour force in any specific society represent the "optimal" occupational adjustment for any group in that society. An independently worked out composite measure, based on occupational participation rates of a number of the most highly industrialized societies, may be a better measure of social adjustment for any collectivity.[1]

The main purpose of this study is not simply to measure the occupational adjustment of Ukrainians to society at large, but to ascertain and to explain how Ukrainians fit into the ethnic stratification system of Canadian society. Ethnic stratification can be defined as the hierarchy which ethnic groups form in relation to each other on the basis of power, wealth and prestige. Occupational participation is only one indicator of the place an ethnic group holds at any given time on the ethnic stratification ladder. Nevertheless, it is an important indicator since occupational structure can be said to be the basis of the social structure of modern societies. Participation in business and professional occupations is especially significant since these are the occupations in modern societies which relate to power, wealth and prestige.

Few attempts have been made to compare the occupational participation of Ukrainians with that of other specific ethnic groups.[2] This paper will deal only with business occupations and will compare Ukrainian participation in them with that of selected other ethnic groups. Only the male labour force will be considered. Because there have been two different labour markets—male and female—it is more accurate to deal with the male and female labour forces separately rather than together.

Published data from the 1971 census of Canada is the basis of this paper.[3] Only those occupational categories are considered in which there is a high chance that primarily business-type occupations are included. Thus, managerial occupations in public administration and in education are excluded, while all sales occupations are considered as business occupations. Occupations listed under categories not designated as managers, but which the occupational classifications manual identifies as proprietary occupations, are also included.[4]

In 1971 the above occupations had 25,960 Ukrainian males or 15.2 per cent of the total Ukrainian male labour force. That is, 15.2 per cent of the Ukrainian male labour force was engaged in business of one type or another. Of the total Canadian male labour force, 17.7 per cent were in business occupations. Thus, Ukrainians were underrepresented in business by 2.5 per cent. That is, Ukrainians participated in business by 14.1 per cent less than the total Canadian male labour force.

If we compare the Ukrainian figure with selected other ethnic groups in Canada, ethnic stratification becomes apparent. The British, French, Germans, Italians, Jews and Asians were all better represented in business than were Ukrainians. Their respective percentages were 18.6, 17.6, 16.0, 15.8, 40.0, 17.6. Those less represented than Ukrainians were other, mostly southern, Europeans (13.3 per cent), Polish (12.7 per cent) and Native Indians (6.2 per cent). The Italians are a much younger ethnic group in Canada and, like Ukrainians, are of rather heavy peasant background, yet in 1971 they were better represented in business occupations than were Ukrainians. Likewise, Germans, who are sociologically somewhat comparable to Ukrainians in terms of their Mennonite rural background, were nevertheless represented in business occupations 2.5 per cent more than were Ukrainians.

To get a better picture of Ukrainian involvement in business occupations, one should look at the type of businesses where Ukrainians work in large proportions. The business occupations used in the 1971 census can be divided into three types: (1) the top status occupations, (2) all sales occupations except top management, and (3) lower status occupations. Type 1 occupations include top management in finance, personnel, sales, purchasing, production, construction and others. Type 2 includes occupations selling commodities and services mainly by sales agents. Type 3 includes mostly small business people, such as hotel and motel managers and owners, custom tailors, photographers with their own studios, etc.[5] The bulk of all ethnic groups is concentrated in Type 2 and Type 3 businesses. Significantly, Ukrainians are equally represented with the total Canadian male labour force only in Type 3 businesses. In this type of business the high status ethnic groups are rather underrepresented. Thus, 6.1 per cent of the Ukrainian male labour force is engaged in this type of business (the figure for the general Canadian male labour force), while only 5.7 per cent of the British, 4.9 per cent of the Jewish and 5.7 per cent of the German male labour force are involved in Type 3 occupations. Instead, the British, Jews and Asians are overrepresented in Type 2 sales occupations, where Ukrainians are underrepresented. The total Canadian percentage in the Type 2 occupations is 10, whereas for Ukrainians it is 8.3. The French and Asians are overrepresented in Type 3 business and underrepresented in Type 2. Yet the French are still better represented (9.4 per cent) in Type 2 businesses than are Ukrainians. Both Asians (10.3 per cent) and Germans (9.0 per cent) are also better represented in Type 2 occupations than are Ukrainians. Italians are like Ukrainians in their participation in Type 2 and Type 3 businesses. They are underrepresented in the former (6.9 per cent) and overrepresented in the latter (8.0 per cent).

In the higher status Type 1 businesses differences are striking. Not only are Ukrainians underrepresented by a factor of 2 to 1 in these occupations in relation to the total labour force, but they have the lowest percentage of participation among all the ethnic groups next to that of Native Indians. There are only 1,305 Ukrainian males in Type 1 occupations or .76 per cent of the Ukrainian male labour force, as compared with 1.6 per cent for the nation, 1.85 per cent for the British, 7.6 per cent for Jews, 1.2 per cent for Germans and 1.04 per cent for Asians.

In summary, in 1971 Ukrainians participated in business at 85 per cent of the participation rate of the total Canadian male labour force. In Type 1 businesses Ukrainians participated at only 47.5 per cent and in Type 2 businesses at 83 per cent of the participation rate of the total male labour force. Only in Type 3 businesses was Ukrainian participation the same as that of the total Canadian male labour force.

The data presented show that Ukrainians in Canada are engaged in business occupations significantly less than are other comparable ethnic groups and less than ethnic groups such as Italians and Asians, who include much larger proportions of recent immigrants.

Why are Ukrainians in Canada not involved in business in larger numbers? There is no simple answer to this question because various factors are involved. How much each factor contributes to the phenomenon requires further research.

1. One factor is the prejudice and discrimination against Ukrainians which discouraged them from venturing into business, especially higher status business. In the wake of the First World War, the rise of Bolshevism in Russia and labour unrest in Winnipeg, urban Ukrainians were often made scapegoats and accused of subversion or potential disloyalty.[6] Indeed, in the 1920s and 30s it was very difficult for Ukrainians to obtain credit. During the Depression most banks, mortgage companies, financial brokers, stock brokers and others discriminated against non-Anglo-Saxons.[7] Many banks considered Ukrainians to be bad risks.[8]

2. The second factor is their delayed migration from farms to cities. In 1941 54.6 per cent of the Ukrainian male labour force was agricultural compared to 31.7 per cent for the Canadian male labour force as a whole. By 1951, the Ukrainian percentage had decreased to 35.3, but the total percentage was down to 19.4. In 1961 the respective percentages were 23 and 12.3 and in 1971, 13.2 and 7.1. Ukrainians have continuously lagged behind the general Canadian population in becoming urbanized. This has slowed down Ukrainian participation in business and in the professions, particularly in the movement from lower to higher status occupations. Ethnic groups with a large continuous immigration, such as the Italians and Asians, have had a better chance of increasing their participation in higher status occupations because they have moved directly to urban areas, even where the background of these immigrants was predominantly rural.

Clifford Sifton wished to get settlers for the stony lands of the prairies and to have them stay on the land as long as possible. When he said that a good settler for Canada was one whose father and grandfather were farmers, he implied that their sons and grandsons should also be farmers. For decades Ukrainians obliged.

The theory of delayed urbanization assumes that occupational mobility is a step-by-step process both in occupational advancement within an individual's lifetime and in occupational mobility from father to son. People do not move from one extreme to another, only one or two notches above their previous occupational level. In this manner, delay in urbanization also delays movement into higher status occupations.

3. A third factor is the ethnic community structure itself. Ivan Light in his perceptive study of ethnic enterprise in America has attempted to explain why the Blacks in the United States have had difficulty in developing business enterprises, whereas the Chinese were able to do it with ease, though both had poor beginnings. His answer was that the Chinese have a structure of community relationships which favours economic interdependence. The Chinese community structure includes networks of quid pro quo relationships upon which individuals or families can rely for economic betterment and organizations and associations aimed at economic betterment of individuals and families.[9] The same can be said of the Jewish ethnic community structure.

Light's thesis about the Blacks is also applicable to the Ukrainian community. The Ukrainian community structure is not economically oriented. Traditionally, it has had very few institutions aimed at assisting individual economic betterment. Two types of economic institutions have developed in the Ukrainian community in Canada— co-operatives and credit unions. The impact of co-operatives has been mainly in agriculture rather than individual business development. The movement to establish credit unions started in the late 1930s, but most have developed and grown after the Second World War.

The main economic impact of credit unions on the Ukrainian community has not been in business development but in purchase of homes and land. Loans for business development have been only a minor part of credit union activities.[10]

Apart from credit unions, virtually all other institutions and organizations in the Ukrainian community have been aimed at cultural preservation and the maintenance of ethnic identity rather than economic development.

4. The fourth factor is socio-psychological. The type of businesses that the bulk of Ukrainians have been engaged in, such as real estate, hotels and motels, general stores, grocery stores, own account truck

drivers, auto repair shops, and barber and beauty shops seem to be low-risk businesses. Quite possibly, Ukrainians shy away from taking high risks. There is an historical basis for this in the Ukrainian social structure developed in Ukraine in which individual ventures were often punished rather than rewarded. The subordinate position the Ukrainian community as a whole has held throughout long historical periods is probably at the root of this attitude. This may also be a contributing factor to the prevalence of Ukrainians in lower level professional occupations. Lower level occupations may often involve less risk taking than do the higher level occupations.

5. The fifth factor is the legacy of the Ukrainian rural community structure. Traditionally, commercial business jobs did not enjoy high prestige in the Ukrainian village. Prestige was accorded to clergymen and teachers. Becoming a teacher meant social mobility. Commercial occupations were often associated with non-Ukrainians, especially Jews, with whom Ukrainian peasants had been accustomed to deal. For the first few decades after their arrival in Canada, Ukrainian settlers often preferred to deal with Jewish merchants. Many Jews in Canada at that time were also immigrants from Ukraine, who knew the language and understood the peasants' customs.

The early businesses established by Ukrainians had to rely mainly on Ukrainian patronage, which was difficult to attract. "Patronize your own" campaigns, appealing to the immigrants' ethnic solidarity, were undertaken. These campaigns became an important aspect of the early development of Ukrainian-owned business, but the need for them prolonged the process of development.[11]

These five factors taken together help to explain why Ukrainians in Canada are less engaged in business occupations than are other comparable ethnic groups. Further sociological and historical research, however, is needed to explain the phenomenon fully.

NOTES

1. For a discussion of the problem of convergence analysis, see Warren E. Kalbach, "Demographic Aspects of Ethnic Identity and Assimilation," in *Sounds Canadian: Languages and Cultures in Multi-Ethnic Society*, ed. Paul M. Migus (Toronto: Peter Martin Associates, 1975), 139–46.

2. See Wsevolod W. Isajiw and Norbert J. Hartmann, "Changes in the Occupational Structure of Ukrainians in Canada: A Methodology for the Study of Changes in Ethnic Status," in *Social and Cultural Change in Canada*, 2 vols., ed. W. E. Mann (Toronto: Copp Clark, 1970), 1:96–112.

3. Statistics Canada, *1971 Census of Canada*, Part 3 (Bulletin 3.3–7) (Ottawa: Queen's Printer, 1975), 3: Table 4.

4. The occupational categories selected include the following occupational codes:

managerial occupations: 1130—general managers and other senior officials; 1135—financial management occupations; 1136—personnel and industrial management occupations; 1137—sales and advertising management occupations; 1141—purchasing management occupations; 1143—production management occupations; 1145—management occupations in construction operations; 1149—other managers and administrators; *sales occupations:* all 513—sales of commodities; all 514—street vendors; all 517—sales of services; all 519—other sales; *service occupations:* 6120—food supervisors and proprietors; 6131—hotel and motel managers; 6141—funeral directors, etc.; 6143—proprietors and managers of barber and beauty shops; *other proprietors and managers:* 3315—photographic studios; 8553—custom tailors, dressmakers; 8561—shoemaking and repairing; 8580—auto repair shops with employees; 8599—own account flower makers; 9170—transport operations with employees; 9173—own account taxi drivers and chauffeurs; 9175—own account truck drivers.

5. The following occupational codes are included in the three types of businesses: Type 1: 1130, 1135, 1136, 1137, 1141, 1143, 1145, 1149; Type 2: all 513 to 519; Type 3: 3315, 6120, 6131, 6141, 6143, 8553, 8561, 8580, 8599, 9170, 9173, 9175.

6. Donald H. Avery, "The Immigrant Industrial Worker in Canada 1896-1919: The Vertical Mosaic as an Historical Reality," in *Identities: The Impact of Ethnicity on Canadian Society,* ed. Wsevolod Isajiw (Toronto: Peter Martin Associates, 1977), 15-29.

7. James H. Gray, *The Winter Years: The Depression on the Prairies* (Toronto: Macmillan of Canada, 1966), 126-7.

8. Mykola Plawiuk, "Ukrainian Credit Unions in Canada," in *Slavs in Canada* (Toronto: Inter-University Committee on Canadian Slavs, 1968), 2:146-8.

9. Ivan H. Light, *Ethnic Enterprise in America: Business and Welfare Among Chinese, Japanese, and Blacks* (Berkeley: University of California Press, 1972).

10. So-Use (Toronto) Credit Union Ltd., *27th Annual Report for 1976,* 12.

11. Ol'ha Woycenko, *The Ukrainians in Canada* (Ottawa: Trident Press, 1967), 53-6; Myrna Kostash, *All of Baba's Children* (Edmonton: Hurtig, 1977), 213-15; Paul Yuzyk, *The Ukrainians in Manitoba: A Social History* (Toronto: University of Toronto Press, 1953), 53-9.

PART III
Social Trends

URBANIZATION OF UKRAINIANS IN CANADA: CONSEQUENCES FOR ETHNIC IDENTITY

Leo Driedger

Because research on urban Ukrainians is limited, this paper shall exploit Canadian census data as much as possible. The census provides demographic longitudinal data over more than a century, well before the first Ukrainians arrived in Canada in 1891.[1]

The objectives of this essay are (1) to outline broadly Canadian urban trends, (2) describe Ukrainian urbanization, (3) discuss the Ukrainian rural prairie hinterland, (4) focus on the major Ukrainian metropolitan centres, and (5) briefly explore how urbanism seems to affect Ukrainian identity.

Canadian Urban Trends

"In 1666 the colony of New France had fewer than 5,000 settlers, while the city of London (England) contained over 400,000 residents. At that time Montreal, Quebec and Trois-Rivières were tiny villages, each with a population of fewer than 1,000. By 1765, Montreal and Quebec had passed the 5,000 mark but no Canadian centre was as large as 20,000." By 1825, Montreal and Quebec had passed the 20,000 mark and York (now Toronto), the capital of Upper Canada, had a population of 2,000 persons. In 1851, over one hundred years ago, about 7 per cent of the population, which later formed the Dominion, were concentrated in cities of 20,000 population or more.[2]

Table 1 indicates that shortly before Confederation about one-sixth of the Canadian population was urban. Since then the proportion of

TABLE 1

Percentage of Urban[a] Population, Canada and Regions, 1851 to 1971

Region	1851	1861	1871	1881	1891	1901	1911	1921	1931	1941	1951	1961	1971
Canada (including Newfoundland)											62.4	69.7	76.1
Canada (excluding Newfoundland)	13.1	15.8	18.3	23.3	29.8	34.9	41.8	47.4	52.5	55.7	62.9	70.2	76.6
Newfoundland											43.3	50.7	57.2
Maritimes	9.0	9.9	11.9	15.3	18.8	24.5	30.9	38.8	39.7	44.1	47.4	49.5	55.5
Quebec	14.9	16.6	19.9	23.8	28.6	36.1	44.5	51.8	59.5	61.2	66.8	74.3	80.6
Ontario	14.0	18.5	20.6	27.1	35.0	40.3	49.5	58.8	63.1	67.5	72.5	77.3	82.4
Prairies						19.3	27.9	28.7	31.3	32.4	44.5	57.6	67.0
British Columbia			9.0	18.3	42.6	46.4	50.9	50.9	62.3	64.0	68.6	72.6	75.7

Source: Leroy O. Stone, *Urban Development in Canada* (Ottawa: Dominion Bureau of Statistics, 1967), 29.

Note: a From 1851 to 1911, the urban population figures refer to incorporated cities, towns and villages 1,000 and over only; from 1921 to 1951, the percentages are estimates of the percentages which would have been reported in the respective censuses had the 1961 census definition and procedures been used; for 1961, the figures are those published according to the 1961 census definition of "urban," and similarly for 1971.

urban population has increased by roughly 5 per cent per decade, although there have been considerable fluctuations. The two world wars brought heavy demands for manufactured products, which seemed to accelerate urban growth, while the Great Depression curbed growth in the thirties.

Rates of growth also vary greatly by provinces and regions. The Maritime provinces have always been less urban than the Canadian average, even though these provinces were a part of early Canadian history. Quebec has approximated the national average very closely, while Ontario has been slightly more urban throughout the past century. British Columbia was slightly more rural in 1881, but now is about as urban as the national average. The Prairies entered Confederation much later with a very rural population, but have doubled their urban population in the past three decades and are presently having their greatest urban growth, especially evident in Alberta and Saskatchewan.

Between 1901 and 1971, urbanization in Canada more than doubled from 35 per cent to 76 per cent, making Canada among the most highly urbanized countries in the world. The urban population of Great Britain was higher, while the urban population in the United States was about the same.

More recently, the ten Canadian provinces have been discussed as five major regions with twenty-two major metropolitan areas.[3] The Prairies and the Maritimes represent a number of provinces with similar characteristics, thus making the five regions somewhat more comparable by size of population, historical background and other socio-economic features. Each of the five regions of Canada was 50 per cent or more urbanized in 1971 with 82 per cent in Ontario, 81 per cent in Quebec, 76 per cent in British Columbia, 67 per cent in the Prairies and 57 per cent in the Maritimes.

The pattern of urbanization in the three most highly urbanized regions is different from that of the other two regions. There are also marked differences between the two least urbanized regions. The Maritimes, together with Quebec, comprise the two oldest of Canada's major regions of European settlement. However, the Maritimes are much more rural than the Canadian average.

While the central provinces were urbanizing rapidly from 1911 to 1941, the Prairies were relatively slow. The Great Depression hit the Prairies especially hard. During the thirty-year period from 1941 to 1971, urbanization in the Prairies has mushroomed. This unusually rapid growth seems to reflect the unusually short history of settlement. Expansion of the oil industry in Alberta and, more recently, the potash industry in Saskatchewan are speeding up urbanization. While rates of

TABLE 2

Total Ukrainian Population in Canada by Provinces, 1901 to 1971

Provinces	1901	1911	1921	1931	1941	1951	1961	1971
Atlantic Provinces	—	300	392	883	735	1,431	2,349	3,215
Quebec	6	458	1,176	4,340	8,006	12,921	16,588	20,325
Ontario	31	3,078	8,307	24,426	48,158	93,595	127,911	159,880
Manitoba	3,894	31,053	44,129	73,606	89,762	98,753	105,372	114,410
Saskatchewan	1,094	22,276	28,097	63,400	79,777	78,399	78,851	85,920
Alberta	634	17,584	23,827	55,872	71,868	86,957	105,923	135,510
British Columbia	23	682	793	2,583	7,563	22,613	35,640	60,145
Yukon and North West Territories	—	1	—	3	60	374	703	1,245
Total Ukrainians in Canada	5,682	75,432	106,721	225,113	305,929	395,043	473,337	580,660
Per cent Ukrainians in Total Canadian Population	0.1	1.1	1.2	2.2	2.7	2.8	2.6	2.7

Percentage of Total Ukrainian Population in Canada by Provinces, 1901 to 1971

Provinces	1901	1911	1921	1931	1941	1951	1961	1971
Atlantic Provinces	—	0.4	0.4	0.4	0.2	0.4	0.5	0.6
Quebec	0.1	0.6	1.1	2.0	3.0	3.3	3.5	3.5
Ontario	0.5	4.1	7.8	11.0	15.7	24.0	27.0	27.6
Manitoba	68.5	41.2	41.3	33.0	29.3	25.0	22.3	20.0
Saskatchewan	19.3	30.0	26.3	28.2	26.1	20.0	17.0	15.0
Alberta	11.2	23.3	22.0	25.0	23.5	22.0	22.4	23.3
British Columbia	0.4	0.9	0.7	1.2	2.5	6.0	8.0	10.3
Yukon and North West Territories	—	—	—	—	—	0.1	0.1	0.2
Total Ukrainians in Canada	100.0	100.0	100.0	100.0	100.0	100.0	100.0	100.0

Source: W. Darcovich and P. Yuzyk. eds., "Statistical Compendium on the Ukrainians in Canada, 1891–1976," (Unpublished typescript, Ottawa 1977), Series 20.41–64, 31–40.

urbanization in the Maritimes may continue to lag and those of the Prairies continue to accelerate, urbanization in Quebec, Ontario and British Columbia may level-off since they are closer to a point of urban saturation.

Ukrainian Urban Trends

Ukrainians came to Canada in three major migrations, the first before the First World War, the second between the two world wars, and the third after the Second World War. Table 2 shows that the Ukrainian population increased by 70,000 in the decade between 1901 and 1911. Due to a second major immigration in the twenties, the Ukrainian population increased from 107,000 to 225,000. The depression of the thirties reduced immigration and population growth. In the fifties the Ukrainian population again increased by about 80,000 (32,104 came as immigrants during 1947–52).[4] Immigration in the seventies declined, so that growth is now more dependent on natural increase and internal migration to urban centers.

Ukrainians in Canada have been located largely in the five most westerly provinces. As shown in Table 2, there are practically no Ukrainians located in the Maritimes and only a few in Quebec, mostly in Montreal. The total 1971 Ukrainian population in the five most easterly provinces was 23,540 or less than 5 per cent. There are a number of reasons for Ukrainian settlement in the West. The first was the availability of farmlands in the West after 1900. Secondly, the period of larger Ukrainian immigrations began less than seventy years ago, when the East was more settled and urban; and thirdly, they were of East European cultural background, and therefore not attracted to dominately French and Anglo-Saxon territories.[5]

In 1971 the 580,660 Ukrainians in Canada represented only 2.7 per cent of the total population. Well over one-half (57.8 per cent) still resided on the prairies. This figure represented one-half of all urban Ukrainians. Since they are located largely in the western provinces where urban growth is now mushrooming, urbanization is influencing Ukrainians profoundly.

Table 3 shows that in 1901 there were still only 5,682 Ukrainians reported by the Canadian census, 97 per cent of them rural. By 1971, the 580,660 Ukrainians in Canada were 75 per cent urban, comparable to the 76.6 per cent national urban figure.

In 1901 almost all rural Ukrainians were located in the three Prairie provinces. In fact, 70 per cent of all Ukrainians in Canada lived in Manitoba in 1901, making rural Manitoba the agrarian base for a majority of the early Ukrainian immigrants. By 1971, 80 per cent of rural

TABLE 3

Total Ukrainian Population in Rural Areas, 1901 to 1971 — Percentage of Ukrainians in Rural Areas, 1901 to 1971

Total Ukrainian Population in Rural Areas, 1901 to 1971

Region	1901	1911	1921	1931	1941	1951	1961	1971
Atlantic Provinces	—	14	22	77	175	285	591	650
Quebec	6	95	48	293	525	552	774	845
Ontario	31	1,230	2,295	6,289	14,523	17,503	15,098	14,220
Manitoba	3,839	25,740	35,587	50,658	58,837	49,406	41,139	35,675
Saskatchewan	1,075	20,985	25,290	53,032	65,086	62,319	48,709	40,275
Alberta	460	15,467	21,705	46,586	58,470	58,854	49,032	40,370
British Columbia	20	586	587	1,692	4,386	7,344	9,144	12,980
Canada	5,485	64,118	85,534	158,635	202,002	196,479	164,811	145,330

Percentage of Ukrainians in Rural Areas, 1901 to 1971

Region	1901	1911	1921	1931	1941	1951	1961	1971
Atlantic Provinces	.0	.0	.0	.1	.1	.2	.4	.5
Quebec	.1	.1	.1	.2	.3	.3	.5	.6
Ontario	.6	1.9	2.7	4.0	7.2	8.9	9.2	9.8
Manitoba	70.0	40.1	41.6	32.0	29.1	25.1	25.0	24.5
Saskatchewan	19.0	32.7	29.6	33.4	32.2	31.7	30.0	27.7
Alberta	8.0	24.1	25.4	29.4	28.9	30.0	30.0	27.8
British Columbia	.4	.9	.7	1.1	2.2	4.0	5.5	8.9
Canada	100.0	100.0	100.0	100.0	100.0	100.0	100.0	100.0

Total Ukrainian Population in Urban Areas, 1901 to 1971

Region	1901	1911	1921	1931	1941	1951	1961	1971
Atlantic Provinces	—	286	370	806	560	1,146	1,758	2,570
Quebec	—	363	1,128	4,042	7,481	12,369	15,814	19,485
Ontario	—	1,848	6,012	18,132	33,635	76,092	112,813	145,665
Manitoba	1	5,313	8,542	22,948	30,925	49,347	64,223	78,740
Saskatchewan	19	1,291	2,807	10,368	14,751	16,080	30,142	45,645
Alberta	—	—	—	9,286	13,398	28,103	56,891	95,140
British Columbia	3	96	206	891	3,177	15,269	26,496	47,165
Canada	197	11,314	21,187	66,478	103,927	198,564	308,526	435,330

Percentage of Ukrainians in Urban Areas, 1901 to 1971

Region	1901	1911	1921	1931	1941	1951	1961	1971
Atlantic Provinces	—	2.5	1.7	1.2	0.5	0.6	0.6	0.6
Quebec	—	3.2	5.3	6.1	7.2	6.2	5.1	3.5
Ontario	—	6.3	28.4	27.2	32.4	38.3	37.0	27.6
Manitoba	—	46.9	40.3	34.5	30.0	25.0	21.0	18.1
Saskatchewan	—	11.4	13.2	15.6	14.2	8.1	10.0	10.1
Alberta	—	—	—	14.0	13.0	14.1	18.3	22.0
British Columbia	—	.8	1.0	1.3	3.1	7.6	9.0	10.3
Canada	—	100.0	100.0	100.0	100.0	100.0	100.0	100.0

Source: Darcovich and Yuzyk, "Statistical Compendium," Series 20.1–29, 26–8.

Ukrainians in Canada still resided on the prairies. The rural Ukrainian base has shifted very little over the past seventy years, and it does not appear that it will shift very much in the future.

Recently, the Ukrainian population has been shifting increasingly toward urban centres. As shown in Table 3, Ukrainian urbanization began most strongly in Manitoba when, in 1911, 47 per cent of urban Ukrainians were urban Manitobans, resident mostly in Winnipeg. By 1941, urban Ukrainians had increased in Ontario with about one-third of urban Ukrainian Canadians living in Ontario and another third in Manitoba. By the end of the Second World War, almost twice as many Ukrainians lived in urban Ontario (76,092) as in urban Manitoba (49,347). By 1971, one-third (34 per cent) of all urban Ukrainians resided in Ontario. However, one-half (50 per cent) of the urban Ukrainians still lived on the prairies. While the rural Ukrainian stronghold has always been on the prairies, the urban Ukrainian population has been divided between the prairies and Ontario.

In 1911 only 9 per cent of all Canadian Ukrainians lived in metropolitan areas; by 1971, 59 per cent were located in the twenty-two Canadian metropolitan areas of 100,000 and over. Over one-half (55.0 per cent) of the metropolitan Ukrainians lived in the three large centres of Winnipeg, Edmonton and Toronto. One-quarter (27.8 per cent) of metropolitan Ukrainians lived in the five centres of Vancouver, Montreal, Calgary, Hamilton and Saskatoon. As illustrated in Table 4, the remaining fourteen metropolitan centres made up only one-sixth (17.5 per cent) of the Ukrainian metropolitan population. Five of the eight largest metropolitan Ukrainian centres were located in the West (four on the prairies). Two of the "Big Three" (Winnipeg and Edmonton) were located on the prairies.

At the beginning of the Second World War, only one-quarter of Ukrainians were located in metropolitan areas. The metropolitan shift did not begin in earnest until after the war, and the trend has continued. The earliest move to an urban centre occurred in Winnipeg before the Second World War; the second large influx occurred in Toronto after the Second World War; and the most recent trend is a large movement to metropolitan Edmonton.

It is important to study concentrations of Ukrainians because we assume that if Ukrainians plan to create urban institutions such as churches, voluntary organizations, parochial schools and communications media, there will need to be numbers large enough to support them. Concentrations of 10,000 to 15,000 should be able to support such institutions. From Table 4, it would appear that about eight metropolitan centres provide a sufficiently large demographic mass to support

TABLE 4

Ukrainian Population in Canadian Metropolitan Areas, 1911 to 1971

Canadian Metropolitan Areas	1971 Canadian Metropolitan Population	Ukrainian Metropolitan Population by Decades						
		1911	1921	1931	1941	1951	1961	1971
Winnipeg	540,000	3,599	7,001	21,459	28,162	41,997	53,918	64,305
Edmonton	496,000	692	547	5,025	6,668	19,111	38,164	62,655
Toronto	2,628,000	61	1,247	5,138	12,313	30,366	46,450	60,755
Vancouver	1,082,000	19	177	759	2,923	11,584	18,712	31,130
Montreal	2,743,000	322	1,092	3,850	6,643	11,238	14,519	18,050
Calgary	403,000	522	153	807	1,164	3,384	8,033	15,850
Hamilton	499,000	36	400	1,390	2,552	7,463	10,931	14,390
Saskatoon	126,000	—	332	1,146	2,499	4,257	9,072	14,390
St. Catharines	303,000	—	97	159	1,363	3,947	5,821	11,585
Thunder Bay	112,000	1,140	2,181	4,384	5,823	8,005	9,609	10,890
Regina	141,000	299	129	1,228	1,619	2,702	5,741	8,755
Windsor	259,000	—	204	1,829	2,246	5,101	5,508	6,975

Sudbury	155,000	—	286	1,192	2,260	3,601	4,942	5,625
Ottawa–Hull	603,000	53	247	482	780	817	2,985	5,400
London	286,000	27	14	67	188	899	1,834	3,360
Kitchener	227,000	15	362	428	749	1,545	2,163	3,210
Victoria	196,000	—	6	7	178	790	1,509	2,615
Halifax	223,000	—	—	28	26	127	432	770
St. John	107,000	—	2	3	10	51	103	135
Chicoutimi	134,000	—	8	1	54	47	67	130
Quebec City	480,000	7	—	1	22	42	60	120
St. John's	131,000	—	—	—	—	—	—	—
Total Metro Population	11,874,000	6,792	14,499	49,383	78,242	157,074	240,573	341,095
Per cent of Canadian Population	55.1	9.0	13.6	22.0	25.6	39.8	51.0	59.0

Source: Darcovich and Yuzyk, "Statistical Compendium," Series 21.243–294, 67–8.

Ukrainian institutions relatively well. The size of a city would be a factor. A population of 60,000 in Toronto will likely fare less well than a similar number in Edmonton, which is one-fifth the size of Toronto. Judging from studies of seven ethnic groups made in Winnipeg, it would seem that "cultural mass" is one important factor.[6]

There have been three periods of Ukrainian immigration. The first was from 1896 to 1914, the second from 1925 to 1930, and the third from 1947 to 1952. The first wave of 170,000 moved heavily onto the prairies. Seventy thousand (41 per cent) came to Manitoba, 12 per cent to Ontario and 9 per cent to Alberta. Two-thirds of the 57,900 Ukrainian immigrants who came in the second wave settled in Manitoba, 13 per cent in Alberta and only 7 per cent in Ontario. The third wave of 32,347 Ukrainian immigrants, who came during 1947–52, represented the smallest of the three immigrations. Almost one-half (47.3 per cent) settled in Ontario, only 12 per cent in Manitoba and 6 per cent in Alberta.[7] One can assume that Ukrainians residing in Winnipeg represent immigrants from the first two immigrations and have been in Canada longer, that Ukrainians in Toronto represent immigrants from both the first two and the most recent immigrations and that the 60,000 Ukrainians residing in Edmonton in 1971 are old settlers or very recent internal Canadian migrants.

By the sixties, Ukrainian immigration from abroad had declined to a mere 3,430 and prospects for a great influx of Ukrainian immigrants in the future are not great. During the sixties the greatest number of rural Ukrainians moved to Edmonton, and this trend will likely continue during the seventies, indicating a large Ukrainian growth in Edmonton.

The Rural Ukrainian Aspen Belt

A few farmers came with Lord Selkirk to the Red River settlement in 1812, but agricultural farming did not flourish until after Manitoba became a province in 1870. Treaties 1, 2 and 3 were signed with the Indians in 1871 and 1873 and soon the Mennonites (1874) and Icelanders (1875) came to join the French and English settlers. The Ukrainians were late in coming. By 1901, most of the better agricultural land in southern Manitoba had been taken, so the Ukrainians were left to choose land north of Winnipeg. The French, Mennonites and others also preceded the Ukrainians to the Northwest Territories (now Saskatchewan and Alberta). Again, Ukrainians were left with land north of Yorkton, Saskatoon and Edmonton.

Due to the late immigration to the prairies and their choice of land, Ukrainians created a rural settlement often referred to as the parkland or the prairie aspen belt. Some scholars claim that Ukrainians, who were used to having a combination of farm land and trees for fuel and shelter in Ukraine, actually chose to settle in the zone between the rich farmlands to the south and the treeline and lakes to the north.[8] Whatever the reasons, they formed a Rural Prairie Aspen Belt anchored east of Winnipeg and extending through the interlake region north of Winnipeg westward through the Dauphin and Yorkton areas and into the regions north of Saskatoon to be anchored in the west by an area to the north of Edmonton. This Rural Prairie Aspen Belt later became an important feeder of Ukrainian migrants into Winnipeg and Edmonton.

As Table 3 showed, the rural Ukrainian population has always been concentrated on the prairies, where 97 per cent of the rural population was located in 1901. Seventy years later 80 per cent of rural Ukrainians still lived there. Ten per cent were located in rural Ontario and another 10 per cent lived in rural British Columbia.

Canadian demographic studies show that 24 per cent of all Canadian residents were rural in 1971, of whom 17.3 per cent were rural non-farm and 6.6 per cent were rural farm. Almost three times as many were non-farm as farm. Table 5 shows that the Canadian-Ukrainian rural non-farm and rural farm ratio in 1951 (73 and 27 per cent respectively) was the reverse of the 1971 Canadian national ratio. However, by 1971, the Ukrainian rural farm and non-farm populations were about the same. Although the Ukrainian non-farm proportion has increased greatly in twenty years, it was still not nearly as heavily non-farm as the national rural population in 1971.

Rural farm and rural non-farm populations vary greatly by regions. The highest proportions of the farm population were located on the prairies (25.2 per cent in Saskatchewan, 14.5 per cent in Alberta and 13.2 per cent in Manitoba). The rural non-farm population made up more than 40 per cent of the total population in the Maritimes and about fifteen per cent in the Prairies and Ontario.

In 1951 about one-fourth of the rural prairie Ukrainians were non-farm and three-fourths were rural farm. By 1971, two-thirds were still rural farm. The high farm quality of the Rural Prairie Aspen Belt will likely continue perpetuating a more conservative Ukrainian community emphasis, replenishing the Ukrainian centres of Winnipeg and Edmonton.

While a small proportion of all rural Ukrainians live in Ontario (10 per cent), by 1971 only one in four was on the farm. The small rural segment of Ukrainians in Ontario was not nearly as firmly anchored in a traditional conservative farm community like the Ukrainian Rural Prairie Aspen Belt, which tends to promote greater rural community solidarity. The traditional farm community seems to be even less

TABLE 5

Percentage Ukrainian Rural Farm (RF) and Rural Non-Farm (RNF) Population, Canada and the Provinces, 1951 to 1971

Region	1951		1961		1971		Total Ukrainian Population in Rural Areas (Farm and Non-Farm)		
	RF	RNF	RF	RNF	RF	RNF	1951	1961	1971
Atlantic Provinces	32.3	67.7	11.0	89.0	19.2	80.8	285	591	650
Quebec	45.0	55.0	30.0	70.0	14.8	85.2	552	774	845
Ontario	46.0	54.0	34.0	66.0	24.0	76.0	17,503	15,098	14,220
Prairie Provinces	78.0	22.0	66.0	34.0	61.0	39.0	170,579	138,880	116,320
British Columbia	20.0	80.0	18.0	82.0	11.3	88.7	7,344	9,144	12,980
Canada	73.0	27.0	60.0	40.0	52.2	47.8	196,479	164,811	145,330

Source: Darcovich and Yuzyk, "Statistical Compendium," Series 20.41-64, 31-40.

established in British Columbia, where only one out of ten Ukrainians reported rural farm status in 1971. The migrants which Vancouver draws from the rural areas are mostly non-farm Ukrainians. In fact, there are only about 13,000 to 14,000 rural Ukrainians to draw from in each of Ontario and British Columbia.

Table 6 shows that over half (58 per cent of all Ukrainians live in the Prairies. They represent 80 per cent of all rural Ukrainians and 50 per cent of all urban Ukrainians. This heavy rural concentration is bound to support Ukrainian identity, as these rural migrants move to prairie cities. In addition these 116,000 rural prairie Ukrainians form a continuous belt which acts as a support system to feed rural Ukrainians into urban centres adjacent to the belt. A very high proportion of these rural migrants moving into these prairie cities are of rural farm background.

TABLE 6
Ukrainian Population in Rural and Urban Areas by Regions, 1971

Region	Rural		Urban		Total	
	N	%	N	%	N	%
Atlantic Provinces	650	.5	2,570	.6	3,220	.6
Quebec	845	.6	19,485	4.5	20,330	3.5
Ontario	14,220	9.8	145,655	33.5	159,885	27.6
Prairies	116,315	80.0	219,525	50.4	335,840	57.8
British Columbia	12,980	8.9	47,165	10.8	60,145	10.3
Yukon and North-west Territories	320	.2	920	.2	1,240	.2
Canada Total	145,335	100.0	435,325	100.0	580,660	100.0

Source: Darcovich and Yuzyk, "Statistical Compendium," Series 22.1–16, 140.

Table 6 also shows that in 1971 one-fourth of all Ukrainians lived in Ontario, representing one-third of all urban Ukrainians and 10 per cent of all rural Ukrainians, of whom three-fourths are non-farm. There are less than 4,000 Ukrainian farmers in Ontario. Ontario Ukrainians have neither a Rural Prairie Aspen Belt for support nor a strong source of traditional farm migrants into their cities. The Ukrainian population in Toronto, one of the three largest Ukrainian urban centres, is scattered in this metropolis of almost three million. Both the shutdown of Ukrainian immigration and the absence of a rural Ukrainian hinterland will make it much more difficult for urban Ukrainians in Toronto to create and perpetuate a Ukrainian identity over time. The situation in British Columbia seems to be very similar.

The "Big Three" Ukrainian Metropolitan Axis

Table 4 clearly showed that the three metropolitan areas of Winnipeg, Edmonton and Toronto (Ukrainian populations of 60,000 each) clearly dominate the Ukrainian demographic scene in Canada. Figure 1 shows that one-third (32.3 per cent) of all Ukrainians in Canada live in these three metropolitan centres. The "Big Three" also include close to one-half (43.1 per cent) of all urban Ukrainians in Canada and represent over half (55.0 per cent) of all metropolitan Ukrainians.

They also form an important metropolitan axis, which appears to be influential demographically and symbolically. Winnipeg has been the largest and most influential Ukrainian urban centre during the past century. Until 1931, more than twice as many Ukrainians resided in Winnipeg as in Toronto and Edmonton combined. This changed by 1971, when the three cities were in a dead heat for first place. Winnipeg's early head start meant that it became the established centre for numerous Ukrainian newspapers, various clubs and organizations, the Ukrainian Catholic and Greek Orthodox dioceses, St. Andrew's College and numerous other cultural and religious institutions.

By 1971, Toronto to the east and Edmonton to the west were becoming increasingly more influential in Ukrainian metropolitan life. As illustrated in Table 4, large numbers of Ukrainian immigrants after the Second World War came to Toronto and more than doubled the population in the latter part of the 1940s and the early 1950s. The presence of these first-generation Ukrainians boosted Ukrainian culture in Toronto, created institutions and even drew away some institutional activities from Winnipeg.

The Ukrainian population grew more slowly in Edmonton. The Edmonton influx began after the Second World War. The population nearly doubled in the 1960s, while populations in Winnipeg and Toronto were levelling off. It now appears that Edmonton has gained a momentum which will easily make it the largest Ukrainian metropolitan centre in Canada by 1981. Like Winnipeg, Edmonton continues to draw rural Ukrainian migrants from the Rural Aspen Belt adjacent to the metropolis. As one of the fastest growing cities in Canada, Edmonton like Toronto, is a strong magnet which draws immigrants from near and far. The oil industry makes Alberta the most affluent province in Canada, thereby continuing to draw Ukrainian migrants.

These three Ukrainian metropolitan centres can be conceived of as the "Big Three" Metropolitan Axis. Winnipeg, in the middle, represents the "old traditional" urban centre, which is becoming less dominant as the influences of Toronto and Edmonton increase. While Winnipeg anchors the east end of the Rural Ukrainian Aspen Belt, Edmonton anchors the

FIGURE 1

The "Big Three" Ukrainian Metropolitan Axis and the Rural Ukrainian Aspen Belt, 1971

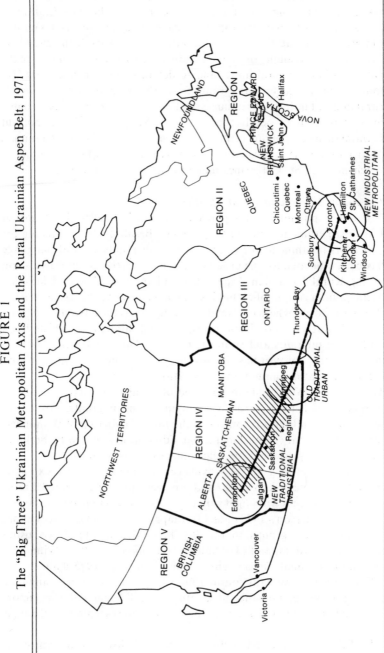

western end of the same belt. Both are clearly fed and influenced by these Ukrainian rural migrants. Edmonton has become the "new traditional industrial" Ukrainian metropolis because it draws on its Ukrainian hinterland and at the same time attracts migrants from elsewhere toward its many opportunities. Ukrainians in Toronto do not have the advantage of the rural hinterland feeder to sustain their culture. No longer replenished by immigrants from abroad and with a negligible rural migrant influx, Ukrainians could increasingly become assimilated in a metropolis of nearly three million. Numerous other important Ukrainian metropolitan centres fall near the "Big Three" Ukrainian Metropolitan Axis. Saskatoon, Thunder Bay, Sudbury, Hamilton, Kitchener and St. Catherines make the axis more influential.

Ukrainian Urban and Rural Identity

It is not possible in this paper to present a detailed discussion of Ukrainian ethnic identity in urban areas. Besides, when searching for indicators of ethnic identity in the census, one finds that only language has been tabulated for the urban criterion. Nevertheless, our discussion of the Rural Ukrainian Aspen Belt and the "Big Three" Ukrainian Metropolitan Axis implies that Ukrainian identity will be stronger in the Prairies than elsewhere in Canada. Winnipeg has the advantage of long established Ukrainian institutions, a rural hinterland which feeds traditional migrants and supports the "Big Three" Ukrainian Metropolitan Axis. Toronto has the advantages of a more recent first- and second-generation immigrant population, of being part of the "Big Three" on the Metropolitan Axis and of being an attractive industrial complex which tends to draw immigrants and migrants. Edmonton seems to have all the advantages of the former two, except Winnipeg's early institutional establishment, but Edmonton seems to be building many vibrant, possible more relevant, recent institutions.

In this section we shall (1) provide census data to show the extent of Ukrainian language knowledge and use over time, (2) compare Ukrainian identity factors with eight other groups in the Rural Prairie Aspen Belt using Anderson's 1972 data, (3) compare Ukrainian identity factors with nine other groups in the Big Five Metropolitan Axis using O'Brien's 1976 data, and (4) examine Ukrainian identity in Winnipeg, the "old traditional" urban centre, using Driedger's 1975 data.[10]

Since many Ukrainians consider knowledge and use of their language as basic to the maintenance of identity, we will begin with this factor. The best longitudinal data is available in the censuses from 1921 through 1971.

In Table 7 we see that before the Second World War almost all

TABLE 7

Percentage of Ukrainians with Knowledge of Their Mother Tongue by Rural-Urban Status in Canada and the Provinces, 1931 to 1971

Region	1931			1941			1951			1961			1971		
	Total	Urban	Rural	Total	Urban	Rural	Total	Urban	Rural	Total	Urban	Rural	Total	Urban	Rural
Atlantic Provinces	82.9	83.4	77.9	65.6	—	—	50.8	52.3	44.9	37.6	37.5	37.7	16.5	17.1	13.8
Quebec	81.8	82.3	86.2	88.0	—	—	80.0	80.5	68.8	70.3	70.8	60.5	53.6	54.3	39.6
Ontario	87.7	89.3	80.5	85.3	—	—	69.4	69.6	68.5	57.9	59.0	49.7	46.4	47.3	37.8
Manitoba	93.9	90.5	95.4	94.9	—	—	84.6	78.3	90.9	69.6	63.4	79.3	57.4	52.8	67.5
Saskatch- ewan	93.6	86.2	95.1	94.1	—	—	87.0	73.4	90.6	72.3	61.3	79.1	57.4	50.2	65.5
Alberta	95.8	80.7	96.8	93.9	—	—	84.6	72.2	90.6	67.8	58.7	78.4	48.1	42.9	60.3
British Columbia	77.7	71.5	—	71.4	—	—	57.5	56.4	54.5	43.8	44.2	42.8	29.2	30.1	26.3
Canada	93.1	—	—	92.1	—	—	79.6	72.0	87.4	64.4	59.3	73.9	48.9	45.9	57.8

Source: Darcovich and Yuzyk, "Statistical Compendium," Series 31.60–75, 237–8.

Ukrainians in Canada (over 90 per cent) were able to speak their Ukrainian mother tongue. We do not have the rural-urban breakdown for the earlier years, but at that time Ukrainians were predominantly rural and a majority remained so until after the Second World War. By 1971, knowledge of the Ukrainian mother tongue had dropped to about one-half (48.9 per cent). Between 1951 and 1971, knowledge of the mother tongue was somewhat greater in rural areas, where it was well over one-half in 1971, in contrast to the urban areas where it dropped below one-half.

This suggests that maintenance of the mother tongue should be strongest in the rural areas of the Prairies, followed by the urban centres of the Prairies, the urban centres of Ontario and finally British Columbia and the Maritimes.

In 1921 regional variations were not yet very great, but the Ukrainian mother tongue was known for its high proportion of maintenance in the Prairies, followed by Ontario, British Columbia and eastern Canada. The regional pattern continued until 1971, although there was a general decline in all regions between 1951 and 1971. The highest proportion of knowledge of the mother tongue existed in the rural prairies, followed by the urban prairies and urban Ontario and Quebec. Less than one-half knew the Ukrainian language in rural Ontario, Quebec, British Columbia and the Maritimes. The Rural Ukrainian Prairie Aspen Belt has the strongest influence followed by the Metropolitan Axis. Outside these areas, knowledge of the Ukrainian language appeared to be minimal by 1971.

Knowledge and use of the Ukrainian language can be compared for Ukrainians of foreign and Canadian birth. It can be assumed that foreign-born Ukrainians would have the highest knowledge of their language, and would use it in their homes the most, followed by knowledgeable Canadian-born. This was found to be the sequence in eight of the largest Ukrainian metropolitan centres. Table 8 shows that almost all the foreign-born knew the Ukrainian language and that about two-thirds to three-fourths of them used it. Only one-third to one-half of the Canadian-born knew their language and almost none used it in their homes.

Although language knowledge and use seemed to be slightly higher in the "Big Three" centres, as expected, the difference was not great. The differences between the "Big Three" and other metropolitan centres where relatively few Ukrainians lived was somewhat greater. Knowledge and use of the Ukrainian language declines fast with each succeeding generation. If language use is indeed the major means of retaining Ukrainian identity, then the future for urban Ukrainian identity looks bleak indeed.

TABLE 8
Knowledge of Ukrainian Mother Tongue and Extent of Use of Ukrainian at Home in the Eight Largest Ukrainian Metropolitan Centres, 1971

Metropolitan Area	Total Ukrainian Population	Foreign Born		Canadian Born	
		% Able To Use Mother Tongue	% Who Speak Ukrainian Most Often At Home	% Able To Use Mother Tongue	% Who Speak Ukrainian Most Often At Home
Winnipeg	64,305	90	70	46	13
Edmonton	62,655	87	65	40	8
Toronto	60,755	86	71	37	16
Vancouver	31,130	72	39	24	3
Montreal	18,050	82	72	40	21
Calgary	15,850	76	46	25	4
Hamilton	14,390	82	66	33	12
Saskatoon	14,390	87	73	46	14

Source: Darcovich and Yuzyk, "Statistical Compendium," Series 31.50–59, 236; 31.178–187, 255.

Unfortunately, except for language use, the information found in the census on ethnic identity is very limited. This necessitates finding other sources of data and more indicators of Ukrainian identity. Excellent comparative data on nine ethnic groups, including Ukrainians, were gathered in rural northern Saskatchewan by Alan Anderson in a thesis mentioned earlier. Anderson studied a number of ethnic bloc settlements north of Saskatoon, using such factors as general attitude toward ethnic identity maintenance, attendance at religious services, extent of endogamy, attitudes toward religious and ethnic intermarriage and language preference.[11]

Table 9 shows that almost all of both the Ukrainian Catholic (82 per cent) and Orthodox (80 per cent) adherents favoured identity preservation. Indeed, except for the German Catholics, a very large majority of all the ethnic groups studied favoured preservation. Almost all of the nine ethnic groups reported knowledge of their mother tongue and two-thirds of both Ukrainian groups used it often at home. Knowledge and use of Ukrainian was much higher in this rural bloc settlement in 1972 than the national Ukrainian rural average in 1971.

Three-fourths of the Ukrainians sampled also attended church regularly—once a week or more. The extent of Ukrainian endogamy was very high (90 per cent). Seventy per cent of the Ukrainian Catholics

TABLE 9

Ukrainian Identity in Rural Northern Saskatchewan (Heart of the Rural Prairie Aspen Belt)
by Attitudes to Identity Preservation, Church Attendance, Language Preference and Use,
and Marriage Preference and Exogamy, in Percentages

Ethnic Groups	Number in Sample	Percentage Favouring Identity Preservation	Language Preference		Church		Intermarriage		
			Knowledge of Mother Tongue	Frequent Use of Mother Tongue	Regular Attendance	Extent of Endogamy	Opposed to Religious Exogamy	Opposed to Ethnic Exogamy
Hutterite	6	100	100	100	100	100	100	100
Polish Catholic	14	92	100	87	53	69	73	40
Doukhobor	17	85	95	70	55	60	35	45
Ukrainian Catholic	126	82	99	67	82	90	70	70
Ukrainian Orthodox	66	80	100	63	70	89	43	41
Mennonite	184	75	97	69	86	98	69	57
Scandinavian	64	74	90	37	87	96	77	52
French	142	70	99	78	91	91	81	46
German Catholic	62	33	93	29	53	90	70	10
Sample Total	681	68	97	60	86	92	70	44

Source: Alan Anderson, "Assimilation in the Bloc Settlements of North-Central Saskatchewan: A Comparative Study of Identity Change Among Seven Ethno-Religious Groups in a Canadian Prairie Region," (Ph.D. thesis, University of Saskatchewan, 1972), 30–120.

were opposed to both religious and ethnic exogamy. However, less than one-half of Ukrainian Orthodox respondents opposed religious and ethnic intermarriage. Endogamy was actually higher for most groups than their opposition to intermarriage, which may mean that exogamy will increase in the future. Indeed, the third-generation Ukrainians did not score as high on all of the identity indicators.

This rural sample of Ukrainians indicates that religious and ethnic identity is still very high in northern Saskatchewan. Compared to other rural ethnic groups in the same area, Ukrainian identity is not as high as that of the Hutterites, but it is considerably higher than that of the German Catholics. Rural Ukrainian-language knowledge, endogamy and church attendance were very high. Although this is only a limited sample of Ukrainians, it does show that this community, in the heart of the Rural Ukrainian Prairie Aspen Belt, is maintaining its identity very strongly. Rural communities such as these feed Ukrainian migrants into Winnipeg, Edmonton and Saskatoon, but are almost non-existent in the Toronto, Montreal and Vancouver areas.

Having sampled a community of Ukrainians in the rural prairies, we now turn to a sample of the five largest Ukrainian metropolitan centres. Ken O'Brien, Jeffrey Reitz and Olga Kuplowska did a metropolitan survey of ten ethnic groups, including Ukrainians in Montreal, Toronto, Winnipeg, Edmonton and Vancouver.[12] Although their major interest focused on non-official language use, they also collected some data on religious beliefs, church attendance, attitudes toward ethnic schools, ethnic newspapers and use of ethnic radio.

The data in Table 10 represent the composite responses in five metro-politan centres from each of the ten groups. Metropolitan Ukrainian knowledge of their mother tongue was high (88.8 per cent) and much higher than the Canadian census report in 1971 (46 per cent), but not as high as the rural sample in Saskatchewan (100 per cent). However, only one-half (49 per cent) used their mother tongue often; more Ukrainians (65 per cent) in the rural sample used it often.

About two-thirds of metropolitan Ukrainians attended church once a week or more (63 per cent), and almost as many indicated that they had strong religious beliefs (60 per cent). About the same proportion (62.9 per cent) favoured more ethnic schools to promote the Ukrainian language. A small proportion made use of the media; about one-fourth (29.7 per cent) read Ukrainian newspapers regularly and about as many (22.1 per cent) listened to Ukrainian radio programmes.

Compared to the other nine ethnic groups sampled in the five selected Canadian metropolitan areas, Ukrainian respondents again ranked in the middle. Groups with more recent immigrants such as the Greeks,

TABLE 10

Ukrainian Identity in Five Metropolitan Centres (Montreal, Toronto, Winnipeg, Edmonton, Vancouver) by Knowledge and Use of Mother Tongue, Church Attendance, Religious Beliefs, and Preference for Ethnic Schools, in Percentages

Ethnic Group	Number in Sample	Language Preference		Religion		Ethnic School	Ethnic Media	
		Knowledge of Mother Tongue	Use of Mother Tongue	Church Attendance	Religious Beliefs	Preference	Newspaper Readership	Radio Regular Listening
Greek	172	99.1	91.7	75.3	78.4	76.7	45.1	67.5
Italian	355	93.7	84.3	82.4	78.1	63.2	46.8	51.2
Portuguese	111	97.7	95.2	86.4	74.8	38.6	35.6	62.4
Chinese	151	96.3	88.0	36.1	28.0	61.2	64.1	34.3
Hungarian	137	90.3	63.1	75.1	53.5	41.3	40.3	19.0
Ukrainian	338	88.8	49.0	63.0	60.2	62.9	29.7	42.0
Polish	278	77.3	46.1	74.1	59.8	43.3	33.4	21.0
German	346	78.5	45.7	69.0	52.9	36.2	34.0	34.9
Dutch	262	82.0	42.0	80.0	59.6	24.6	33.6	18.6
Scandinavian	283	52.3	13.9	55.4	46.7	27.4	18.7	3.4
Sample Total	2,433	86.3	62.6	72.1	63.2	47.0	38.4	41.6

Source: G. K. O'Brien, J. G. Reitz and O. M. Kuplowska, *Non-Official Languages: A Study in Canadian Multiculturalism* (Ottawa: Supply and Services, Canada, 1976), 50–150.

Italians and Portuguese ranked higher, while the Dutch, German and Polish respondents ranked lower on most identity factors. Ukrainian identity in the metropolis, as measured by this sample, was considerably lower than in the rural sample, but nevertheless fairly substantial.

While we have discussed a number of ethnic variables and the extent to which these influence Ukrainians in rural and urban centres, none of these have been developed into a more comprehensive Ukrainian ethnic identity index or scale. Driedger first attempted an Ethnic Cultural Identity Index using both attitudinal and behavioural items by comparing seven groups of ethnic university students in Winnipeg in 1975.[13] He also developed a Self Identity Index using the same seven groups.[14] By means of a factor analysis, he also developed six Ethnic Cultural Behavioural Identity (ECBI) index items.[15]

In Table 11 we see that Ukrainian university students scored moderately high in comparison to other ethnic groups on many of the six cultural behavioural factors (religious attendance, endogamy, language use, participation in ethnic organizations, attendance at ethnic schools and choice of ingroup friends). French and Jewish identity was highest; Scandinavian and British identity was lowest. This moderate Ukrainian identification seems to be consistent with observations in both the Anderson and the O'Brien studies. Three-fourths of Ukrainian students reported that no one in their immediate family had married a non-Ukrainian, which, although not as high as in the rural sample, was quite high. Somewhat less than one-half of students sampled attended church at least twice a month (43.6 per cent) and had attended a Ukrainian school for at least a year or more (41.1 per cent). Ukrainian student use of their language at home (22 per cent), participation in at least one Ukrainian organization (23 per cent) and choice of Ukrainian as a majority of ingroup best friends (16 per cent) was relatively low.

Ukrainian university students in Winnipeg have a moderate degree of ethnic cultural identity compared to other ethnic students. The Winnipeg study also shows that the endogamy factor is much more important for most students than language use. Even church attendance and attendance at ethnic schools was reported more often by students than use of their ethnic language at home. One cannot assume that the census reports of declining language use is sufficient to assess the overall identity of Canadian Ukrainians. Even though the Winnipeg research is a study of only one city, the number of factors used to assess Ukrainian identity are more adequate than those in the census.

Conclusion
Demographic data show that, in 1971, three-fourths of all Ukrainians

TABLE 11

Ukrainian Identity in Winnipeg Compared with Six Other Groups by Six Identity Factors
(Religion, Endogamy, Language, Organizations, Parochial Education, Friends)

Ethnic Groups	Number in Sample	Composite Identity Rank	Behavioural Identity Factors (Percentages)					
			Religious Attendance	Endogamy	Language Use	Ethnic Organization Participation	Ethnic School Attendance	Choice of Friends
1 French (F)	86	55.0	55.6 (G)	91.3 (J)	60.5 (F)	28.6 (J)	79.1 (F)	62.5 (J)
2 Jewish (J)	112	44.2	53.5 (F)	75.6 (U)	29.4 (G)	22.9 (U)	74.0 (J)	48.8 (F)
3 German (G)	160	40.8	46.4 (P)	72.0 (B)	21.8 (U)	22.6 (F)	57.1 (P)	44.6 (B)
4 Ukrainian (U)	188	36.8	43.6 (U)	65.4 (F)	14.3 (P)	16.3 (G)	44.3 (G)	36.3 (G)
5 Polish (P)	56	31.5	22.9 (B)	62.8 (G)	1.8 (J)	12.7 (P)	41.1 (U)	15.9 (U)
6 British (B)	157	29.3	14.7 (S)	57.1 (S)	0 (S)	10.0 (B)	27.4 (B)	5.4 (P)
7 Scandinavian (S)	61	16.4	7.2 (J)	53.2 (P)	0 (B)	2.0 (S)	24.5 (S)	0 (S)
Sample Total	820							

Source: Leo Driedger, "In Search of Cultural Identity Factors: A Comparison of Ethnic Students," *Canadian Review of Sociology and Anthropology* 12 (1975): 150–62.

in Canada were urban, a figure similar to the Canadian population. A majority of Ukrainians have always lived in the Prairies. By 1971, more than one-half still lived in the Prairie provinces, but one-fourth were in Ontario due to more recent immigration and migration.

The Prairies have always represented the major rural Ukrainian region. Eighty per cent of all rural Ukrainians were still located there in 1971. The Rural Ukrainian Prairie Aspen Belt, which began to form in 1901, continues to dominate rural Ukrainian life and continues to act as a traditional feeder to adjacent urban centres such as Winnipeg and Edmonton.

After the Second World War, Ukrainians migrated primarily to the "Big Three" Ukrainian Metropolitan Axis of Winnipeg, Toronto and Edmonton. While Winnipeg Ukrainian institutions and media have dominated in the past, recent immigrant populations have increased the importance of Toronto and Edmonton. Edmonton is destined to be the future dominant Ukrainian metropolitan centre because it is supported by the Rural Prairie Aspen Belt, which draws immigrants and migrants alike to its influential, industrial development. Today one-third of all Ukrainians in Canada live in the "Big Three" Ukrainian Metropolitan Axis and over one-half of all metropolitan Ukrainians live in Winnipeg, Edmonton and Toronto.

This strong movement of Ukrainians to the city, especially after the Second World War, has had consequences for Ukrainian identity. Knowledge of the Ukrainian language before the Second World War was high. After the war it declined. By 1971, only about one-half of Ukrainians knew their language. The decline of Ukrainian-language use in the home is even more pronounced among Canadian-born Ukrainians. Ethnic language knowledge and use seems to have remained fairly high among Ukrainians in the Rural Prairie Aspen Belt, although third-generation Ukrainians use it less. Foreign-born Ukrainians in the metropolitan areas are still fluent in the language and use it often; however, a majority of the Canadian-born Ukrainians no longer know their language and very few use it at home. If Ukrainian identity depends on ethnic language use, then the future for metropolitan Ukrainian identity is not encouraging.

Some studies suggest that Ukrainian endogamy and church attendance in the Rural Aspen Belt is high. Rural segregation, endogamy, religious commitment and ethnic language use seem to reinforce each other, so that Ukrainian identity is still fairly strong and will likely remain alive despite urban influences for some time to come. Ukrainian endogamy, church attendance and ethnic schools also seem to be influential among students in Winnipeg, for example, but use of the

Ukrainian language seems to be minimal. Ukrainian identity appears to be on trial in the two prairie centres of the "Big Three" Metropolitan Axis. Hope for the survival of Ukrainian identity among Canadian-born Ukrainians in metropolitan Toronto seems even more tenuous. The data used in this study did not lend themselves to an exploration of the extent to which urban Ukrainians are shifting their identity from traditional cultural factors to new institutional and symbolic identity factors such as those suggested by Glazer and Moynihan.[16] Unless this shift is indeed taking place among Ukrainians in the metropolitan centres, their current identity will be difficult to maintain for very long. Research needs to be designed to explore the extent to which urban Ukrainians are developing an identity "beyond the cultural melting pot." A new urban Ukrainian identity may be emerging, but we will need to look elsewhere than to the census to find it.

NOTES

1. Much of the Canadian census data used in this paper are taken from an unpublished typescript in four volumes, "Statistical Compendium on the Ukrainians in Canada, 1891–1976," edited by William Darcovich and Paul Yuzyk. The Compendium consists largely of special census cross-tabulations with a special focus on Ukrainians.
2. Leroy O. Stone, *Urban Development in Canada: An Introduction to the Demographic Aspects* (Ottawa: Dominion Bureau of Statistics, 1967), 14.
3. Twenty-two urban centers were designated metropolitan areas in 1971. A population of 100,000 or more was the major criterion. Since the ten provinces of Canada are unequal in size and population, five regions are often used for comparison: the Atlantic region or the Maritimes (Newfoundland, Nova Scotia, New Brunswick, Prince Edward Island); Quebec; Ontario; the Prairies (Manitoba, Saskatchewan, Alberta); and British Columbia. There are three metropolitan centres in the Atlantic region, three in Quebec, nine in Ontario, five in the Prairies and two in British Columbia.
4. Darcovich and Yuzyk, Series 50.62–77, 492.
5. Leo Driedger, "Toward a Perspective on Canadian Pluralism: Ethnic Identity in Winnipeg," *Canadian Journal of Sociology* 2 (1977): 77–95.
6. Leo Driedger and Glenn Church, "Residential Segregation and Institutional Completeness: A Comparison of Ethnic Minorities," *Canadian Review of Sociology and Anthropology* 11 (1974): 30–52.
7. Darcovich and Yuzyk, Series 50.62–77, 492–3.
8. Ol'ha Woycenko, *The Ukrainians in Canada* (Winnipeg: Trident Press, 1967).
9. *Canada Year Book* (Ottawa: Queen's Printer, 1975), 165.
10. Alan Anderson, "Assimilation in the Bloc Settlements of North-Central Saskatchewan: A Comparative Study of Identity Change Among Seven Ethno-Religious Groups in a Canadian Prairie Region" (Ph.D. dissertation, University of Saskatchewan, 1972); K. G. O'Brien, G. Reitz and O. M. Kuplowska, *Non-Official Languages: A Study in Canadian Multiculturalism* (Ottawa: Ministry of Supply and Services, Canada, 1976); Leo Driedger, "In Search of Cultural Identity Factors: A Comparison of Ethnic Students," *Canadian Review of Sociology and Anthropology* 12 (1975): 150–62.
11. Alan Anderson collected his data during 1969–71 in eighteen ethno-religious bloc settlements (seven French Catholic, one German Catholic, two Mennonite, two

Hutterite, one Ukrainian Orthodox, one Ukrainian Catholic, one Polish Catholic, one Russian Doukhobor and two Scandinavian Lutheran) located in the region between Saskatoon, North Battleford and Prince Albert (Census Divisions 15 and 16). A 2 per cent controlled quota sample was stratified by age, generation and sex to represent as closely as possible the demographic structure of the total population of each settlement. One in every fifty persons of the relevant ethnic and religious category was interviewed in each settlement. This sampling technique yielded a thousand cases. These respondents were located in the heart of the Rural Ukrainian Aspen Belt between Edmonton and Winnipeg, north of Saskatoon.

12. K. G. O'Brien, J. G. Reitz and O. M. Kuplowska in *Non-Official Languages* made their study of ten groups (Chinese, Dutch, German, Greek, Hungarian, Italian, Polish, Portuguese, Scandinavian and Ukrainian) in five metropolitan centres (Montreal, Toronto, Winnipeg, Edmonton and Vancouver). Each metropolitan area was stratified by ethnic-language groups, using 1971 census data and tracts as units. This data is especially useful, because it includes the three metropolitan centres of the "Big Three" Ukrainian Metropolitan Axis and the five metropolitan centres in which there are the largest number of Ukrainians.

13. See footnote 15.

14. Leo Driedger, "Ethnic Self Identity: A Comparison of Ingroup Evaluations," *Sociometry* 39 (1976): 131-41.

15. Leo Driedger has published numerous articles based on a random sample of 1,560 questionnaires which were collected from 76 classes at the University of Manitoba. The following seven groups were represented: British (157), French (86), Germans (160), Jews (112), Poles (56), Scandinavians (61) and Ukrainians (188). This data is useful because it was gathered in Manitoba and Winnipeg, the old traditional Ukrainian areas of settlement in the heart of the Rural Ukrainian Aspen Belt, and it also includes the Big Three Ukrainian Metropolitan Axis. The study used a series of Cultural, Identity, Self-Identity, and Religous Identity indexes in a more sophisticated way than had previously been done in Canada.

16. Nathan Glazer and Daniel Patrick Moynihan, *Beyond the Melting Pot: The Negroes, Puerto Ricans, Jews, Italians and Irish of New York City* (Cambridge, Mass.: Harvard University Press—MIT, 1970).

LANGUAGE RETENTION PATTERNS AMONG UKRAINIAN CANADIANS

Olga M. Kuplowska

This essay presents a profile of urban Ukrainians in Canada with respect to Ukrainian language knowledge, use and support, as indicated by the data collected for the Non-Official Languages (NOL) Study.[1] The urban centres from which the sample was selected were: Montreal, Toronto, Winnipeg, Edmonton and Vancouver.

Sample Description

Ukrainians living in these five urban centres account for 40.8 per cent of all Ukrainians living in Canada. More than half live in other urban centres and rural areas. Thus the profile of Ukrainians generated by this study is limited to Ukrainians in these five cities and those eighteen years

TABLE 1
Sample Distribution of Ukrainians in Five Cities

City	Sample Percentage
Montreal	5.3
Toronto	25.7
Winnipeg	32.1
Edmonton	24.0
Vancouver	12.0
TOTAL	100.0

of age or older. Both elements were required qualifications for an interview. The sample distribution of Ukrainians across the five cities in Table 1 closely reflects the actual distribution of Ukrainians in these cities, based on 1971 census data.

In comparison to the other ethnic groups in the NOL study, Ukrainians had a good representation of each generation in their sample, as shown in Table 2. The first generation (immigrant), however, was overrepresented with 34.9 per cent. According to the 1971 census, 17.7 per cent of Ukrainian Canadians were born outside Canada.

TABLE 2

Percentage of Respondents in Each Generational Group, by Ethnic Group

Ethnic Group	First Generation	Second Generation	Third & Older Generations	N
Ukrainian	34.9	44.3	20.9	181,656
Chinese	88.7	8.6	2.8	57,636
Dutch	70.3	15.2	14.5	76,637
German	62.8	17.6	19.5	303,874
Greek	95.8	3.5	0.8	88,640
Hungarian	83.0	15.0	2.0	34,866
Italian	81.7	13.8	4.6	382,499
Polish	48.4	40.9	10.6	91,066
Portuguese	99.5	0.0	0.5	57,365
Scandinavian	34.6	44.5	20.9	69,353
TOTAL	67.8	20.8	11.4	1,343,586

A closer look at the immigrants reveals that they came to Canada either between 1946 and 1953 (22.3 per cent) or before 1945 (21.5 per cent). A still larger number (37.8 per cent) claimed to have grown up in Canada. The image created is one of a group whose members, for the most part, have had a long Canadian experience. As a result, the connotation usually associated with the term "immigrant" would be misleading if applied even to first-generation Ukrainian Canadians.

The age distribution of the Ukrainian sample was fairly well spread throughout all age categories, with the heaviest concentration (32.6 per cent) falling in the thirty-six to fifty year-old bracket. However, a little over 40 per cent were between the ages of eighteen and thirty-five, and 27 per cent were over fifty.

TABLE 3

Percentage of Ukrainians in Each Age Group (A) and by Generation (B)

	18–25 years	26–35 years	36–50 years	51–60 years	Over 60	N
A Overall Sample	19.4	20.9	32.6	12.8	14.3	179,217a
B First Generation	9.9	12.0	35.5	13.8	28.7	63,092
Second Generation	13.0	19.9	40.1	18.0	9.1	78,789
Third Generation	49.1	38.3	11.7	0.0	1.0	37,336

Note: aThe number of missing observations is 2,432.

A generational breakdown of the age distribution reveals that most of the younger respondents were third-generation Ukrainians, whereas the first generation had large percentages in the thirty-six to fifty, and over sixty, age groups. Second-generation Ukrainians tended to be middle-aged, although one-third were between eighteen and thirty-five years old.

Most of the first-generation respondents lived in Toronto and Montreal, where they comprised about one-half of each city sample. Winnipeg and Edmonton, on the other hand, had larger representations of the third and older generations (one-fourth to one-third of each city sample). Table 4 indicates that there were no third-generation Ukrainians in the Montreal or Toronto samples.

TABLE 4

Percentage of Ukrainians in each Generational Group by City

City	First Generation	Second Generation	Third & Older Generation	N
Montreal	46.1	46.6	—a	9,569
Toronto	54.4	37.7	—	46,741
Winnipeg	27.1	42.8	30.2	58,349
Edmonton	27.1	46.9	26.1	45,163
Vancouver	25.3	55.9	18.7	21,834

Note: aIn this and other tables very small Ns are not computed but are denoted by a dash (—).

A little over 80 per cent were married, one-half to Ukrainian spouses. Montreal and Vancouver had the highest intermarriage rate with only about one-third of the married respondents reporting a Ukrainian spouse. In each of the other three cities, over one-half of the married respondents were married to Ukrainians. From the data available, there does not seem to be any particular group into which Ukrainians are marrying.

Generation is definitely a major factor in the intermarriage rate. Among first-generation respondents, about one out of every four who were married had a non-Ukrainian spouse. Among second-generation respondents, the intermarriage rate had increased to one out of every two married couples. By the third generation, most of the married respondents had non-Ukrainian spouses.

Language Knowledge

In discussing language retention patterns among these urban Ukrainians, this paper has maintained the same approach as that used in the NOL study. First, it looks at the reported knowledge of Ukrainian among urban Ukrainians; secondly, it examines the use of Ukrainian in terms of frequency and context; and thirdly, it looks at support for the retention of Ukrainian among urban Ukrainians.

Table 5 shows that a majority of Ukrainians (72.4 per cent) reported Ukrainian as their mother tongue. Ukrainian was the mother tongue for 94 per cent of first-generation respondents and 76 per cent of second-generation respondents. By the third generation, however, only 29 per cent reported Ukrainian as their mother tongue. The others claimed English was the language they first learned.

TABLE 5
Percentages Reporting Mother Tongue, by Ethnic Group

Ethnic Group	Ethnic	English or French	Other	N
Ukrainian	72.4	27.0	0.6	181,656
Chinese	91.8	6.9	1.4	57,636
Dutch	74.1	23.1	2.8	76,637
German	69.1	29.5	1.4	303,872
Greek	91.2	2.0	6.8	88,640
Hungarian	85.6	9.9	4.5	34,866
Italian	87.9	11.0	0.3	382,499
Polish	63.8	24.2	12.1	91,066
Portuguese	97.1	2.9	0.0	57,365
Scandinavian	33.5	60.5	6.2	69,353
TOTAL	78.2	20.5	1.3	1,343,580

While overall mother tongue percentages were high, only 30.7 per cent claimed to be fluent in the language, while 58.1 per cent claimed some knowledge. It should be remembered that the respondents were asked to assess their own level of fluency in Ukrainian. Although there may be certain flaws in such self-reports, still they have an advantage, since "perceived" levels of fluency can also be influential factors in attitudes toward language and other cultural issues.

TABLE 6

Reported Percentages at Each Level of Knowledge of Ukrainian (A), by Generation (B) and by City (C)

		Level of Language Knowledge			
		Fluent	Some Knowledge	No Knowledge	N
A	Overall Sample	30.7	58.1	11.2	181,656
B	First Generation	63.6	36.4	—	63,378
	Second Generation	18.9	73.8	7.3	80,423
	Third Generation	0.7	61.8	38.5	37,855
C	Montreal	26.7	49.2	24.1	9,569
	Toronto	51.1	44.6	4.3	46,741
	Winnipeg	22.9	59.1	18.0	58,349
	Edmonton	23.7	70.1	6.2	45,163
	Vancouver	24.1	63.5	12.4	21,834

The first generation claimed a majority of the fluent speakers, although a very large percentage among the second generation (92.7 per cent) claimed at least some knowledge of the language. To be classified fluent, the respondents had to have indicated that they spoke, understood, read and wrote in their ethnic language "very well." Everybody else fell into the "some knowledge" classification. By the third generation, hardly anyone is fluent in Ukrainian and over one-third claim to have no knowledge at all of Ukrainian.

A comparison of mother tongue knowledge percentages with level of knowledge percentages across generations reveals that mother tongue knowledge drops mostly between the first and second generations. This makes the transition period from the first to the second generation the crucial one for language loss.

Toronto had the highest percentage of fluent speakers (one-half). All other cities had one-fourth of their respondents claiming fluency. A generational breakdown, however, provides interesting revelations. When one looks at first-generation Ukrainians in each city, at least one-half of the respondents claim to be fluent (with the exception of Winnipeg), and both Edmonton and Vancouver report slightly higher fluency rates than does Montreal. At the second-generational level, fluency among Toronto Ukrainians dropped from 83 to 15 per cent. Winnipeg Ukrainians report the least decrease with a drop from 42 to 25 per cent. Among second-generation respondents, this was the highest fluency rate. While the overall fluency rates for Winnipeg are not high, the carryover to the second generation is greater than Toronto's where the overall fluency rate is high. Similar East-West differences will be noted for other variables.

TABLE 7
Reported Percentages and Numbers (N) of Respondents
Fluent in Ukrainian in Five Cities at Two Generational Levels

City	Fluent Speaking			
	First Generation	N	Second Generation	N
Montreal	50.4	4,409	7.4	4,457
Toronto	83.3	25,418	15.4	17,644
Winnipeg	42.4	15,793	25.7	24,945
Edmonton	58.3	12,225	16.8	21,169
Vancouver	56.1	5,533	17.7	12,207

Note: There was a negligible percentage fluent in the third and older generations. It is not listed in the above table.

Education, Income and Language Knowledge

Prior research suggested a negative relation between language retention and higher education and income levels. The overall NOL survey findings point to only a slight relationship between income and language retention, while lending moderate support to the view that there is a negative relation between higher education and language retention. What relationships exist between these variables for Ukrainians?

The educational profile for Ukrainians, as shown in Table 8, is quite interesting. While about one-half of the entire Ukrainian sample reported having nine to twelve years of education (one-fourth had thirteen or more years of education and another fourth had eight years or less), the generational breakdown reveals that the main differences among generations are the percentages reporting lower and middle levels of education. One-half of the first generation has eight years or less of education and this percentage decreases across generations to 4 per cent for the third and older generations. This pattern is reversed for those with the middle level of education. Here percentages increase across generations from 29 per cent for the first generation to 67 per cent for the third and older generations. Little difference occurs in generational representation at the highest educational level. Between 21 per cent to 27 per cent reported having thirteen years or more of education at each generational level.

TABLE 8

Percentages at Three Levels of Education, by Generation

	Levels of Education			
Generation	13 years or more	9 to 12 years	8 years or less	N
First Generation	21.0	29.2	49.8	63,378
Second Generation	29.1	51.2	19.6	80,423
Third Generation	27.6	67.7	4.7	37,855
TOTAL	26.0	47.0	27.0	181,656

The fluency rates across educational levels for Ukrainains are different from those for the entire NOL sample. Among Ukrainian respondents, fluency is highest among those with eight years or less of education and lowest for those with nine to twelve years of education. Those with university education fall in between. Altogether, there was a more consistent negative correlation between fluency in the ethnic tongue and level of education for the entire NOL sample.

When controlling for generation, a different pattern emerges. Among first-generation respondents, those with the highest educational level have the highest fluency rates (73 per cent), followed closely by those with the lowest education (65 per cent). Respondents with nine to twelve years of education reported 55 per cent of their group as fluent. At the second-generational level, the pattern is similar to that of the entire Ukrainian sample. Those with the lowest education have the highest fluency rates, and those with the middle level of education have the lowest fluency rates. In general, however, for second-generation Ukrainians there is a drop in fluency regardless of educational level.

TABLE 9

Percentages at Three Levels of Knowledge of Ukrainian,
by Years of Education

| | Levels of Language Knowledge | | | |
Years of Education	Fluent	Some Knowledge	No Knowledge	N
13 years or more	31.1	56.9	12.0	47,207
9 to 12 years	18.5	65.4	16.2	85,326
8 years or less	51.6	46.7	1.7	49,123
TOTAL	30.7	58.1	11.2	181,656

TABLE 10

Percentages at Three Levels of Knowledge of Ukrainian,
by Generation and Years of Education

| | Levels of Language Knowledge | | | |
Years of Education	Fluent	Some Knowledge	No Knowledge	N
First Generation				
13 or more	73.0	27.0	0.0	13,327
9 to 12	55.1	43.2	1.7	18,485
8 or less	64.7	35.3	0.0	31,567
Second Generation				
13 or more	21.0	68.2	10.8	23,434
9 to 12	12.9	78.8	8.2	41,208
8 or less	31.2	68.8	0.0	15,781
Third Generation				
13 or more	0.0	69.9	30.1	10,446
9 to 12	1.0	59.6	39.4	25,634
8 or less	—	—	—	1,775

Note: Dashes (—) denote small Ns.

These different fluency patterns between the first and second generations can be explained if we know where each generation received most
of its education. One may assume that the second-generation studies
were primarily in Canada, but no such assumption can be made about
the first generation. If there is truly a negative relationship between

higher education and language retention (as noted to some extent in the overall NOL sample and among second-generation Ukrainians), a number of questions should be raised. Are the educational and economic aspirations of those who do retain an ethnic language different from those who do not? Does the education and economic system in Canada work against ethnic language acquisition and retention? What are the implications for the ethnic community where those possessing greater skills and awareness as a result of education are likely to be less conversant in its language than the less formally educated persons in the same ethnic group?

TABLE 11
Percentages at Three Levels of Income, by Generation

Generation	Levels of Income				
	Less than $7000	$7000–13,999	$14,000 or more	Refused/ Don't know	N
First Generation	22.9	29.9	8.4	38.7	63,378
Second Generation	20.4	31.0	28.6	19.9	80,423
Third Generation	15.6	50.1	18.9	15.4	37,855
TOTAL	20.3	34.6	19.5	25.5	181,656

TABLE 12
Percentages at Three Levels of Knowledge of Ukrainian, by Income

Income	Levels of Language Knowledge			
	Fluent	Some Knowledge	No Knowledge	N
Less than $7000	35.1	58.3	6.6	36,903
$7000 to $13,999	25.5	61.4	13.1	62,893
$14,000 or more	13.8	71.4	14.7	35,512
TOTAL	30.7	58.1	11.2	181,656

The income of Ukrainians in the sample tended to increase across generations (Table 11), and fluency in Ukrainian decreased with income (Table 12). If one controls for generation, the differences in fluency rates between the various income levels become more pronounced, suggesting a negative relationship between higher income and knowledge of Ukrainian (Table 13). Among first-generation Ukrainians, fluency is much more prevalent among those earning $13,999 or less, than among those earning $14,000 or more. While fluency rates drop drastically for second-generation respondents, overall the fluency rate is still twice as much for those earning less than $7,000 than for those at the highest income level. In contrast with the findings for the entire NOL sample, income seems to be an influential factor in determining the language retention rates of Ukrainians.

TABLE 13

Percentages at Three Levels of Knowledge of Ukrainian,
by Generation and Income

Income	Fluent	Some Knowledge	No Knowledge	N
First Generation				
Less than $7000	57.8	42.2	0.0	14,544
$7000 to $13,999	63.7	36.3	0.0	18,967
$14,000 or more	29.9	64.2	5.9	5,329
Second Generation				
Less than $7000	27.6	72.4	0.0	16,443
$7000 to $13,999	15.9	76.6	7.5	24,959
$14,000 or more	13.4	73.5	13.2	23,026
Third Generation				
Less than $7000	0.0	58.7	41.3	5,916
$7000 to $13,999	0.0	66.4	33.6	18,967
$14,000 or more	3.5	70.2	26.4	7,157

Intermarriage and Language Knowledge

With respect to intermarriage and language retention, Table 14 indicates that there is some relationship between one's knowledge of the ethnic tongue and the ethnicity of one's spouse, although at this point not enough data has been collected to say whether it is a cause or effect. In any case, knowledge of Ukrainian is much higher among those with Ukrainian spouses than among those with non-Ukrainian spouses. In the former case, over one-half reported being fluent while only 9 per cent of those intermarried claimed to be fluent. Interestingly, among single Ukrainians fluency is quite low. Almost one-fourth know no Ukrainian.

TABLE 14

Ethnicity of Spouse, by Three Levels of Knowledge of Ukrainian

Ethnicity of Spouse	Levels of Language Knowledge			
	Fluent	Some Knowledge	No Knowledge	N
Ukrainian spouse	54.1	43.6	2.2	77,869
Non-Ukrainian spouse	9.4	74.5	16.1	67,744
Single (not married)	21.0	56.7	22.2	33,233
TOTAL	30.7	58.1	11.2	181,656

Language Use

In contrast to the relatively high rates of knowledge of Ukrainian, the percentage who use the language on a daily basis is quite low. Overall, 35.2 per cent claim to speak Ukrainian every day, 13.8 per cent speak it often, 14.3 per cent occasionally and 11.9 per cent rarely or never. Almost one-fourth felt that their knowledge of Ukrainian was insufficient for personal use (Table 15).

Of those who are fluent in Ukrainian, frequent use of the language in speaking is nearly universal (Table 16). Among those reporting only "some knowledge" of Ukrainian, three-fifths report little or no use of the language. Thus while one-third of those with at least some conversational knowledge of Ukrainian do use the language on a frequent basis, its use resides mainly with fluent speakers.

As expected, daily and frequent use of the language decreases with each generation (Table 16). While over 80 per cent of the first generation use Ukrainian everyday or often, by the second generation, about 40 per cent use it with such frequency. At best, most of the third-generation speakers use it only occasionally.

When looking at the generational effect on language use for people having the same knowledge of Ukrainian, the drop in language use from generation to generation is slightly reduced (Table 17). Nonetheless, the data indicate that in the second and third generations, Ukrainian tends to fall into a degree of disuse even among those who know it well.

Some very interesting differences among cities can be observed. When overall frequencies of use were compared, Montreal, Toronto and Winnipeg reported similar percentages (between 33 and 37 per cent of the sample speak Ukrainian every day). Edmonton reported the highest percentage of daily use (42 per cent), even though this city claimed a

TABLE 15
Percentages of Non-Official Language Use, by Ethnic Group

Ethnic Group	Frequency of Use				Insufficient Conversational Knowledge	N
	Every Day	Often	Occasionally	Rarely or Never		
Ukrainian	35.2	13.8	14.3	11.9	22.6	181,656
Chinese	82.7	5.3	5.7	1.4	4.9	57,636
Dutch	31.5	8.5	23.6	13.2	21.9	76,637
German	35.6	10.1	15.4	10.4	27.7	303,876
Greek	89.5	2.2	2.8	2.4	2.3	88,640
Hungarian	55.9	7.2	13.8	9.6	10.7	34,866
Italian	78.5	5.8	2.9	3.0	9.4	382,500
Polish	39.6	6.5	15.7	7.7	28.8	91,066
Portuguese	89.1	6.1	0.8	0.6	2.3	57,365
Scandinavian	8.0	5.9	13.9	11.3	59.7	69,353
TOTAL	54.7	7.9	10.2	7.2	19.0	1,343,583

TABLE 16

Percentages Using Ukrainian with Various Degrees of Frequency, by Levels of Language Knowledge (A) and by Generation (B)

	Frequency of Use				Insufficient Conversational Knowledge	N
	Every Day	Often	Occasionally	Rarely or Never		
A Fluent	78.1	14.3	5.3	2.2	0.0	55,757
Some Knowledge	19.3	16.2	21.8	19.2	19.6	105,561
B First Generation	69.8	14.4	7.4	2.7	5.8	63,378
Second Generation	22.7	17.2	18.7	19.7	17.9	80,423
Third Generation	3.9	5.4	16.5	10.6	60.7	37,855

TABLE 17

Percentages Using Ukrainian with Various Degrees of Frequency, by Generation and Levels of Language Knowledge

Generation	Levels of Language Knowledge	Frequency of Use				Insufficient Conversational Knowledge	N
		Every Day	Often	Occasionally	Rarely/ Never		
First Generation	Fluent	83.2	12.1	2.5	2.2	0.0	40,328
	Some Knowledge	46.9	18.7	16.2	3.6	14.6	22,735
Second Generation	Fluent	65.8	18.9	12.9	2.4	0.0	15,181
	Some Knowledge	13.9	18.5	22.1	26.1	14.2	59,321
Third Generation	Fluent	—	—	—	—	—	248
	Some Knowledge	6.3	7.7	26.6	17.0	39.8	23,506

Note: Dashes (—) denote small Ns.

TABLE 18

Percentages Using Ukrainian with Various Degrees of Frequency, by City (A) and by Levels of Language Knowledge in Each City (B)

City		Frequency of Use				Insufficient Conversational Knowledge	N
		Every Day	Often	Occasionally	Rarely/ Never		
A Montreal		32.6	10.5	13.3	13.0	30.5	9,569
Toronto		35.1	22.0	12.1	15.8	15.0	46,741
Winnipeg		36.6	10.3	13.3	3.8	29.5	58,349
Edmonton		42.0	11.9	15.2	13.9	16.4	45,163
Vancouver		18.9	10.8	20.2	20.5	29.6	21,834
B Montreal	Fluent	87.1	12.9	0.0	0.0	0.0	2,550
	Some Knowledge	19.1	14.3	27.1	26.4	13.0	4,712
Toronto	Fluent	66.4	27.2	6.4	0.0	0.0	23,905
	Some Knowledge	2.5	18.1	19.9	35.5	23.9	20,833
Winnipeg	Fluent	91.4	3.8	0.0	4.8	0.0	13,350
	Some Knowledge	26.5	16.0	22.5	4.5	19.4	34,496
Edmonton	Fluent	88.3	6.1	0.0	5.6	0.0	10,689
	Some Knowledge	30.1	14.9	21.7	17.8	14.5	31,661
Vancouver	Fluent	72.4	0.0	27.6	0.0	0.0	5,262
	Some Knowledge	2.2	17.0	21.4	32.4	27.1	13,859

smaller percentage of fluent speakers. Vancouver, on the other hand, which had slightly more fluent speakers than did Edmonton, reported only 18.9 per cent using Ukrainian daily. These city differences become even more intriguing when only the fluent speakers in each city are considered. Winnipeg, Edmonton and Montreal report an exceptionally high frequency of use of Ukrainian (87 to 91 per cent). Vancouver reports 72.4 per cent using Ukrainian daily. Toronto, with the highest percentage of fluent speakers, uses Ukrainian least frequently. Even among those with only some knowledge of the language, daily use of Ukrainian occurs more frequently in Winnipeg, Edmonton and Montreal than in Toronto.

Similar results are obtained when looking at the frequency of use in each city by generation (Table 19). Edmonton and Winnipeg report the highest percentages of daily use in both the first and second generations. While a majority of first-generation respondents in Montreal, Toronto and Vancouver do use Ukrainian daily, almost no daily use is recorded by second and older generations in these three cities.

These findings imply that while generation is by far still the most important factor in language retention or loss, other factors peculiar to each city are at play. At times, they act to partially neutralize or reduce the effects of generation.

In various types of language studies, reference is often made to language domains, that is to situations or places where one language has preference over another for whatever reason. This may help to explain the discrepancies between the cities. The use of Ukrainian, even if it is not in perfect form, may have become more ingrained into the daily lives of Edmonton Ukrainians than into the daily lives of Toronto Ukrainians. If Ukrainian is not used at home in Toronto, it is even less likely to be used outside the home than in Edmonton.

Work being done by Jeffrey G. Reitz on language maintenance in urban ethnic communities indicates that retention and use of the ethnic tongue among children depends more on external influences than the family or immediate ethnic community.[2] Unless the ethnic community becomes more relevant to the daily needs of its members, the gap between the general and ethnic communities increases to the point that members are forced to choose one over the other, instead of being able to bridge the two comfortably. Perhaps the Ukrainian community in Edmonton impinges more strongly on its members' lives than does the Ukrainian community in Toronto.

Among those who do tend to speak Ukrainian on a regular basis, one expects the greatest use will be found in the home among members of the immediate family or with close relatives. But to what extent is it being used beyond the home?

TABLE 19

Percentages Using Ukrainian with Various Degrees of Frequency by City at Two Generational Levels

Generation	City	Frequency of Use				Insufficient Conversational Knowledge	N
		Every Day	Often	Occasionally	Rarely/ Never		
First Generation	Montreal	63.6	0.0	15.3	0.0	21.1	4,409
	Toronto	64.5	16.8	8.6	2.2	7.8	25,418
	Winnipeg	77.5	14.0	5.3	3.3	0.0	15,793
	Edmonton	79.2	13.3	2.7	4.9	0.0	12,225
	Vancouver	56.1	18.3	12.2	0.0	13.4	5,533
Second Generation	Montreal	7.1	22.5	13.5	28.0	28.9	4,457
	Toronto	0.0	34.0	19.7	28.8	17.4	17,644
	Winnipeg	31.8	13.4	18.0	4.5	21.3	24,945
	Edmonton	42.5	10.3	16.4	21.7	7.8	21,169
	Vancouver	8.3	10.9	24.6	31.2	25.0	12,207

As expected, the greatest use of Ukrainian takes place among family members. Two out of three Ukrainian respondents use at least some Ukrainian in that context. Outside the home, the greatest use is with clergy and close friends. Much smaller percentages use Ukrainian with their grocer, their doctor and their co-workers or classmates. This suggests that Ukrainian is used primarily in informal contexts, with the exception of the church.

Among fluent speakers, these percentages are increased considerably. At least some Ukrainian is used 94 per cent of the time with families, 86 per cent of the time with friends and 84 per cent of the time with clergy. Use of at least some Ukrainian among fluent speakers also rises considerably with doctors, classmates and co-workers. The latter may indicate that a person who is fluent in his/her ethnic tongue may seek out situations where he/she can use it.

While a relatively high percentage reported using Ukrainian with clergy, other data on the church membership of Ukrainians and on the languages used in these churches indicate that the Ukrainian churches are no longer "keepers" of the Ukrainian language nor do its members see that as the church's role. One-fourth of the Ukrainian sample claimed no association with any church. Of those who did belong, 37 per cent said both Ukrainian and English were used in church services, 32 per cent said only Ukrainian was used and 25 per cent said that only English or French was used (Table 21). While most of those attending "Ukrainian language only" churches tend to be first generation, a large percentage of the first generation also belongs to bilingual Ukrainian churches. As expected, the second and older generations have large percentages attending churches where only English or French is used; very few attend churches where only Ukrainian is used. In general, membership in a church declines with generation.

Montreal and Toronto had the highest percentage attending churches where only Ukrainian was used, while Winnipeg and Edmonton tended to attend bilingual churches. Surprisingly, Vancouver reported the highest percentage of Ukrainians (about one-half of its membership) attending English-language churches. When respondents were asked what languages should be used in church, the responses given tended to reflect the actual situation. In other words, those who attended Ukrainian-only churches tended to say that only Ukrainian should be used, while those attending bilingual churches tended to support the use of both English and Ukrainian in church. Cross-tabulations by degree of fluency in Ukrainian, by generation and by city showed that these variables had little influence on responses. It seems that the church with which one associates is a good indicator of one's position on the language used in church.

TABLE 20

Percentages Reporting Some Use of Non-Official Languages in Speaking to Various Types of Persons, by Ethnic Groups

Ethnic Group	Family[a]	Close Friends	Clergy	Grocer	Doctor	Classmates/ Co-Workers	N
Ukrainian	66.5	40.5	40.9	8.2	13.9	16.3	181,654
Chinese	92.3	77.8	27.5	36.4	37.3	45.5	57,636
Dutch	68.9	27.3	5.0	0.6	6.3	0.6	76,637
German	61.5	29.8	14.8	6.7	9.2	9.3	303,637
Greek	93.5	81.1	84.0	37.2	32.7	33.0	88,642
Hungarian	85.0	46.0	36.7	8.0	31.3	15.7	34,866
Italian	89.7	67.4	49.9	43.1	33.1	26.9	382,501
Polish	63.7	35.4	20.9	6.5	8.8	7.2	91,066
Portuguese	97.7	88.3	62.7	52.4	34.6	37.3	57,365
Scandinavian	32.6	12.6	7.2	0.0	0.3	0.7	69,353
TOTAL	74.9	49.6	35.5	21.9	20.4	18.0	1,343,590

Note: [a]The percentages include respondents reporting some use, or exclusive use, with at least one family member.

TABLE 21

Percentages Reporting Languages Used and Which Should be Used
in Churches They Attend

Language(s)	Language(s) Currently Used in Church	Language(s) Which Should be Used in Church
Ukrainian only	24.0	22.2
English/French only	18.9	19.9
Ukrainian & English	27.3	28.7
Other	2.4	1.9
Not associated with any church	26.5	26.8

Since fluent speakers are the prime patrons of Ukrainian-only churches and the prime supporters of Ukrainian use in these churches, one could deduce that unless language loss with each generation is curtailed, Ukrainian-language churches will gradually disappear. On the other hand, since a large percentage of fluent speakers also attend bilingual churches and are supportive of them, it is possible that factors other than lack of fluency in Ukrainian determine one's choice of church. An analysis of the various churches' characteristics by the languages used would provide at least some direction to speculation about the future of Ukrainian churches.

Support for Language Retention

Over 75 per cent of Ukrainian respondents said they were either very or somewhat desirous of having Ukrainian maintained and used in Canada (Table 22). This is interesting in the light of previous findings on fluency and use. Furthermore, when asked to rate the seriousness of various problems confronting ethnic groups, language loss was mentioned most frequently as a very serious problem. Loss of ethnic customs and traditions and loss of interest in traditional religion were also perceived as problems. However, problems such as job discrimination and social isolation received negligible mentions.

When asked to give reasons why they support Ukrainian language retention, over one-third said they were in favour of retaining Ukrainian because it would help them maintain traditions and customs. While very few claimed they favoured language retention for communication purposes, about 24 per cent said they saw its value as a second language.

(This area is worthy of further investigation since maintaining a language for traditional purposes only is almost a guarantee of its downfall.)

TABLE 22
Attitudes Toward Non-Official Language Retention, by Ethnic Groups in Percentages

Ethnic Group	Attitude Toward Language Retention				
	Very Desirable	Somewhat Desirable	Indifferent	Somewhat or Very Undesirable	N
Chinese	38.8	40.3	10.5	10.5	57,636
Dutch	8.5	41.6	35.2	14.7	76,637
German	21.9	43.9	25.1	9.2	303,670
Greek	54.3	28.4	9.8	7.5	88,642
Hungarian	17.3	51.2	20.0	10.8	34,866
Italian	39.8	36.7	14.9	8.7	380,570
Polish	19.5	52.3	21.6	6.5	91,066
Portuguese	29.2	39.2	16.1	11.8	57,365
Scandinavian	14.1	39.6	33.3	13.0	69,223
Ukrainian	30.3	45.8	19.8	4.1	181,165
TOTAL	29.9	41.1	20.1	8.8	1,340,833

Source: G. K. O'Brien, J. G. Reitz and O. M. Kuplowska, *Non-Official Languages: A Study in Canadian Multiculturalism* (Ottawa: Minister of Supply and Services, Canada, 1976), 75.

Among those who expressed opposition to the retention of the Ukrainian language (4.1 per cent), most gave no particular reason for feeling that way. Among respondents from the other ethnic groups who were also opposed to the retention of their respective language, many felt that language retention prevents mixing with others, but this feeling was not very strong among Ukrainians. Either Ukrainians really had no particular reason for opposing retention (which undercuts the seriousness of their position) or they did not care to express their true feelings about the issue.

Support for language retention is high regardless of level of knowledge of Ukrainian or generation, although stronger among the fluent speakers and first-generation Ukrainians.

In a city-by-city breakdown, Toronto reports the highest incidence of fluent speakers in Ukrainian; Edmonton reports Ukrainian used most often on a daily basis; and Montreal records the highest support for its

TABLE 23

Attitudes Toward Retention of the Ukrainian Language,
by Level of Language Knowledge (A) and Generation (B) in Percentages

	Attitude Toward Language Retention				
	Very Desirable	Somewhat Desirable	Indifferent	Not Very, or Not at all, Desirable	N
A Fluent	48.4	35.0	12.4	4.2	55,757
Some Knowledge	25.0	49.0	21.6	4.3	105,561
No Knowledge	7.9	59.0	30.5	2.6	20,338
B First Generation	43.9	37.6	12.8	5.8	63,092
Second Generation	26.3	50.4	20.4	2.9	78,789
Third Generation	13.7	50.6	31.5	4.1	37,336

TABLE 24

Attitudes Toward Retention of the Ukrainian Language, by City,
and by City at Three Generational Levels in Percentages

City		Very Desirable	Somewhat Desirable	Indifferent	Not Very or Not at all Desirable	N
A Montreal		42.9	47.0	6.7	3.4	9,569
Toronto		24.7	56.6	17.4	1.2	46,741
Winnipeg		29.4	41.1	21.7	7.8	58,349
Edmonton		33.2	42.3	21.6	2.9	45,163
Vancouver		33.3	42.1	21.4	3.2	21,834
B First	Montreal	48.9	43.6	0.0	7.4	4,409
Generation	Toronto	33.9	42.1	21.8	2.2	25,418
	Winnipeg	39.9	32.0	10.4	17.7	15,303
	Edmonton	48.7	44.2	7.2	0.0	12,225
	Vancouver	86.5	13.5	0.0	0.0	5,533
Second	Montreal	35.5	57.7	6.7	0.0	4,457
Generation	Toronto	14.2	74.0	11.8	0.0	17,644
	Winnipeg	32.2	39.1	24.6	4.1	24,945
	Edmonton	34.2	40.0	22.7	3.0	21,169
	Vancouver	14.8	54.5	24.8	5.8	12,207
Third	Winnipeg	16.1	51.8	27.5	4.5	17,611
Generation	Edmonton	15.4	44.4	34.5	5.8	11,769

Attitude Toward Language Retention

retention. In all, 89 per cent of Montreal Ukrainian respondents said they were very or somewhat supportive of retaining the Ukrainian language. Toronto followed closely with 81.3 per cent expressing strong support, followed by Edmonton and Vancouver with 75 per cent. Winnipeg recorded the lowest support in comparison with other cities —70.5 per cent.

When one looks at the support expressed in each city at each generational level, however, different patterns emerge. All first-generation Vancouver respondents expressed strong support for the retention of Ukrainian, as did over 90 per cent of the first generation in Montreal and Edmonton. Between 70 and 76 per cent of the first generation in Winnipeg and Toronto expressed similar support.

At the second-generation level, strong support for the retention of Ukrainian remained relatively the same as among first-generation respondents in Montreal and Winnipeg, but it increased for Toronto Ukrainians and decreased for Vancouver and Edmonton Ukrainians. In all cases, however, percentages expressing strong support were in the majority.

An attempt was made to depict graphically the relationship among the five cities with respect to three variables—knowledge of Ukrainian, its use and support for its retention (Figure 1). When overall figures across all generations were used, no clear pattern among these three variables evolved. In each case, fluency rates were the lowest, support rates the highest and frequency rates in the middle.

Applying the same formula to both first- and second-generation figures, the patterns become even more unclear, especially for the first generation. Among first-generation respondents in each of the cities, frequency of use rates tend to be higher in some cases than the support rates, and, for Toronto, expressed support is even lower than expressed language knowledge. While one can speculate about these patterns, in the author's opinion more information is needed and perhaps a larger sample as well.

One question which arises is whether support for retention of Ukrainian is simply a reflection of ethnic group self-identity, a variable which is usually considered to be strongly related with generational status. For the Ukrainian sample, ethnic self-identification does not seem to be strongly related with generation but is with degree of support of the language.

Even among first-generation Ukrainians, the tendency is to refer to oneself as being a "Ukrainian Canadian," or a "Canadian of Ukrainian origin" (59 per cent) or even "Canadian" (26.6 per cent) rather than as a "Ukrainian only" (12.3 per cent). In the second and third generations,

FIGURE 1
Patterns of Ukrainian Language Knowledge, Use and Support among Ukrainians in the Five Cities

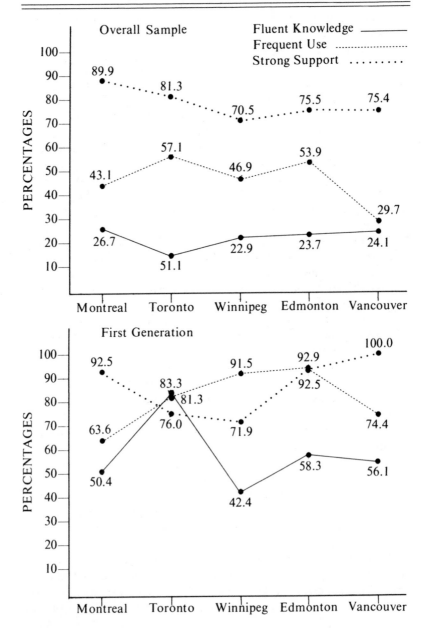

FIGURE 1—*Concluded*

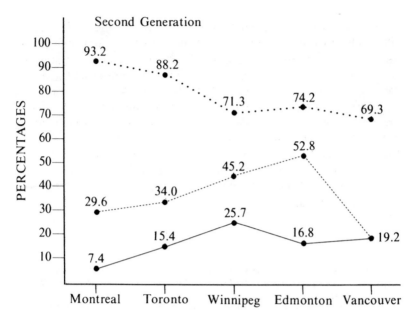

hardly anyone refers to himself as a "Ukrainian" and the split is almost even between calling oneself a "Ukrainian Canadian" or just a "Canadian." A stabilizing factor seems to have set in after the first generation, and one is tempted to say that identification was merely a preferential choice at the time of the interview.

However, when one looks at the degree of support for the Ukrainian language expressed by those who call themselves "Ukrainian Canadians" and by those who call themselves "Canadians," there is more to the way respondents identify themselves than just chance. Whereas 84 per cent of "Ukrainian Canadians" expressed strong support for language retention, only 64 per cent of "Canadians" did so. Furthermore, 28 per cent of "Canadians" expressed an indifference to retention. That these differences were not totally the result of generational influence is indicated by the results obtained when the generation factor is controlled. Among first-generation respondents "Ukrainian Canadians" express much stronger support for retention than do "Canadians." This also occurs among second-generation respondents. It would seem that ethnic identity is an important factor in the whole question of support for language, regardless of generation, even though some influence may still be coming from that area as well.

Conclusion

Generation is the principal correlate for knowledge of Ukrainian, although other factors such as income, education and ethnicity of spouse contribute to the overall result. While generational status also affects language use, decrease in language use is not primarily due to language loss from generation to generation but occurs because of other facilitating and motivating conditions. As indicated earlier, the highest frequencies of use were not always located where there were high fluency rates. The emphasis should be on social conditions which facilitate and encourage the use of Ukrainian. Otherwise, the language falls into disuse just as surely as if it were not known at all. Support for retention, in turn, is primarily determined by ethnic identification, generation and language knowledge.

NOTES

1. K. G. O'Brien, J. G. Reitz and O. M. Kuplowska, *Non-Official Languages: A Study in Canadian Multiculturalism* (Ottawa: Ministry of Supply and Services, Canada, 1976), 24–41.
2. J. G. Reitz, *Survival of Ethnic Groups* (Toronto: McGraw-Hill Ryerson, 1980).

TRENDS IN MARITAL STATUS AND FERTILITY OF UKRAINIANS IN CANADA

Jean E. Wolowyna

The family is one of the primary human institutions. It performs many functions for individual family members, for the family as a group and for society. Included in these functions are the production of economic goods and services, the giving of status, education and religious training of the young, recreation, protection and affection. The family is important both for reproducing and maintaining the species and larger social structures.

Marital status and fertility are two demographic characteristics which are related to family formation and functioning. A change in marital status usually precedes the formation or dissolution of the family. In Canada fertility is related to marital status in that unmarried individuals have few children compared to married persons. Consequently, the "age at first marriage" and the "proportion married" influence fertility. Furthermore, a large proportion of marital dissolutions tend to reduce fertility.

This paper examines trends in the marital status and fertility of Ukrainian Canadians and Canadians of all ethnic origins between 1931 and 1971. For the most part, it is descriptive. Trends for the Ukrainian ethnic group are traced through time and comparisons noted between Ukrainian Canadians and the remainder of the population. At the end of the paper an exploratory multivariate analysis is presented, which examines the relationship between several socio-economic and demographic variables and family size while holding constant the effects of the remaining factors.

Data

Data used in this analysis are mainly from "A Statistical Compendium on the Ukrainians in Canada, 1871–1976" supplemented by data from the "1971 Canadian Census 1/100 Public Use Sample Tape: Individual Province File."[1] The two defined groups are Ukrainian Canadians and Canadians of all origins. The group "Canadians of all origins" includes the entire Canadian population including the Yukon, the Northwest Territories and Newfoundland after 1949. Defining the Ukrainian ethnic group is somewhat more difficult and complex. Since the data from the Compendium come from both the census and vital statistics, the definitions used in these two sources and their changes through time must be considered. It is important that vital statistics and census definitions of ethnicity be comparable since the births obtained from vital statistics and the population totals obtained from the census comprise the numerators and denominators of fertility measures.

Warren Kalbach has summarized the instructions given to census enumerators and the questions used to obtain ethnic origin in censuses over the years.[2] In the 1971 and 1961 censuses a question was asked regarding the ethnic or cultural group to which the respondent or the respondent's ancestor on the male side belonged upon coming to this continent. In the 1951 census a question was asked about "origin," while in 1941 and 1931 a question was asked about "racial origin." In all cases the instructions to enumerators were to ascertain origin on the male side of the family. Although instructions to enumerators were similar for all census years, variations in the wording of the question may have influenced whether or not the respondent identified himself as "Ukrainian."

The instructions for ethnic origin in the vital statistics were similar to those given to the census enumerators. Origin again was traced through the male side. The major difference between the ethnicity question in the census and in vital statistics is that the "informant" for vital statistics is usually one of the parents unaided by an enumerator (until 1971 when the census became self-enumerated). Therefore, errors of misclassification may occur in both vital statistics and the census.

Marital Status

The major waves of Ukrainian immigration to Canada began after 1890. The first phase consisted of about 170,000 pioneers who arrived in Canada between 1896 and 1914. The second phase brought about 58,000

Ukrainians from about 1921 to 1939. From about 1947 to the early 1950s about 38,000 more Ukrainian immigrants arrived in Canada.[3]

Immigration can influence patterns of marital status. Immigration waves, particularly the earlier ones, usually contain a large proportion of young, single men who come to the country in search of land and work. If the man is single, a certain amount of time elapses before he is able to become established and find a spouse. This tends to result in a later age at marriage. Single women, on the contrary, are less likely to emigrate unless they are very young and come with their families.

Evidence has shown that the pressure to marry within the ethnic group is strong, especially in the case of first- and second-generation immigrants. This is true not only of Ukrainians but of other ethnic groups.[4] When there is community pressure to marry within the ethnic group, a marriage market of eligible candidates becomes important. To the extent that there is a relative shortage of women of marriageable age who belong to that ethnic group, women's age of first marriage tends to be reduced.

It has been found that the sex ratio of Ukrainians near the turn of the century was higher than for Canadians as a whole. In 1911 the sex ratio for Canadians was about 113 and for Ukrainians about 135. By 1961, the sex ratio for Canadians had declined to 102, which was similar to the Ukrainian sex ratio of 109.[5] These figures indicate that there was a greater shortage of Ukrainian women early in the century than recently and that the difference in the proportion of males and females was more pronounced for Ukrainians than for the entire Canadian population. In addition, the degree of intermarriage for Ukrainians has been increasing over the century.[6]

Two types of comparisons of marital status distribution can be done. First, the distribution of individuals by marital status for Ukrainians and Canadians can be compared at each year (1931, 1941, 1951, 1961 and 1971) to see whether any differences occur in the distributions at each of these times and whether these differences change over time. The other comparison is to follow the Ukrainian and Canadian distributions through time to see if any changes take place. For both of these comparisons, age and sex must be controlled since both influence the distribution of marital status.

First, the distributions of marital status for Ukrainians and Canadians of all origins are compared over time. In other words, the distribution of marital status by age for Ukrainian males is compared with that of Canadian males in 1931, 1941, 1951, 1961 and 1971. The comparisons are then repeated for females. When this is done, few differences are found between the distribution of marital status by age for Ukrainian and Canadian males over the years 1931 to 1971. There is a tendency for larger percentages of male Ukrainians twenty-five years and over in 1931, thirty-five years and over in 1941, fifty-five years and over in 1951 and sixty-five years and over in 1961 to be married and lower percentages to be single when compared with all Canadians. For the younger age groups in all these years and for all ages in 1971, a larger proportion of Ukrainians are single and a smaller proportion married when compared with all males in Canada. This appears to be a cohort effect since those who are most affected age at each successive time period. However, none of these differences are large. The same sort of pattern is seen in the Prairie provinces. In the central provinces of Quebec and Ontario the distribution of marital status for males is very similar for Ukrainians and all Canadians over the years. There is a slight tendency for larger percentages of Ukrainians to be single and smaller percentages to be married when compared with all Canadians. In the provinces, as with Canada as a whole, none of the differences are pronounced.

Even these small differences in marital status are unexpected, if one takes into consideration the sex ratio for Ukrainians early in the century. In 1931 Ukrainian males still outnumber the females at almost every age. One possible explanation for the marital status difference may be that Ukrainian men were more likely than Ukrainian women to marry outside the ethnic group. In addition, some Ukrainian men who came to Canada may have been married before they emigrated but left their spouses in Europe.

Similar comparisons were carried out for females. Fairly large differences were found between Ukrainians and Canadians in 1931. (Figure 1 and Appendix A). Ukrainian women at all ages were more likely to be married and less likely to be single when compared with Canadians of all origins. For example, in the age group 20–24 years in 1931, 37.4 per cent of Ukrainian women were single and 62.2 per cent married compared with Canadian women of all origins, of whom 63.1 per cent were single and 36.6 per cent married. The same differences appear in 1941. In 1951 and 1961 the larger percentages married and the smaller percentages single occur only in the older age groups. By 1971, the two distributions were quite similar (Figure 2). For example, in the age group 20–24 years in 1971, 45.7 per cent of Ukrainian women were single and 52.5 per cent married, which is similar to the Canadian women of all origins who were 43.8 per cent single and 55.5 per cent married.

The same sort of differences are found in the central provinces, except there the differences are even more pronounced than for Canada as a whole. In the Prairie provinces the same differences occur again between

FIGURE 1

Percentage Distribution of Single and Married Ukrainian Women and Women of All Origins by Age for Canada, 1931

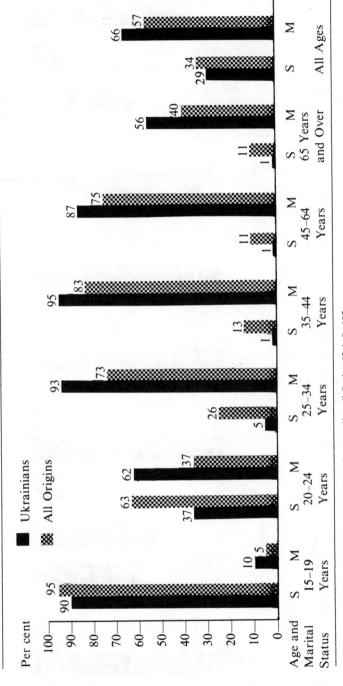

Source: Darcovich and Yuzyk, "Statistical Compendium," Series 62.1–8, 692.

FIGURE 2

Percentage Distribution of Single and Married Ukrainian Women and Women of all Origins by Age for Canada, 1971

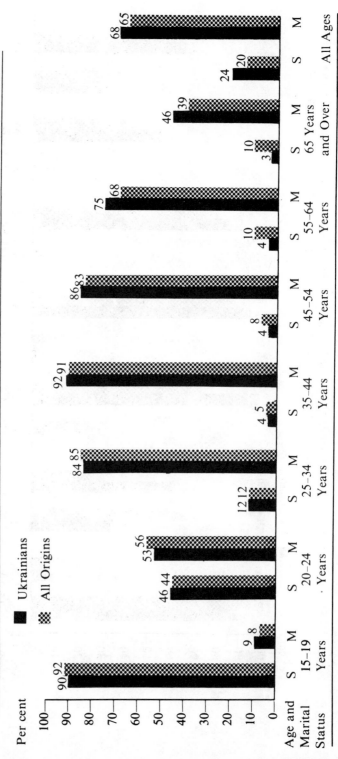

Source: Statistics Canada, "1971 Canadian Census 1/100 Public Use Sample Tape; Individual Province File," (Ottawa: Statistics Canada, n.d.)

the Ukrainian and Canadian women, but the differences are somewhat less pronounced than those seen for Canada and for the central provinces. It would appear that Ukrainian women married younger and that a larger proportion of them married in the early part of the century, when compared with Canadian women of all origins. In the Prairie provinces, however, all women, both Ukrainians and Canadians of all origins, married younger and in larger proportions than was the case in the rest of Canada and in the central provinces. These differences for Ukrainian women are not too surprising considering the sex ratio at that time and the community encouragement of intermarriage. These differences for women may provide an additional explanation for the unexpected findings on men. Particularly in 1931, large proportions of Ukrainian women married, often at an early age, and may have contributed to a slight lowering in the proportions of single Ukrainian men compared to all Canadian men about that time.

The second comparison is the distribution of marital status traced through time. For Canadians of all origins, both male and female, there is a decrease in the percentage single and an increase in the percentage married over time in the 20–24 year and the 25–34 year age groups (Tables 1 and 2). This is true for both Canada as a whole and for the central and Prairie provinces. This probably reflects the decreasing age of first marriage. Similarly for Ukrainian males there is a decrease in the percentage single and an increase in the percentage married in the same two age groups. This is the same in the central and Prairie provinces. No trends are found for other age and marital status groups over time.

A somewhat different pattern occurs for Ukrainian women (Table 2). Unlike the above results, there is no trend in the distribution of marital status by age from 1931 to 1971. This is probably due to the very large percentage of Ukrainian women already married in the 20–24 year age group. For example, in 1931, 36.6 per cent of the Canadian women aged 20–24 years were married compared to 62.2 per cent of Ukrainian women. These patterns are the same for Canada as a whole, the Prairie provinces and the central provinces included. This finding supports the previous suggestion that Ukrainian women married earlier than the rest of the Canadian women around 1931. As the age of marriage for Canada as a whole decreased, however, the distribution of marital status for Ukrainian women became more similar to that of Canadian women of all origins.

Fertility

Before 1921, it was impossible to compile comprehensive birth

TABLE 1
Percentage Distribution of Single and Married Ukrainian
and Canadian Males Ages 20 to 24 Years and 25 to 34 Years,
Canada, 1941, 1951 and 1961

Ethnic Origin, Age and Year			Marital Status		
			Single	Married	N
Canadians	Male	20 to 24 years			
	1941		83.7	16.1	517,956
	1951		74.4	25.5	537,535
	1961		69.5	30.4	587,139
Canadians	Male	25 to 34 years			
	1941		40.0	59.0	919,931
	1951		27.6	72.0	1,065,369
	1961		23.3	76.3	1,258,304
Ukrainians	Male	20 to 24 years			
	1941		88.2	11.7	15,672
	1951		80.4	19.6	16,587
	1961		72.5	27.4	14,301
Ukrainians	Male	25 to 34 years			
	1941		43.4	55.8	25,272
	1951		34.4	65.3	37,090
	1961		25.7	73.9	32,737

Source: Darcovich and Yuzyk, "Statistical Compendium," Series 62.29–44, 701–4; 62.45–60, 705–8.

statistics for Canada since there was incomplete registration, a lack of uniformity in classification and presentation and an absence of a co-ordinating body for vital statistics. Under the Statistics Act of 1918, however, each province was to co-operate in recording uniform vital statistics. Under the Act, the Dominion Bureau of Statistics (now Statistics Canada) was to co-ordinate, analyze and publish the statistics. In 1921 vital statistics were published for eight provinces. In 1926 Quebec, in 1951 the Northwest Territories and the Yukon and in 1949 Newfoundland were included. Before 1944, births were classified by place of occurrence and only after that date were they classified by place of residence of the mother. This should have no effect on the results of this analysis, however, since only data for certain provinces and Canada as a whole will be used.

TABLE 2
Percentage Distribution of Single and Married Ukrainian
and Canadian Females Aged 20 to 24 Years and 25 to 34 Years,
Canada, 1931, 1941, 1951 and 1961

Ethnic Origin, Age and Year			Marital Status		
			Single	Married	N
Canadians	Female	20 to 24 years			
	1931		63.1	36.6	447,449
	1941		61.0	38.5	514,470
	1951		48.5	51.2	551,106
	1961		40.5	59.2	596,507
Canadians	Female	25 to 34 years			
	1931		25.9	72.7	716,973
	1941		27.5	70.4	890,905
	1951		17.4	81.3	1,108,580
	1961		12.9	86.0	1,222,803
Ukrainians	Female	20 to 24 years			
	1931		37.4	62.2	9,772
	1941		49.2	50.2	16,327
	1951		43.4	56.4	17,518
	1961		38.0	61.7	14,999
Ukrainians	Female	25 to 34 years			
	1931		5.4	93.0	13,454
	1941		12.7	84.8	24,698
	1951		12.3	86.4	36,245
	1961		9.7	89.1	33,163

Source: Darcovich and Yuzyk, "Statistical Compendium," Series 62.29–44, 701–4; 62.45–60, 705–8.

Birth statistics for Ukrainians are defined by the ethnic origin of the mother. This definition is used since nearly all the statistics presented in the Compendium classify births by the ethnic origin of the mother rather than the father. In addition, classifying births according to the ethnic origin of the mother makes the definition quite comparable to the "children ever born" question on the census, which considers the children born to mothers of Ukrainian ethnic origin.

Ethnicity was ascertained for vital statistics until the 1950s when questions were raised about the usefulness of these data. As a result, Ontario discontinued recording ethnicity in 1960. In the same year

British Columbia reported only Indian, Eskimo, Negro, Chinese, Japanese and East Indian origins. Alberta discontinued recording ethnicity in 1968 and Manitoba in 1969. Newfoundland has never recorded ethnicity. Because the coverage of the Ukrainian ethnic group is different after 1960 than before, this essay will calculate fertility using vital statistics for 1931, 1941 and 1951. By using census years, exact counts of Ukrainians are available for population totals. Since population figures for intervening years are only estimates, fluctuations in the actual Ukrainian population could reduce the accuracy of fertility measures. Since vital statistics data on births are available for Ukrainians only for a few provinces after 1951, the 1971 census measure of "children ever born" will be used to supplement the data.

The first fertility measure calculated is the crude birth rate shown in Table 3. (Computing formulas for fertility are presented in Appendix B.) The crude birth rates for both Ukrainians and Canadians of all origins for Canada and provincial groupings follow similar patterns over time. The birth rate was high in 1931, dropped in 1941 and rose again in 1951. This is the same pattern found in many of the industrialized countries during that time period. When the crude birth rate for Ukrainians is compared with that for Canadians of all origins, the Ukrainian crude birth rate in 1931 was much higher. By 1941, the two crude birth rates

TABLE 3

Crude Birth Rates for Ukrainians and Canadians in Canada,
the Central and Prairie Provinces, 1931, 1941 and 1951

Geographical Area and Ethnic Origin	Year		
	1931	1941	1951
Canada			
All origins	23.2	22.2	26.3
Ukrainians[a]	30.4	23.8	25.8
Central Provinces (Ontario and Quebec)			
All origins	24.2	22.7	27.2
Ukrainians	29.7	24.7	30.1
Prairie Provinces (Manitoba, Saskatchewan and Alberta)			
All origins	22.5	20.9	27.0
Ukrainians	30.6	23.3	24.7

Source: Darcovich and Yuzyk, "Statistical Compendium," Series 60.17–32, 611–14.
Note: [a]Ukrainian births are defined by ethnic origin of mother.

were more similar but the Ukrainian one was still the higher of the two. By 1951, however, the Ukrainian crude birth rate was higher than that for Canadians of all origins only in the central provinces.

While the crude birth rate is a useful measure of comparison, it is, as its name suggests, a crude measure of fertility because it relates the number of births to the total population, while only women between about the ages of fifteen and forty-nine are capable of giving birth. Even within these ages the number of births varies by the age of the mother. Consequently, if the proportion of the population represented by women in the childbearing years or the age distribution of these women changes markedly from one year to another, or from one population group to another, spurious changes in the crude birth rate may result. A distribution of age specific fertility rates overcomes some of these shortcomings.

TABLE 4

Age Specific Fertility Rates[a] for Canadians of All Ethnic Origins and Ukrainians in Canada, 1931, 1941 and 1951

Ethnic Origin and Age	Year		
	1931	1941	1951
All origins			
15 to 19	24.4	25.5	37.9
20 to 24	130.3	130.6	174.3
25 to 29	171.4	155.6	189.9
30 to 34	143.0	120.0	138.7
35 to 39	101.5	78.5	83.1
40 to 44	43.4	31.0	29.7
45 to 49	5.2	3.5	2.8
Total Fertility Rate	3096	2724	3282
Ukrainians[b]			
15 to 19	40.9	29.9	39.8
20 to 24	216.6	147.2	170.2
25 to 29	227.3	142.7	165.2
30 to 34	193.6	103.9	111.8
35 to 39	121.9	70.1	55.2
40 to 44	60.7	32.2	18.8
45 to 49	12.9	5.1	2.0
Total Fertility Rate	4370	2506	2815

Source: Darcovich and Yuzyk, "Statistical Compendium," Series 60.103–122, 630.
Notes: [a]Births to married women only are included.
[b]Ukrainian births are defined by ethnic origin of mother.

In Table 4 age specific fertility rates are calculated only for Canada since no age specific figures are available for the provinces. In 1931, at every age, the fertility of Ukrainians was substantially higher than for Canadians. In 1941 Ukrainian fertility was somewhat higher for the two youngest age groups and the two oldest age groups, but it was lower for the three intermediate groups. However, none of the differences is large. In 1951 Ukrainian fertility was lower in all age groups except the 15–19 year age groups when compared with Canadians.

From these age specific fertility rates a total fertility rate may be calculated. The total fertility rate provides an effective summary measure of age- and sex-adjusted fertility, facilitating year-to-year and area-to-area comparisons (Appendix B). Because the total fertility rate combines fertility rates over all childbearing ages in a given year, it may also be viewed as representing the completed fertility of a synthetic cohort of women. In Table 4, for example, the total fertility rate of 3,096 for Canadians of all origins in 1931 may be interpreted to mean that a cohort of 1,000 women would have, on the average, 3,096 children in their lifetime, assuming that they bear children at each age at the rates prevailing in Canada at that time and that none of the women die before reaching the end of the childbearing period.

Similar to the crude birth rate, the total fertility rate for both groups in 1931 was high, decreased in 1941 and increased again by 1951. When age and sex are adjusted, the Ukrainian total fertility rate is lower than that of Canadians of all origins in both 1941 and 1951. Although Ukrainian fertility increased in 1951 over the 1941 level, it did not reach its 1931 level. In comparison, the Canadian total fertility rate in 1951 exceeded the 1931 level.

In summary, it appears that in 1931 the Ukrainian fertility was higher than Canadian fertility at all ages. By 1941, the younger and older Ukrainian women still had higher fertility than Canadian women of all origins, but this was not true of the intermediate age groups. The overall level of fertility as measured by the total fertility rate was lower for Ukrainians than for Canadians of all origins. By 1951, the fertility of Ukrainians was generally lower than Canadian fertility. The fertility rates were similar for both groups in the ages 15–19 years and 20–24 years, whereas Ukrainian fertility was lower than that of Canadians of all origins in all the remaining age groups. Both in 1941 and in 1951 it appears that Ukrainian women were beginning their families as early as, or a little earlier than, Canadian women of all origins. Fewer Ukrainian women, however, were having large families when compared with Canadian women.

The 1971 measure of the number of "children ever born" is available from the "Canadian Census 1/100 Public Use Sample Tape." It must be kept in mind that the measure of "children ever born" available in the census is a very different measure from the number of births available in vital statistics. The major difference is that annual fertility rates from the vital statistics consider all the births in a particular year, while the number of "children ever born" provides a measure of past fertility performance of all "ever married" women in the population at the census date. The rates based on census data do not include the children of women who have died or emigrated, yet these children are included in the vital statistics. On the other hand, the children of women who immigrated are included in the census but not in the vital statistics figures. One advantage of the census measure is that if only women who have completed childbearing are selected, then "children ever born" becomes a measure of completed family size which can be related to various social and economic characteristics of the family and mother (Appendix C).

In Table 5 the distribution of "children ever born" is cross-tabulated with the age of the "ever married" women. Three age groups are defined—15–39 years, 40–54 years and 55 years and over. The first age group represents women still in their childbearing ages, while the rest have, for the most part, completed their families. Since the measure "children ever born" relies on memory, older women, who may inaccurately recall their number of children were placed in a separate category. In addition, respondents 40–54 years of age were in their childbearing years from about 1932 to 1951 and thus would have been bearing children at the dates for which vital statistics data were available.

It can be seen in Table 5 that the distribution of "children ever born" for Ukrainian women 15–39 years is very similar to that for Canadian women of all origins. In the age group 40–54 years, however, Ukrainian women are more likely to have smaller completed family sizes than Canadian women of all origins (that is, 0, 1 and 2 children compared with the 3 or more children of Canadian women). Although in 1931 all Ukrainian women and in 1941 some Ukrainian women had higher fertility than the Canadian women of all origins, this appears not to have resulted in greater completed family size. In Table 5 the distribution of "children ever born" to women fifty-five years of age and over is different from other age groups. Ukrainian women in this age group are somewhat less likely to be childless and just as likely to have large families as Canadian women of all origins.

Although the distribution of "children ever born" provides interesting insights, a summary measure such as "mean children ever born"

TABLE 5

Percentage Distribution of Children Ever Born and Mean Number of Children Ever Born
for Ever Married Ukrainian Women and Women of All Origins, Canada, 1971

Ethnic Origin and Age	Children Ever Born						Mean Number of CEB	N
	0	1	2	3 to 4	5 to 6	7+		
All Origins								
15 to 39	22.9	20.0	25.0	24.9	5.5	1.7	1.98	2,454,000
40 to 54	9.4	11.0	20.8	33.4	14.8	10.6	3.42	1,720,000
55 Years and Over	15.6	14.6	18.8	25.4	13.3	12.3	3.28	1,576,000
All Ages	16.9	15.8	22.1	27.6	10.4	7.3	2.77	5,750,000
Ukrainians								
15 to 39	20.8	22.1	25.5	26.6	4.4	0.6	1.90	68,700
50 to 54	9.7	13.3	31.6	30.3	11.8	3.2	2.67	55,700
55 Years and Over	10.0	14.2	21.2	29.4	12.3	12.9	3.42	55,100
All Ages	14.0	16.9	26.1	28.6	9.1	5.2	2.61	179,500

Source: "1971 Canadian Census 1/100 Public Use Sample Tape: Individual Province File" (Ottawa: Statistics Canada, 1971).

facilitates more detailed comparisons. The mean number of "children ever born" is calculated by adding the total number of children reported and dividing by the total number of "ever married" women. Another interpretation of the "mean number of children ever born" is the average size of the family at the time of the census. Thus the "mean number of children" ever born in Table 5 can be used to draw the same conclusions as those reached when distributions were examined. The fertility of Ukrainian women aged 15–39 years is very similar to that of Canadian women of all origins. The completed family size of the Ukrainian women is smaller for the age group 40–54 years and larger for the age group fifty-five years and over when compared with Canadian women of all origins.

Several controls can now be introduced. It is known that generation, education, age at first marriage, family income and place of residence are related to fertility (Appendix C). Table 6 shows the "mean number of children ever born" for Ukrainians and Canadians of all origins, controlling for age and generation. If intergenerational comparisons are made first in the age group 15–39 years, the pattern is similar. The first generation has the smallest family size, followed by the third generation and finally the second generation with the largest family size. In the age group 40–54 years, the first generation, both Ukrainian and Canadians of all origins, has the smallest completed family size. For Ukrainians the second and third generations have very similar family sizes, whereas for Canadians of all origins the family size of the third generation is larger than the second generation. For women fifty-five years of age and over of both groups the second generation has the smallest family size. While first-generation Ukrainians have the largest family size, it is third-generation Canadians that have the largest family size. With only two exceptions, for those fifty-five years of age and over in the first and second generations, the fertility of Ukrainians is lower than that of Canadians of all origins.

In Table 7 place of residence and age are considered. As would be expected for all the age groups for both Ukrainians and Canadians of all origins, the family size of rural residents is larger than that of urban residents. In only one case, those women aged fifty-five years of age and over who are rural residents, does Ukrainian family size exceed the family size of Canadians of all origins. For this same age group the urban family size for the two groups is almost identical.

In Table 8 controls are introduced for age and the education of the mother. As expected, for both Ukrainians and Canadians of all origins and all age groups, the higher the education the smaller the family size. Only for the 15–39 year age group with eight years or less of education

TABLE 6
Mean Number of Children Ever Born to Ever Married
Ukrainian Women and Women of All Origins by Age and Generation
of Mother, Canada, 1971

Age and Generation	Mean Number of Children Ever Born			
	Ukrainians		All Origins	
	Mean	N	Mean	N
First Generation				
15 to 39	1.48	4,400	1.78	424,000
40 to 54	2.31	12,500	2.65	346,000
55 Years and Over	3.83	28,800	3.06	464,000
All Ages	3.19	45,700	2.51	1,234,000
Second Generation				
15 to 39	2.13	32,300	2.26	426,000
40 to 54	2.78	39,100	3.05	472,000
55 Years and Over	2.91	23,100	2.63	272,000
All Ages	2.59	94,500	2.67	1,170,000
Third or Higher Generation				
15 to 39	1.73	32,000	1.96	1,604,000
40 to 54	2.73	4,100	3.91	902,000
55 Years and Over	3.41	3,200	3.60	840,000
All Ages	2.00	39,300	2.90	3,346,000

Source: "1971 Canadian Census 1/100 Public Use Sample Tape: Individual Province File" (Ottawa: Statistics Canada, 1971).

does Ukrainian family size exceed that of women of all origins. Family size is the same for the two groups for the 15–39 year age group with high school education. In the 40–54 year age group with elementary education the completed family size of Canadians of all origins is very large (4.15 children) compared to that of Ukrainian (2.76 children).

In Table 9 family income and age are considered. For the youngest age group there is little difference in family size from one income group to another, although the lowest income group tends to have the largest family size. For the Ukrainians of both the 40–54 year and 55 year and over age groups the highest and lowest income groups have the largest family sizes. This is not true for Canadians of all origins where the relationship is more complex, although the lowest income group has the largest family size. If the two groups are compared (excepting those 15–39 years with $8,000–$14,999 income and those 55 years of age and

TABLE 7

Mean Number of Children Ever Born to Ever Married Ukrainian
Women and Women of All Origins by Age and Place of Residence,
Canada, 1971

Age and Place of Residence	Mean Number of Children Ever Born			
	Ukrainians		All Origins	
	Mean	N	Mean	N
Urban Residence				
15 to 39	1.81	55,500	1.84	1,950,000
40 to 54	2.54	42,500	3.10	1,340,000
55 Years and Over	3.13	41,000	3.12	1,246,000
All Ages	2.42	139,000	2.56	4,536,000
Rural Residence				
15 to 39	2.32	13,200	2.52	504,000
40 to 54	3.11	13,200	4.54	380,000
55 Years and Over	4.26	14,100	3.88	330,000
All Ages	3.25	40,500	3.53	1,214,000

Source: "1971 Canadian Census 1/100 Public Use Sample Tape: Individual Province
File" (Ottawa: Statistics Canada, 1971).

over with $15,000 or more income), the Ukrainians have smaller family
sizes than Canadians of all origins. For those 40–54 years of age in the
lowest income group the Canadian completed family size is much larger
(4.56 children) than the Ukrainian family size (3.27 children).

In Table 10 the age at first marriage and age of mother are considered.
As age at first marriage increases the size of family decreases.
Ukrainians have a smaller family size than Canadians with the
exception fifty-five years of age and older who were married between
the ages of 15–19 years and those 15–39 years who were married between
the ages of 25–29 years. However, neither of these differences is large.

Examining the mean family size in various categories indicates that
in many cases distributions are similar for both Ukrainians and Canadians of all origins. For both groups the average family size decreases
with increasing education, decreases with older age at first marriage and
is larger for rural than urban residence. For both groups the relationship between family size and family income is more complex, although
the lowest income group has the largest family size. For Ukrainians the
lowest and highest income groups tend to have the largest families,
which is not true for Canadians of all origins. The relationship between

TABLE 8
Mean Number of Children Ever Born to Ever Married Ukrainian Women and Women of All Origins by Age and Education of Mother, Canada, 1971

Age and Education	Mean Number of Children Ever Born			
	Ukrainians		All Origins	
	Mean	N	Mean	N
Elementary (Grade 8 or less)				
15 to 39	2.74	8,500	2.51	556,000
40 to 54	2.76	25,500	4.15	686,000
55 Years and Over	3.68	45,000	3.87	884,000
All Ages	3.29	79,000	3.61	2,126,000
Secondary (Grades 9–13)				
15 to 39	1.88	52,600	1.87	1,648,000
40 to 54	2.64	27,300	2.99	924,000
55 Years and Over	2.25	8,900	2.53	628,000
All Ages	2.15	88,800	2.32	3,200,000
University				
15 to 39	1.17	7,600	1.51	250,000
40 to 54	2.21	2,900	2.44	110,000
55 Years and Over	2.08	1,200	2.41	64,000
All Ages	1.52	11,700	1.89	424,000

Source: "1971 Canadian Census 1/100 Public Use Sample Tape: Individual Province File" (Ottawa: Statistics Canada, 1971).

family size and generation differs for the two groups. This is probably influenced by the period of immigration and the characteristics of immigrants. For example, first-generation Ukrainian women fifty-five years of age and over had a larger family size than Ukrainians in the same age group but who were of second or more generation. These first-generation women were among the immigrants who settled in the rural prairies and tended to have large families.

Some interesting differences also occur when comparisons are made between Ukrainians and Canadians of all origins in comparable categories. With some exceptions, Ukrainian family size is smaller than the family size of Canadians of all origins. A larger Ukrainian family size does occur repeatedly for those fifty-five years of age and over. Women fifty-five years of age and over, who are first- or second-generation rural residents and who married early with high family income, have larger

TABLE 9

Mean Number of Children Ever Born to Ever Married Ukrainian Women and Women of All Ethnic Origins by Age and Family Income, Canada, 1971

Age and Family Income	Mean Number of Children Ever Born			
	Ukrainians		All Origins	
	Mean	N	Mean	N
Less Than $4,000				
15 to 39	2.20	7,400	2.26	326,000
40 to 54	3.27	8,300	4.56	188,000
55 Years and Over	3.63	14,700	3.86	280,000
All Ages	3.18	30,400	3.37	794,000
$4,000 to $7,999				
15 to 39	1.94	17,300	2.09	718,000
40 to 54	2.73	14,600	3.47	402,000
55 Years and Over	2.48	11,700	3.13	276,000
All Ages	2.35	43,600	2.69	1,396,000
$8,000 to $14,999				
15 to 39	1.93	33,600	1.86	1,066,000
40 to 54	2.43	21,200	3.30	656,000
55 Years and Over	2.92	7,200	3.14	274,000
All Ages	2.22	62,000	2.51	1,996,000
$15,000 and Over				
15 to 39	1.80	7,900	2.09	260,000
40 to 54	2.84	8,100	3.35	392,000
55 Years and Over	3.43	2,100	2.88	116,000
All Ages	2.45	18,100	2.85	768,000

Source: "1971 Canadian Census 1/100 Public Use Sample Tape: Individual Province File" (Ottawa: Statistics Canada, 1971).

completed family size than do Canadians of all origins. Although previous vital statistics measures show that in 1941 Ukrainian fertility was higher than that for Canadians of all origins in some age groups, this did not seem to result in a larger completed family size. In the age group 40-54 years the Ukrainian family size was smaller than that for Canadians of all origins.

Up to this point various social and economic variables have been related to "mean number of children ever born." For the younger age

TABLE 10

Mean Number of Children Ever Born to Ever Married Ukrainian
Women and Women of All Origins by Age and Age of First Marriage
of Mother, Canada, 1971

Age and Age of First Marriage	Mean Number of Children Ever Born			
	Ukrainians		All Origins	
	Mean	N	Mean	N
First Married Between 15 and 19 Years of Age				
15 to 39	2.14	24,500	2.41	838,000
40 to 54	3.49	13,400	4.51	378,000
55 Years and Over	4.56	18,900	4.47	308,000
All Ages	3.26	56,800	3.35	1,524,000
First Married Between 20 and 24 Years of Age				
15 to 39	1.80	36,600	1.81	1,276,000
40 to 54	2.66	26,300	3.50	844,000
55 Years and Over	3.28	20,500	3.74	598,000
All Ages	2.44	83,400	2.76	2,718,000
First Married Between 25 and 29 Years of Age				
15 to 39	1.71	6,200	1.61	294,000
40 to 54	2.28	10,900	2.90	332,000
55 Years and Over	2.74	8,800	2.82	354,000
All Ages	2.30	25,900	2.48	980,000
First Married when 30 Years of Age or Older				
15 to 39	1.36	1,400	1.64	46,000
40 to 54	1.41	5,100	1.52	166,000
55 Years and Over	1.57	6,900	1.75	316,000
All Ages	1.49	13,400	1.64	528,000

Source: "1971 Canadian Census 1/100 Public Use Sample Tape: Individual Province
File" (Ottawa: Statistics Canada, 1971).

group (15–39 years) women are still in their childbearing years, and so
the measure cannot be considered as one of completed family size. After
the age of forty years, however, "mean children ever born" can be
considered to be completed family size. Using the age group 40–54 years,

FIGURE 3
Deviations From Overall Mean of Number of Children Ever Born to Ukrainian Women 40-54 Years of Age by Family Income, Generation and Place of Residence, Canada, 1971

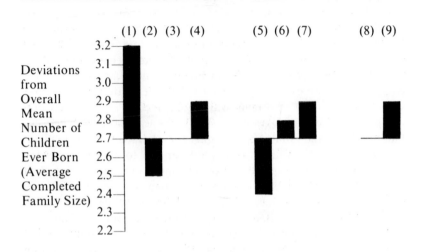

Source: "1971 Canadian Census 1/100 Public Use Sample Tape; Individual Province
File" (Ottawa: Statistics Canada, 1971).

Notes:

FAMILY INCOME	GENERATION	PLACE OF	
(1) Less than $4,000—3.2	(5) First—2.4	RESIDENCE	N = 52,200
(2) $4,000-$7,999—2.7	(6) Second—2.8	(8) Urban—2.7	
(3) $8,000-$14,999—2.5	(7) Third or	(9) Rural—2.9	
(4) $15,000 or More—2.9	Higher—2.9		

an exploratory multiple classification analysis was undertaken. The relationship between religion, family income, education, place of residence, and generation and the number of children ever born was ascertained while controlling for age at first marriage. In this way the independent effects of each of these variables can be assessed while holding the effects of other variables constant. The technique of multiple classification analysis enables the family size of each category of each variable to be expressed as a deviation from the overall mean family size of the group.

Figure 3 shows that the overall mean family size for Ukrainian women 40-54 years of age is 2.7 children. Only three variables—family income, generation and place of residence—are significantly related to family size when age at first marriage as well as other independent variables are controlled. For example, one can say that family income exerts an independent effect on completed family size of Ukrainians. An income of less than $4,000 is related to an increase in family size of 0.5 children from the overall group average, while an income of $15,000 or more is related to a 0.2 children increase in family size. For Canadian women of all origins aged 40-54 years (Figure 4) all five variables exert an independent effect on family size, after adjusting for age at first marriage. Since there is an interaction between place of residence and family income, and between place of residence and religion, the exact deviations from the overall mean should be interpreted cautiously.

A comparison of the findings in Figure 3 and Figure 4 shows that place of residence exerts the greatest independent effect on the family size of Canadians of all origins, while family income exerts the greatest independent effect for Ukrainians. The U-shaped relationship between family income and family size is similar for Ukrainians and Canadians of all origins. In addition, generation appears to have a somewhat different meaning for the two groups. The smaller family size of the first generation for both Ukrainians and Canadians is consistent with the findings of other researchers who report an across-the-board lower fertility for immigrants. Being of second or third generation relates to a larger family size than is average for Ukrainians, although the differences are not large. This is true only for third-generation Canadians.

The overall family size is smaller for Ukrainians (2.7 children) than for Canadians of all origins (3.5 children). There is also more homogeneity among Ukrainians than among the Canadians of all origins. For Ukrainains the largest deviation from mean family size is 0.5 children, and only three of the five variables included in the analysis exert an independent effect on family size. By comparison, the largest deviation from the mean family size is 0.8 children for Canadians of all origins, and all five variables included are significantly related to family size. A more detailed analysis and a comparison with other ethnic groups would be needed to determine if this homogeneity is unique to the Ukrainian group. Further analysis is also needed to investigate whether the relationships between the independent variables and family size are similar for other ethnic groups.

Summary

This essay examined trends in the marital status and fertility of Ukrainian Canadians and Canadians of all ethnic origins between the years 1931 and 1971. For the most part the paper was descriptive and

FIGURE 4

Deviations From Overall Mean Number of Children Ever Born of Canadian Women of All Origins 40–54 Years of Age by Education, Family Income, Generation, Place of Residence and Religion, Canada, 1971

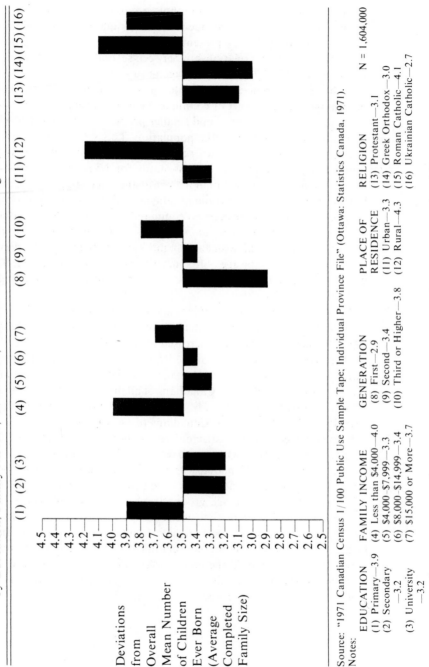

Source: "1971 Canadian Census 1/100 Public Use Sample Tape; Individual Province File" (Ottawa: Statistics Canada, 1971).

Notes:

EDUCATION	FAMILY INCOME	GENERATION	PLACE OF RESIDENCE	RELIGION	N = 1,604,000
(1) Primary—3.9	(4) Less than $4,000—4.0	(8) First—2.9	(11) Urban—3.3	(13) Protestant—3.1	
(2) Secondary —3.2	(5) $4,000–$7,999—3.3	(9) Second—3.4	(12) Rural—4.3	(14) Greek Orthodox—3.0	
(3) University —3.2	(6) $8,000–$14,999—3.4	(10) Third or Higher—3.8		(15) Roman Catholic—4.1	
	(7) $15,000 or More—3.7			(16) Ukrainian Catholic—2.7	

traced trends for the Ukrainian ethnic group through time and made comparisons with the remainder of the population. An exploratory multivariate analysis was presented briefly at the end of the paper to begin to examine the relationship between several social and economic variables and family size for one age group.

Although differences were small, there was a tendency for larger percentages of the cohort of Ukrainian men aged twenty-five years and older in 1931 to be married and smaller proportions to be single when compared with the rest of the population. This would not have been anticipated considering the sex ratio of Ukrainians at that time. It was found that the pattern of marital status for Ukrainian women was different from that of Canadian women of all ethnic origins. It appeared that early in the century Ukrainian women married younger and a larger proportion of them were married compared to other Canadian women. This was less pronounced on the prairies where it appeared that marriage patterns of all women were more similar to those of Ukrainian women. Thus when the age of first marriage in Canada decreased, there was no such trend for Ukrainian women since the age at first marriage had previously been low.

The fertility trends of Ukrainians and of other Canadians were found to follow the same general pattern through time. Fertility was high in 1931, decreased in 1941 and increased again in 1951. In 1931 and 1941 for Canada as a whole and for the Prairie and central provinces at all three points in time (1931, 1941 and 1951), the Ukrainian crude birth rate was higher than that of Canadians of all origins. When age and sex were controlled, however, only in 1931 was Ukrainian fertility consistently higher than that of Canadians of all origins.

Using the measure of "mean children ever born" or "mean family size" it was again found that, with some exceptions, Ukrainian family size was smaller than that of Canadians of all origins. The smaller Ukrainian family size was particularly pronounced for the low income and low education groups in the age group 40–54 years. Ukrainians fifty-five years of age and over of first or second generation, rural residence, young age at first marriage and high family income tended to have larger family sizes than the comparable Canadian group. A multivariate analysis explored the independent effects of several social and economic variables on family size for the age group 40–54 years, and a further analysis was proposed.

185

APPENDIX A
Percentage Distribution of Ukrainian and Canadian Females by Marital Status and Age, Canada, 1931 and 1971

Year, Ethnic Origin and Age	Single	Married	Widowed and Divorced	N
1931—Canadians				
15 to 19	94.9	5.1	0.1	514,331
20 to 24	63.1	36.6	0.3	447,449
25 to 34	25.9	72.7	1.5	716,973
35 to 44	12.5	82.7	4.8	627,685
45 to 64	10.6	75.2	14.2	790,500
65 years and over	10.9	40.2	48.9	281,419
All Ages	34.0	57.3	8.6	3,378,357
1931—Ukrainians				
15 to 19	90.3	9.7	0.1	14,122
20 to 24	37.4	62.2	0.4	9,772
25 to 34	5.4	93.0	1.6	13,454
35 to 44	1.1	95.2	3.7	10,533
45 to 64	0.8	86.5	12.7	8,488
65 years and over	0.7	55.9	43.3	2,430
All Ages	29.4	65.8	4.7	58,799
1971—Canadians				
15 to 19	92.0	8.0	0.1	963,237
20 to 24	43.8	55.5	0.7	966,570
25 to 34	12.1	85.1	2.8	1,406,526
35 to 44	5.4	91.2	3.4	1,176,549
45 to 54	7.9	82.9	9.2	1,306,536
55 to 64	10.4	67.5	22.1	829,917
65 years and over	9.8	39.3	50.9	916,575
All Ages	24.1	64.6	11.3	7,565,910
1971—Ukrainians				
15 to 19	90.4	8.6	1.1	28,000
20 to 24	45.7	52.5	1.8	22,100
25 to 34	11.9	84.4	3.7	40,500
35 to 44	4.0	91.8	4.2	37,900
45 to 54	3.8	85.9	10.2	39,100
55 to 64	4.3	75.4	20.3	30,500
65 years and over	3.4	45.5	51.1	26,800
All Ages	20.2	67.5	12.3	224,900

APPENDIX B

Computing Formulas

$$\text{Crude Birth Rate} = \frac{\text{Total Births}}{\text{Total Population}} \times 1,000$$

$$\text{Age Specific Fertility Rate} = f_a = \frac{b_a}{p_a^f} \times 1,000 \quad \text{where}$$

f_a = fertility of a specific age group

b_a = number of births to women in a specific age group

p_a^f = number of women in a specific age group

$$\text{Total Fertility Rate} = \text{TFR} = 5 \sum_{a=15-19}^{a=45-49} f_a \quad \text{where}$$

f_a = fertility of a specific age group

Source: Henry Shyrock and Jacob S. Siegel, *The Methods and Material of Demography* (New York: Academic Press, 1976), 276–87.

APPENDIX C

Definitions

Age   Respondents were asked to state their age, in completed years, as of their last birthday before the census date.

Generation   This is a variable created using two questions. The respondent was asked where he was born. This refers to province of birth if born in Canada, and to country of birth according to boundaries at the census date if born outside Canada. Respondents were categorized into Canadian-born and non-Canadian-born.

The respondent was further asked if his parents were born inside Canada. Respondents were categorized into those with both parents born in Canada, and those with one or both parents born outside Canada.

On the basis of these two definitions the respondent was defined as first generation if he was born outside Canada, second generation if he was born in Canada but one or both of his parents were born outside Canada and third or subsequent generation if both the respondent and his parents were born in Canada.

Religion   This refers to the specific religious body, denomination, sect or community reported in answer to the question "What is your religion?" The resulting answers were grouped into Greek Orthodox including only Greek Orthodox, Roman Catholic including only Roman Catholic, Ukrainian Catholic including only Ukrainian Catholic, Protestant including Anglican, Baptist, Lutheran, Pentecostal, Presbyterian, United Church, no religion and other.

Education   This refers to the highest grade or year of elementary, secondary or university attended. This variable was categorized into Grade 8 or less (elementary), Grade 9–13 (secondary) and more than Grade 13 (university).

Family Income   This refers to the sum of incomes received by all members of a family fifteen years and over from all sources during the calendar year 1970. Included are wages and salaries, net income from business and professional practice, net income from farm operations, transfer payments, retirement pensions, investment income and other miscellaneous sources.

Number of Children Ever Born   This refers to the number of children born alive, either of the present marriage or any previous marriage.

Respondents were instructed to include children who died after birth as well as those residing elsewhere at census time and to exclude adopted and stepchildren. "Children ever born" is reported for women fifteen years and over who reported themselves as having been married at one time. If fourteen or more children are reported, then fifteen is the number used in the calculations.

Age at First Marriage This age was derived by combining information on date of first marriage with date of birth. This is reported for persons fifteen years and over who have ever been married.

Place of Residence This refers to the place where a person normally lives and sleeps.

Urban This includes all persons living in incorporated cities, towns and villages with a population of 1,000 or over; unincorporated places of 1,000 or over having a population density of at least 1,000 per square mile; the urbanized fringe of either of the above. All the remaining population is rural.

NOTES

1. William Darcovich and Paul Yuzyk, eds., "Statistical Compendium on the Ukrainians in Canada, 1891-1976" (Unpublished typescript, Ottawa, 1977); "1971 Canadian Census 1/100 Public Use Sample Tape: Individual Province File" (Ottawa: Statistics Canada, n.d.).
2. Warren E. Kalbach, *The Impact of Immigration on Canada's Population* (Ottawa: Dominion Bureau of Statistics, 1970).
3. V.J. Kaye, "Three Phases of Ukrainian Immigration," in *Slavs in Canada*, ed. Yar Slavutych, 3 vols. (Edmonton: Inter-University Committee on Canadian Slavs, 1966), 1: 33–43; Paul Yuzyk, *Ukrainian Canadians: Their Place and Role in Canadian Life* (Toronto: Ukrainian Canadian Business and Professional Federation, 1967).
4. William M. Kephart, *The Family, Society and the Individual* (Boston: Houghton Mifflin Co., 1977); W. P. Wakil, *Marriage and the Family in Canada* (Calgary: *The Journal of Comparative Family Studies,* Department of Sociology, University of Calgary, 1976).
5. Warren E. Kalbach, "Some Demographic Aspects of Ukrainian Population in Canada," in *Slavs in Canada,* ed. Yar Slavutych, 3 vols. (Edmonton: Inter-University Committee on Canadian Slavs, 1966), I: 54–68.
6. Ivan Tesla, "Z demografichnych doslidiv Ukrainskoyi ludnosty Kanady" in *Ukrainians in American and Canadian Society,* ed. Wsevolod W. Isajiw (Jersey City, N.J.: M. P. Kots Publishing, 1976), 23–36.

THE CHANGING STATUS OF UKRAINIAN WOMEN IN CANADA, 1921-1971

Marusia K. Petryshyn

In the past decade there has been a burgeoning of studies on women and ethnocultural groups. However, few studies have combined feminist and ethnocultural perspectives. If one examines Canadian women's studies, one finds that very little attention has been paid to the question of immigrant women and almost none to that of women of minority and ethnocultural groups. Likewise, when one examines ethnocultural group studies, specifically those of Ukrainian Canadians, one finds few references to the specific history and experience of women. Recent sociological studies of social transitions among Ukrainian Canadians have primarily treated this group as male-defined and neglected the specific experiences of women.[1]

It was not until the publication of Helen Potrebenko's *No Streets of Gold* and Myrna Kostash's *All of Baba's Children* that a feminist perspective was applied to the ethnocultural history of Ukrainian Canadians.[2] By relating the problems of women and ethnocultural group life, Kostash and Potrebenko have posed a challenge to students of both Ukrainian-Canadian studies and women's studies. Ukrainian-Canadian studies can no longer present the Ukrainian-Canadian male as representative of Ukrainian Canadians as a whole. Conversely, women's studies can no longer ignore immigrant and ethnocultural group experiences which are of considerable significance in shaping particular groups of Canadian women.

How, then, does one deal with the question of Ukrainian-Canadian women? The position of women in every society must be studied historically, sociologically and economically. Juliet Mitchell has suggested four key structures which must be examined: production, reproduction, sexuality and the socialization of children.[3] The study of Ukrainian-Canadian women must deal with an additional factor—ethnicity. One must be able to assess the degree to which the experiences of women from a particular immigrant-ethnic group are distinct from the experiences of women in society as a whole.

Using statistics from the Compendium, as well as data from historical and sociological literature, this essay provides a social and demographic framework for the study of Ukrainian-Canadian women.[4] The first section documents the changes in basic social characteristics of Ukrainian-Canadian women revealed by census data from 1921 to 1971. The focus is then narrowed to document and discuss the participation of Ukrainian-Canadian women in the paid work force.

In documenting the changing status of Ukrainian-Canadian women in the work force from 1921 to 1971, a constant comparison with the total female Canadian work force has been provided to ascertain the extent to which the status of the Ukrainian-Canadian female can be explained by processes affecting all women and the extent it is affected by ethnicity. Changing occupational patterns are also examined in comparison to entrance-status occupations of Ukrainian-Canadian women to assess the degree to which such women are experiencing ethnic as well as gender impediments in attaining proportional distribution across all occupational categories. This paper concludes with a discussion of the relative weight of economic, gender and ethnic factors in influencing Ukrainian-Canadian female participation in the work force.

Ukrainian-Canadian Women

"Ukrainian-Canadian women," as a census definition, are women claiming Ukrainian male ancestry, but not necessarily members of Ukrainian-Canadian ethnocultural communities. This broad definition is adequate since mere membership in a group, regardless of conscious awareness or attachment, is enough to affect an individual's status. In describing the broad outlines of the social profile of Ukrainian-Canadian women, their social characteristics as a Canadian group will first be examined, followed by a discussion of their characteristics as immigrants.

The census of 1971 reports 284,935 women of Ukrainian ethnic origin.

Table 1 shows that approximately 83 per cent were Canadian-born. This reflects the steadily increasing native-born character of this group, which in 1921 was only 58 per cent Canadian-born. Among Ukrainian-Canadian women, only a minority are foreign-born. Of the latter, most have been Canadian residents for years.

TABLE 1
Percentage of Ukrainian-Canadian Female Population
Born in Canada, 1921 to 1971

Year	Percentage	Total Number of Ukrainian-Canadian Females
1921	58.4	48,867
1931	62.2	102,341
1941	69.3	143,329
1951	73.2	186,749
1961	79.2	226,817
1971	82.9	284,935

Source: Based on Darcovich and Yuzyk, "Statistical Compendium," Series 52.1–13, 559–61.

Table 2 shows the changing pattern in the regional distribution of the Ukrainian-Canadian female population. In 1921, 91 per cent of Ukrainian-Canadian women were concentrated in the Prairie provinces, with Manitoba having the largest number. With time the population migrated to British Columbia and Ontario at the expense of

TABLE 2
Provincial Distribution of Ukrainian-Canadian Female Population,
in Percentages, 1911 to 1971

Province	1911	1921	1931	1941	1951	1961	1971
Yukon and N.W.T.	—	—	—	.01	05	.1	.2
British Columbia	.2	.6	1.0	2.4	5.8	7.6	10.5
Alberta	23.4	22.4	25.3	23.7	22.1	22.4	23.4
Saskatchewan	30.8	26.4	28.4	26.2	19.9	16.6	14.6
Manitoba	43.1	42.3	33.4	29.9	25.5	22.6	19.9
Ontario	1.6	6.8	9.9	14.9	23.0	26.5	27.2
Quebec	.3	1.0	1.5	2.4	3.1	3.4	3.3
Maritimes	.2	.3	.3	.2	.3	.5	.6

Source: Based on Darcovich and Yuzyk, "Statistical Compendium," Series 20.65–82, 41–4.

Saskatchewan and Manitoba. By 1971, Ontario had the greatest concentration of the Ukrainian-Canadian female population (27 per cent). According to the census of 1971, the Prairie provinces still housed the majority of Ukrainian-Canadian women (58 per cent).

One of the most dramatic demographic shifts affecting Ukrainian-Canadian women has been their urban-rural distribution, illustrated in Table 3. In 1931, 56 per cent of Canadian females of all origins lived in urban areas, yet only 29 per cent of Ukrainian-Canadian females were urban dwellers. However, by 1971 the process of urbanization had affected the Ukrainian-Canadian population more than the general population, resulting in Ukrainian-Canadian females and all females being almost equally urbanized. It is interesting to note that Ukrainian-Canadian females were proportionately more urbanized than Ukrainian-Canadian males, of whom only 74 per cent lived in urban areas in 1971.[5]

TABLE 3

Urban-Farm Distribution of Ukrainian-Canadian Female Population and Total Canadian Female Population, in Percentages, 1931 to 1971

Year	Urban		Farm	
	Ukrainian-Canadian Females	Canadian Females	Ukrainian-Canadian Females	Canadian Females
1931	29.0	56.0	—	—
1941	35.2	56.6	—	—
1951	51.9	63.6	35.0	18.7
1961	66.5	71.0	19.8	10.5
1971	76.0	77.1	12.1	6.1

Source: Based on Darcovich and Yuzyk, "Statistical Compendium," Series 22.1–16, 140–2.
Note: Rural non-farm omitted

A regional examination of urban-rural distribution for the period 1951–71 shows that the greatest movement of Ukrainian-Canadian women to the cities occurred in Alberta and Saskatchewan. Ontario with 91 per cent and Quebec with 96 per cent have consistently had a highly urbanized Ukrainian-Canadian female population. Of all rural females a greater proportion of Ukrainian-Canadian females than Canadian females of all origins reside on farms. Saskatchewan has been and remains the province with the greatest proportion of Ukrainian-Canadian farm females. The Prairie provinces have the lowest proportions of Ukrainian-Canadian urban females and the highest proportions of Ukrainian-Canadian females who reside on farms. However, even in the Prairie provinces the females residing in rural areas constitute a minority.

TABLE 4

Urban-Farm Distribution of Ukrainian-Canadian Female Population, by Province, in Percentages, 1951 and 1971

Province	Urban		Farm	
	1951	1971	1951	1971
British Columbia	71.2	79.4	10.6	2.3
Alberta	34.2	71.8	50.9	17.8
Saskatchewan	22.1	54.5	59.6	28.3
Manitoba	52.4	70.6	36.2	14.8
Ontario	82.8	91.3	8.5	2.0
Quebec	95.8	96.1	1.6	.7
Maritimes	—	76.6	—	2.3

Source: Based on Darcovich and Yuzyk, "Statistical Compendium," Series 22.1–16, 140–2.
Note: Rural non-farm omitted

An examination of the age structure of the Ukrainian-Canadian female population in 1971 indicates that it is slightly older than the total Canadian female population. There is an overrepresentation of females in the 35–69 year bracket.[6]

By 1971, in terms of education there is a narrowing, though significant lag. When compared to the total Canadian female population, Ukrainian-Canadian women were about 8 per cent overrepresented in the category of those having 5 to 8 years as their highest level of schooling. They were underrepresented in all higher educational categories.[7] However, when compared to 1951 figures, we find the 1971 figures indicate a dramatic improvement. In 1951, Ukrainian-Canadian women were overrepresented by approximately 8 to 10 per cent in the categories of "no schooling" and "1 to 4 years schooling." In the category "5 to 8 years schooling" they closely approximated the total Canadian female population and were underrepresented in the remaining higher education categories.[8]

The data from 1921 and 1931 provide even more severe contrasts. In 1921, 56 per cent of Ukrainian-Canadian females were illiterate, while only 32 per cent of Ukrainian-Canadian males were illiterate and only 5 per cent of Canadian females of all origins were illiterate. By 1931, the percentage of illiterate Ukrainian-Canadian women had decreased to 30. At the same time, only 16 per cent of Ukrainian-Canadian men were illiterate and 4 per cent of Canadian women of all origins.[9]

In 1971, therefore, the Ukrainian-Canadian female population was primarily urban, Canadian-born and slightly older than the total Canadian female population. By 1971, Ukrainian-Canadian females approximated Canadian females in education more closely. This must be kept in mind when analysing their position in the paid work force. This is not to say that the rural prairie women are to be excluded from the analysis. That would merely reverse the distortion of earlier images of the Ukrainian-Canadian woman, where she was portrayed as exclusively rural and immigrant.

To state that the majority of Ukrainian-Canadian women are Canadian-born does not exhaust their description. Canadian birth implies a greater influence of Canadian, in contrast to foreign experience. However, Ukrainian-Canadian experience in the past (and to a certain extent in the present) has been much influenced by social and cultural patterns originating in Ukraine, which, in turn, have influenced those in Canada.

To understand the historical development of Ukrainian-Canadian women, it is necessary to focus briefly on their immigrant conditions and experiences. Figure 1 shows that the waves of Ukrainian female immigration coincided roughly with the waves of Ukrainian male immigration, although the female proportion of the total immigration was much smaller. The magnitude of disproportion between genders, figures from Table 5 further show gender disproportions as they emerged in Canada's regions in 1911.

TABLE 5

Percentage of Males in the Ukrainian-Canadian Population, by Province, 1911

British Columbia	Alberta	Saskatchewan	Manitoba	Ontario	Quebec	Maritimes
89.7	57.5	55.6	54.8	82.5	76.6	96.6

Source: Based on M. H. Marunchak, *Istoriia Ukraintsiv Kanady* (Winnipeg: Ukrainian Free Academy of Sciences in Canada, 1968), 63.

The first and largest wave of immigration, which with descendants constitutes the majority of Ukrainian Canadians, arrived between

FIGURE 1

Ukrainian Male and Female Immigration to Canada, 1896 to 1961

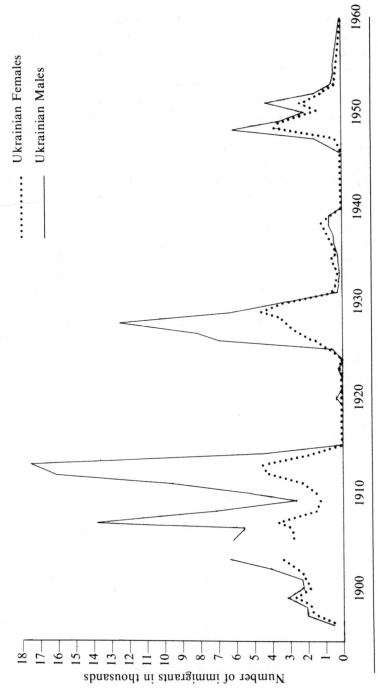

Source: Darcovich and Yuzyk, "Statistical Compendium," Series 50.94–103, 495.

1896 and 1914. This wave included approximately 41,000 females. The second immigration consisted of approximately 21,000 females, the bulk of whom arrived between 1926 and 1930. The post-Second World War immigration consisted of approximately 13,000 women.[10]

Although more research is needed on the social origins and characteristics of Ukrainian immigrant women, census and other historical materials do provide some information. Historical studies of Ukrainian Canadians have deduced that 97 per cent of first wave immigrants originated in Galicia and Bukovyna, the provinces of western Ukraine under Austro-Hungarian rule; only 3 per cent originated in eastern Ukrainian lands under Russian rule.[11] Emigration from both areas occurred for the same reasons, but Tsarist restrictions limited the number of emigrants.

What were the social origins of the Ukrainian women who emigrated? The bulk of the first wave of female immigrants was composed of wives of peasants, but single women from both the peasantry and the emerging working class also came. There is evidence that some single women used money saved for their dowries to come to Canada.[12] The shortage of men in the Austrian Empire made immigration a relatively attractive proposition.[13] The opportunities for employment for peasant women who did not marry were restricted to agricultural labour, domestic service or small craft industries in the towns of Galicia or Bukovyna —all of which were very low-paying and insecure employment opportunities. Many single women who emigrated were likely employed in these occupations, as they coincided with the "entrance status" of the Ukrainian female immigrant in Canada.

Many of the women in the first wave of immigration were illiterate; the remainder had only the rudiments of an education. This is not surprising since the year of birth of the first wave immigrants, when averaged, was 1865.[14] It was only in 1872 that an elementary four-year education was made mandatory for girls in Galicia, and the ruling was not widely implemented by the Austro-Hungarian authorities, especially among the poorer peasants in eastern Galicia. There were no Ukrainian *gymnasia* or secondary schools for girls until the end of the nineteenth century.[15] Education for women in Russian Ukraine was not much better. The Tsarist census of 1897 records a female literacy rate of 13 per cent.[16]

The situation of immigrants is a combination of the conditions they left behind and the social positions they occupy in their host country. The positions Ukrainians occupied were those not filled by Canadians or by more "preferred" immigrants. Their low-level occupations, due to the underdeveloped economy of their home country, filled the needs of

Canada's expanding economy for workers in the back-breaking frontier jobs on the land and in industry. As Ukrainian women entered the work force, they too were located in the low-level occupations of agriculture and domestic service.

Females in the interwar immigration came either as dependents of men who had already settled in Canada, or to fill immigration quotas for farm labourers and domestics. By and large they came from Galicia and Bukovyna, where in 1931, 88 per cent of the Ukrainians were still farmers, and only 6 per cent were in manufacturing, 1.5 per cent in trade and 1.2 per cent in office and service work.[17] The Compendium reports that from 1926–30 most Ukrainian women immigrants stated "domestic service" or "farmer" as their actual or intended occupation. When immigration was restricted during 1936–7, 24 per cent stated they were farmers and 5 per cent that they were domestics.[18]

Although the reasons for the second wave of emigration were also economic and political, this wave differed from the first in that it was somewhat better educated. The First World War and technological progress had certainly equipped males with some knowledge and skills, while education for women improved as well.[19] Most women came to join families on the farms. Others took agricultural work as a temporary occupation for the transitional period until jobs in the city were available.

The post-1945 immigration of Ukrainians had more skilled workers, professionals and intellectuals than did the previous two immigrations, but the precise proportion of the immigration that they constituted has yet to be adequately established.[20] The exact occupational distribution of the Ukrainian women immigrants among them is not yet available either, because it cannot be determined from census data. The occupational and educational status of these immigrants may have been higher than that of the previous two immigrations, partly due to the improvement in educational opportunities for women and men in western Ukraine. However, due to discrimination and the depressed economy in that area, university education among the Ukrainian population was still relatively rare. The amount of time this immigration spent in refugee camps in Germany and Austria and the fact that some came from Soviet Ukraine accounts in part for the higher educational level of this third wave of immigration. The growth of the Canadian economy and post-secondary education in Canada in the period after the Second World War meant that the educated proportion of this immigration spent a relatively short time in "entrance status" occupations. It must be kept in mind that, because of its small size relative to the first two Ukrainian immigrations, the slightly higher occupational status of the post-Second World War immigrants has had only a small influence on the overall picture of Ukrainian-Canadian women in the work force.

In examining the changing occupational status, and especially the recent situation, it is well to bear in mind that by 1971 only 17 per cent of all Ukrainian-Canadian females were foreign-born. Of these, 61 per cent arrived before the Second World War and 39 per cent arrived thereafter.[21] The regional distribution of Ukrainian foreign-born females given in Table 6 shows that 44 per cent of foreign-born Ukrainian-Canadian females lived in the Prairie provinces, while Ontario contained 41 per cent. In these provinces they constituted approximately 13 to 26 per cent of the total Ukrainian-Canadian female population. The foreign-born women were concentrated in urban areas: only 7 per cent lived on farms. Of the pre-Second World War immigration, 74 per cent lived in cities, while 92 per cent of the post-Second World War immigration lived in urban areas. While the foreign-born portion of the Ukrainian-Canadian female population has been small, it is significant. Since the greater portion has consisted of pre-Second World War immigrants (that is, immigrants who entered at a low occupational status), this would undoubtedly affect the present socio-economic configuration of Ukrainian-Canadian women.

TABLE 6
Distribution of Ukrainian-Canadian Female Foreign-born Population, by Province, in Percentages, 1971

Province	Ukrainian-Canadian Foreign-born Females	Foreign-born Percentage of Total Ukrainian-Canadian Female Population by Province
British Columbia	6.6	10.7
Alberta	17.0	12.4
Saskatchewan	10.5	12.2
Manitoba	16.6	14.2
Ontario	41.5	25.9
Quebec	7.1	35.9
Maritimes	.4	11.2

Source: Based on Darcovich and Yuzyk, "Statistical Compendium," Series 52.1–13, 559–61.

Women in the Work Force

The study of Ukrainian-Canadian women in the work force involves two basic phenomena. The first is the influx of women into the work force; the second is their changing position in that work force. It is naive to believe that the entry of women into the work force is synonymous with either liberation or equal power for women in society. Rather, it is more directly related to the growth and needs of the economy. There is evidence that women are used as reserve labour—pulled into the economy when needed and pushed back into the home when the economic demand is no longer there.[22] However, this is no reason to deplore the growth of female participation in the work force. The growing number of female heads of households, single women and the demand of married women to have an option to work for either economic or personal reasons, all require a growing female work force. In the past the lack of employment opportunities for females led to such disastrous consequences as prostitution and poverty.[23] The unprecedented growth since 1951 of participation in the economy of Canadian women (and Ukrainian-Canadian women in particular) has fundamentally altered their position in society.

There are various approaches to establishing position in the social order using occupational patterns and status. The methodological approach which provides the most fruitful assessment of class and power is the corporate elite approach as exemplified by Wallace Clement, whose findings on the status of women in the upper sector of the economy are presented here.[24] However, the available data can be treated best within the framework of stratification studies which rank occupations in order to establish relative differences in status. This approach will be used in assessing the position of Ukrainian-Canadian women in the non-elite sector of the Canadian economy.

For Ukrainian-Canadian women another factor must be taken into account when commenting on their position in the work force. This factor is "entrance status," which John Porter defined as "the lower level occupational roles and subjection to processes of assimilation, laid down and judged by the charter group."[25] This status is certainly applicable to the first two waves of Ukrainian immigration. The Canadian economy at the turn of the century and in the interwar period needed and obtained low-level occupational labourers. Although Canadian immigration authorities attempted to attract "preferred" immigrants for agricultural and labourer positions, including domestic labour, these were not forthcoming. The needs of the economy were met by an eastern European immigration. Consequently, the "entrance status" of Ukrainian-Canadian women is the result of a complex interaction of economic processes in the home and host countries and not an automatic concomitant of immigration.

Given the assumption of equality of opportunity, one would expect that over time the position of "entrance status" would improve. Where the contrary exists, it is important to examine the extent to which social factors such as class, gender and ethnicity act as impediments to occupational mobility.

The Changing Position of Ukrainian-Canadian Women in the Work Force, 1921–71

The participation of all women in the work force has increased dramatically over the past fifty years, a trend shared by Ukrainian-Canadian women. Table 7 shows that from 1941 to 1971 the participation of all eligible women in the work force doubled, whereas that of Ukrainian-Canadian women tripled. From a position of proportional underrepresentation in the work force during the period 1921–41, Ukrainian-Canadian women equalled the participation of all women by 1951. Since 1951, Ukrainian-Canadian women have been proportionately overrepresented in the work force in comparison to the total Canadian female population.

TABLE 7

Female Labour Force Participation of Ukrainian-Canadian Women and Canadian Women, in Percentages, 1921 to 1971

Year	Ukrainian-Canadian Women	Canadian Women
1921	4.4	15.2
1931	10.6	17.0
1941	15.3	20.1
1951	24.6	23.5
1961	36.3	29.5
1971	44.6	38.7

Source: Darcovich and Yuzyk, "Statistical Compendium," Series 40.15–30, 377–8.
Note: Definition of labour force is not constant for all years: in 1971 and 1961 it was fifteen years and over; in 1951 and 1941, fourteen years and over; in 1931 and 1921, ten years and over.

Prior to the Ukrainian immigration, growing industrialization in Canada increased the number of jobs available to women. For example, during 1860–8 the number of jobs for women doubled.[26] In part this explains the higher rate of participation for Canadian women of all origins in the paid work force when compared to Ukrainian-Canadian women in the 1921 census. Those women who had been in Canada longer and resided in urban areas could enter the new jobs because of industrialization, whereas Ukrainian women immigrants settled mostly in rural areas and were not in a position to participate to the same extent.

The two world wars also had a profound influence on pulling women into the labour force. During the First World War women were a reserve labour force. Labouring under difficult conditions, women achieved official government recognition of the principle of equal pay for equal work.[27] During the Second World War the government introduced such measures as government-subsidized day care centres, which made women's entry into the labour force more attractive. After the war the measures were dropped and women's rate of participation in the labour force also dropped, not to reach its 1947 level until 1956.[28] Despite such fluctuations, women in the work force steadily increased from 1921 to 1971.

What was the cause of this increased participation, especially after the Second World War? Basically, women continued to enter occupations in response to shortages in the labour supply. "The rapidly growing areas of work have been those in which technological advances have had less impact on productivity, where more work has required more workers, and where labour costs have accounted for a high proportion of total costs. As a result, salaries tend to be low and these are the sectors where women work."[29] The greater proportion of the increase is accounted for by married women. There has also been an increase in the number of women acting as heads of households. In part, therefore, the increase in participation by Ukrainian-Canadian women in the paid work force has reflected trends for all women. However, in 1951, 1961 and 1971, Ukrainian-Canadian women participated proportionately more than the total Canadian female population. Data from 1961 show that the rate of participation of Ukrainian-Canadian women was greater than that of all other ethnocultural groups, except for the Hungarians.[30] The reason, however, is not immediately evident from the census data. The low average income of the Ukrainian-Canadian male in the labour force may in part account for this fact.[31]

But the entry of women into the work force has not been the same across all job categories or classes. The participation of women in the highest and most powerful reaches of our economy is summarized by Clement's statement that "Women are probably the most underrepresented type in the economic elite."[32] The Royal Commission on the Status of Women in Canada studied both the participation of women in the corporate elite and in the trade union structure. Results indicate that in 1971 out of a total of 5,889 directorships only 40 were given to women; out of 1,469 executive positions in corporations, women occupied only 8.[33] The situation in trade unions was found to be only slightly better. A few women have been leaders or high officials in unions but neither the proportion of women elected to offices nor the proportion of women named to collective bargaining committees has begun to represent the proportion of women in the total union membership. Consequently, when considering the economic position of women in general and Ukrainian-Canadian women in particular, they must be considered outside the corporate elite.

The *Report of the Royal Commission on the Status of Women in Canada* sums up the position of women in the paid work force rather succinctly: "Women generally work in a few occupations labelled 'female,' earn less money than men and rarely reach the top. This has been the situation for so long that society takes it for granted."[34] Census figures do not provide a sufficiently detailed outline of the precise positions occupied by women in the broad census occupational categories. They tend to mask the fact of the feminization of specific sectors of the economy, the fact that women are clustered in certain occupations or within sectors of those occupations which are most poorly paid.

In the 1860s the ten leading occupations for women were servant, dressmaker, teacher, farmer, seamstress, tailoress, saleswoman, house-keeper, laundress and milliner. From the latter part of the nineteenth century, shifts occurred in the nature of the labour force and the development of the economy. Lower salary level clerical and teaching jobs changed from men's work to women's work. In the clerical sector, for example, the invention of the typewriter opened the field for the emergence of low-paid female secretaries. Nursing continued as a traditionally poorly paid female profession.[35] From 1941 to 1971 the ten occupations which had the most female workers were stenographer and typist, sales clerk, babysitter, maid and related service worker, school teacher, tailoress, waitress and bar tender, graduate nurse, nursing assistant and aide, telephone operator, janitor and cleaner. In 1971 these occupations accounted for 46 per cent of all female workers.[36] Even in these predominantly female occupations women earned less than men. Pat and Hugh Armstrong, in a recent book, have called this location of women in the feminized sectors of the economy *The Double Ghetto.* Ukrainian-Canadian women in the work force will be assessed as experiencing the triple restraints of immigration, low entrance status and non-charter group ethnicity—the triple ghetto.

The 1921 census figures for the occupations of Ukrainian-Canadian women in the labour force and the social histories of the period establish the entrance status occupations of Ukrainians as domestic and agricultural labourers. From 1921 to 1941 approximately three-quarters of Ukrainian-Canadian women were located in these two occupational categories. This is qualified by the fact that the proportion of eligible Ukrainian-Canadian women in the paid work force was still small. As Ukrainian-Canadian women entered the work force in greater numbers, there occurred a diversification of their occupations. However, overrepresentation in the entrance status occupations, although declining, was still significant. In 1971 Ukrainian-Canadian women were still 9 per

TABLE 8

Distribution of Ukrainian-Canadian Female Workers and
Canadian Female Workers[a], in Selected Occupations,
in Percentages, 1921 to 1971

	1921	1931	1941	1951	1961	1971
Proprietary, Managerial[b]				2.2 (3.1)	2.6 (3.4)	1.3 (1.9)
Professional, Technical	6.7 (20.2)	5.8 (17.6)	5.9 (15.5)	6.6 (14.2)	8.3 (15.4)	13.1 (17.7)
Clerical		3.0 (17.5)	4.8 (18.6)	21.1 (27.6)	24.3 (28.8)	29.4 (31.7)
Sales[c]	5.8 (15.7)	2.7 (8.1)	6.2 (9.8)	10.4 (10.2)	7.4 (8.3)	8.4 (8.3)
Service, Recreation[d]	47.0 (30.3)	62.9 (34.5)	60.1 (34.7)	27.8 (21.0)	25.5 (22.4)	19.7 (15.8)
Crafts, Manufacturing[e]	8.4 (21.4)	5.2 (12.7)	13.6 (15.5)	16.6 (14.8)	10.5 (11.6)	6.0 (7.5)
Agriculture	30.7 (3.6)	18.0 (3.6)	7.3 (2.2)	10.2 (2.7)	16.5 (4.2)	9.0 (3.6)

Source: Based on Darcovich and Yuzyk, "Statistical Compendium," Series 40.59–70, 381–2; Series 40.71–86, 383–4; Series 40.87–102, 385–6; Series 40.103–118, 387–8; Series 40.119–134, 389–90; Series 40.135–140, 391.
Notes: [a]Figures for Canadian women given in parenthesis.
  [b]Occupations with very low proportions excluded.
  [c]In 1971 category includes process, machining and product fabricating workers.
  [d]Professional and public service workers have been subtracted and put into separate category for 1941, 1931 and 1921.
  [e]Includes trade and commercial workers.

cent overrepresented in the entrance status occupations. The Compendium does not provide data which would indicate whether this overrepresentation is attributable to ethnicity or to immigrant entrance status.

In 1921, 54 per cent of Ukrainian-Canadian women in the labour force were engaged in service occupations, compared to 51 per cent of the total Canadian female work force. Of the women in service occupations, 7 per cent of Ukrainian-Canadian women and 20 per cent of all Canadian women were in professional services.[37] Agriculture engaged 31 per cent of Ukrainian-Canadian women and only 4 per cent of all Canadian women. In 1921, 14 per cent of Ukrainian-Canadian women were engaged in manufacturing and trade, compared to the total Canadian female work force of 20 per cent.

Table 8 shows that by 1931 the concentration of Ukrainian-Canadian women in the entrance status occupations had grown to 80 per cent. However, the number of women in agriculture declined in favour of women in the service sector. At this time the total Canadian female work force was also concentrated in the service occupations, but there were significant proportions in the clerical, sales and manufacturing sectors. However, this type of diversification continued to be lacking in the Ukrainian-Canadian female work force.

A detailed occupational breakdown by N. J. Hunchak of Ukrainian-Canadian women from the 1941 census shows the changes which had occurred since 1931. Table 8 shows an 11 per cent decline from 1931 to 1941 in the proportion of Ukrainian-Canadian women in agriculture. Hunchak reports that, in 1941, 835 Ukrainian-Canadian females were farmers and stockraisers and 288 were agricultural labourers.[38]

In 1941 the proportion of Ukrainian-Canadian women engaged in the service sector had declined slightly from 1931, but it still engaged the majority of them. Since the service category included professional and public servants, Hunchak's data is essential to obtaining a true picture of the position of Ukrainian-Canadian women in this broad occupational category. In the service category, 905 or 6 per cent of Ukrainian-Canadian women were professionals.[39] Of these, about half were teachers and one-quarter graduate nurses or nurses in training; 6 per cent were religious professionals. Despite this homogeneity of professional employment in 1941, there were eight artists, two librarians, one author, three chemists or metallurgists, two physicians and surgeons and ten social workers. The bulk of salaried Ukrainian-Canadian women (9,221) were located in the personal service sector. Of these, about one-half were domestic servants, 16 per cent waitresses, 11 per cent housekeepers, 6 per cent lodging housekeepers and 4 per cent worked in laundries. There were 57 managers of hotels, laundries or restaurants.

The proportion of Ukrainian-Canadian women found in manufacturing in 1941 had increased to 13 per cent. Most produced clothing and textile products, the rest produced food and metal products.[40] Of 955 Ukrainian-Canadian women employed in the trade sector in 1941, 569 were salespersons, 198 packers and wrappers, 125 retail owners and managers and 46 inspectors and graders. Of the 755 Ukrainian-Canadian women employed in the clerical sector in 1941, 383 were stenographers and typists, 214 office clerks, 115 bookkeepers and cashiers, 14 accountants, 11 appliance operators and 18 shipping clerks.[41] According to Hunchak's data, the following were the main paid occupations for Ukrainian-Canadian women in 1941 in decreasing order of numerical strength: domestic servant, waitress, clothing and textile product manufacturing, housekeeper, farmer, lodging housekeeper, salesperson, teacher, laundry worker, stenographer and typist.

The influx of Ukrainian-Canadian women into the paid work force in 1951, 1961 and 1971 was accompanied by a diversification of their occupational profile, approximating the occupational profile of the total Canadian female work force. There has been a steady increase in the proportion of Ukrainian-Canadian women in the professional and technical occupations with the greatest increase occurring between 1961 and 1971. Table 8 shows that, although the total Canadian female work force has consistently had a greater proportion of women in the technical and professional occupations than have Ukrainian-Canadian women, the latter have experienced a more dramatic and steady increase of their proportion in this sector. In 1971 Ukrainian-Canadian women remained 5 per cent underrepresented in this occupational category.

Compendium data allow for a more detailed examination of Ukrainian-Canadian females in the professional and technical occupations. In this sector we can observe several trends. The religious profession and teaching have declined as the dominant professions. Whereas in 1921, 90 per cent of Ukrainian-Canadian professional women were in these two professions, by 1971 only 37 per cent were still here.[42] As the proportion of teaching and religous professionals declined, the proportion of Ukrainian-Canadian women who entered the medical and related professions increased. In general, the trends from 1951 to 1971 indicate a differentiation of the professional and technical work force when compared to the situation in 1921. However, in 1971, 80 per cent of Ukrainian-Canadian women professionals were in nursing and associated medical professions and in teaching, whereas only two-thirds of the total Canadian female work force were engaged in these two professional categories.[43] This may be interpreted as evidence of ethnic enclaves within occupational categories that are independent of the effects of entrance status.

The clerical sector, one of the sectors of the economy which has grown significantly since the Second World War, has attracted Canadian women of all origins. Table 8 shows a dramatic 16 per cent increase of Ukrainian-Canadian women in the clerical sector from 1941 to 1951. This sector has increased steadily in the two subsequent censuses. By 1971 the clerical sector was the largest and engaged similar proportions of Ukrainian-Canadian and Canadian women.

The service sector is the next largest sector for women. Although the proportion of Ukrainian-Canadian women employed in the service sector has dropped dramatically since 1941, Ukrainian-Canadian women are still 4 per cent overrepresented in this category. This indicates a weakening but still significant influence of entrance status.

From 1951 to 1971 there has been a decline in the proportion of Ukrainian-Canadian women in the remaining sectors of manufacturing and agriculture. By 1971, Ukrainian-Canadian women were similar to the total Canadian female work force in terms of their proportions in manufacturing but still remained overrepresented in the agricultural sector. In this latter area 89 per cent of Ukrainian-Canadian women were farm labourers rather than farmers or stockraisers.[44] Their over-representation in this low-status category reflects a continuing influence of entrance status.

Ukrainian-Canadian women, like all Canadian women, are exposed to the conditions and restrictions which give rise to the "double ghetto" —low paid, female-segregated jobs. Their position is distinct from that of men in general and Ukrainian-Canadian men in particular. Within the "double ghetto" Ukrainian-Canadian women have moved into those sectors of the economy that have opened up since the Second World War and have attracted all women. These are the clerical, hospital and education sectors.

However, even within the "double ghetto," Ukrainian-Canadian women have occupied distinct positions. The 1921, 1931 and 1941 census data show that from two-thirds to four-fifths of Ukrainian-Canadian women were located in the entrance status occupations of agriculture and service. In comparison to Canadian females of all origins, Ukrainian-Canadian women were overrepresented in these occupational categories by 43 per cent in 1921 to 31 per cent in 1941. The concentration of Ukrainian-Canadian women in these entrance status occupations has declined since the Second World War; in 1971 Ukrainian-Canadian women were overrepresented in these occupations by only 8 per cent.

As a small proportion of Ukrainian-Canadian women gradually enter the higher status occupations in the professional and technical sectors, they are concentrated in specific occupations. This provides a basis for the hypothesis that ethnicity may still be a factor in occupational mobility and location, though clearly its influence is less powerful than that of immigrant entrance status.

Although Ukrainian-Canadian women are more closely approximating the occupational profile of Canadian women of all origins, they do occupy a distinct position in the "double ghetto." This specific position can be attributed to the combined effect of immigrant entrance status and ethnicity, and it points to the existence of a "triple ghetto." Further research is required to determine the weight of entrance status as compared to ethnicity in the formation of the "triple ghetto." The influence may not be one which gives rise to class stratification of a complete ethnic group, but it may contribute to different ethnic job concentrations within broad occupational categories.

Conclusion

Statistics on the social characteristics of Ukrainian-Canadian women presented in this study show that from 1921 to 1971 this group has become increasingly more native-born and urban. The concentration of the Ukrainian-Canadian female population in the Prairie provinces has declined. Data from 1971 shows the Ukrainian-Canadian female group as being older than the total Canadian female population. Statistics on Ukrainian female immigrants show gender disproportions in the three immigrations, whose description from historical sources has provided the background needed to understand their occupation and education characteristics.

Demographic statistics help to provide the background for understanding the position of Ukrainian-Canadian women in the work force and are meant to prevent simplistic explanations of occupational status through the concept of ethnic speciality. Major demographic changes coupled with changes in the economy contribute to changes in the occupational profile of Ukrainian-Canadian women.

The occupational profile of Ukrainian-Canadian women in the work force from 1921 to 1971 has changed from being very distinctive to one more closely approximating the profile of all Canadian women. Despite this approximation, there is evidence of the existence of a "triple ghetto" or a specific location in the work force due to the restraints of class and sex augmented by ethnicity and immigrant entrance status. The effects of the "triple ghetto" are easily discernible in census data from 1921, 1931 and 1941, but are less evident in subsequent census data. Further research is needed to ascertain the weight of entrance status as opposed to ethnicity in contributing to the "triple ghetto." The effects of ethnicity appear to be much more subtle than those of entrance status and require a more detailed breakdown of occupational statistics in order to trace its effects.

Ukrainian-Canadian female workers can no longer be stereotyped as domestic and farm workers; but neither are they doctors, lawyers or school principals, let alone leaders in the corporate sector. As women continue to enter the work force and grow in power and influence in Canadian society, Ukrainian-Canadian women will not only have to join the efforts of other Canadian women as a whole to overcome the effects of class and sex discrimination in our society, they will have to exert a special effort to overcome the additional restraints of immigrant entrance status and possibly ethnicity.

NOTES

1. Wsevolod W. Isajiw and Norbert J. Hartman, "Changes in the Occupational Structure of Ukrainians in Canada: A Methodology for Study of Changes in Ethnic Status," in *Social and Cultural Change in Canada*, 2 vols., ed. W. E. Mann (Toronto: Copp-Clark, 1969), 2:96–112; W. Roman Petryshyn, "The Ukrainian Canadians in Social Transition," in *Ukrainian Canadians, Multiculturalism and Separatism: An Assessment*, ed. Manoly R. Lupul (Edmonton: University of Alberta Press, 1978), 73–97.
2. Helen Potrebenko, *No Streets of Gold: A Social History of Ukrainians in Alberta* (Vancouver: New Star Books, 1977); Myrna Kostash, *All of Baba's Children* (Edmonton: Hurtig, 1977).
3. Juliet Mitchell, *Woman's Estate* (New York: Pantheon Books, 1971).
4. William Darcovich and Paul Yuzyk, eds., "Statistical Compendium on the Ukrainians in Canada, 1891–1976" (Unpublished typescript, Ottawa, 1977).
5. Ibid., Series 22.1–16, 140.
6. Ibid., Series 22.17–56, 145–6.
7. Ibid., Series 32.121–136, 293–4.
8. Ibid., Series 32.93–106, 286.
9. Ibid., Series 32.1–12, 273.
10. Ibid., Series 50.94–103, 495–6.
11. Michael H. Marunchak, *The Ukrainian Canadians: A History* (Winnipeg: Ukrainian Free Academy of Sciences, 1970), 22; N. J. Hunchak, *Canadians of Ukrainian Origin: Population* (Winnipeg: Ukrainian Canadian Committee, 1945).
12. Anne B. Woywitka, "A Pioneer Woman in the Labour Movement," *Alberta History* 26 (Winter 1978): 32–55.
13. Martha Bohachevsky-Chomiak, "Socialism and Feminism: The First Stages of Women's Organizations in the Eastern Part of the Austrian Empire" (Paper read at the "Women in Eastern Europe and the Soviet Union" conference, 26–28 October 1978, University of Alberta), 25.
14. C. W. Hobart, W. E. Kalbach, J. I. Borhek, A. P. Jacoby, "Persistence and Change: A Study of Ukrainians in Alberta" (Toronto: Ukrainian Canadian Research Foundation, 1978), 85.

15. Martha Bohachewsky-Chomiak, "Kobrynska: A Formulation of Feminism," mimeographed (1978), 18.
16. "Zhinocha Osvita," in *Ukrainska Radianska Entsyklopedia* (Kiev: Akademia Nauk Ukrainskoi Radianskoi Sotsialistychnoi Republiky, 1961), 5:83.
17. V. Kubijovyč and H. Selehen, "Chyslo i budova liudnosty Ukrainy," in *Entsyklopedia Ukrainoznavstva* (Munich and New York: Naukove Tovarystvo im. Shevchenka, 1949), 1:138.
18. Darcovich and Yuzyk, Series 50.135–162, 499–500.
19. Ol'ha Woycenko, *The Ukrainians in Canada* (Winnipeg: Trident Press, 1967), 13.
20. Marunchak, 571; Woycenko, 14.
21. Darcovich and Yuzyk, Series 51.61–68, 540.
22. Pat Armstrong and Hugh Armstrong, *The Double Ghetto: Canadian Women and Their Segregated Work* (Toronto: McClelland and Stewart, 1978), 19.
23. Charles H. Young, *The Ukrainian Canadians: A Study of Assimilation*, ed. Helen R. Y. Reid (Toronto: Nelson and Sons, 1931), 123.
24. Wallace Clement, *The Canadian Corporate Elite: An Analysis of Economic Power* (Toronto: McClelland and Stewart, 1975).
25. John Porter, *The Vertical Mosaic: An Analysis of Social Class and Power in Canada*, 2d. ed. (Toronto: University of Toronto Press, 1969), 63–4.
26. *Report of the Royal Commission on the Status of Women in Canada* (Ottawa: Information Canada, 1970), 53. Herafter *RCSWC*.
27. Christina M. Hill, "Women in the Canadian Economy," in *(Canada) Ltd.: The Political Economy of Dependency*, ed. Robert Laxer (Toronto: McClelland and Stewart, 1973), 84–106.
28. *RCSWC*, 54.
29. Armstrong, 27.
30. *Report of the Royal Commission on Bilingualism and Biculturalism, Book IV: The Cultural Contribution of the Other Ethnic Groups* (Ottawa: Queen's Printer, 1970), 270.
31. Petryshyn, 87.
32. Clement, 266.
33. *RCSWC*, 64.
34. Ibid., 53.
35. Hill, 95.
36. Armstrong, 32–3.
37. Darcovich and Yuzyk, Series 40.161–172, 394.
38. Hunchak, 21.
39. Ibid.
40. Ibid., 17.
41. Ibid., 23.
42. Darcovich and Yuzyk, Series 40.161–172, 394.
43. Armstrong, 36.
44. Darcovich and Yuzyk, Series 40.193–204, 404.

PART IV
Political Participation

POLITICAL MOBILITY OF UKRAINIANS IN CANADA

Roman R. March

The rise of a variety of "ethnic consciousnesses" that no longer accept the old assimilation model are a recent and fascinating North American phenomenon. While "Black Power" and "Quebecois nationalism" have been extensively examined, various forms of "Slavic consciousness" have received only minimal scholarly treatment. This essay is a contribution to this relatively new, but increasingly important, area of study and activity.

Commenting on the phenomenon of developing Ukrainian communities in the United States and Canada, Myron B. Kuropas of the Ukrainian National Association said:

> Both of our communities were founded by pioneers who arrived in North America with little appreciation for their Ukrainian ethno-national heritage. Occupied and divided by foreign powers for centuries, Ukrainians had little opportunity to raise the level of their national consciousness and to develop a national will which reflected the sentiment of all segments of the population.... The ethnic climate in the United States began to change dramatically a few years ago as the result of the rise of Black Power. Other ethnic groups benefited from this development because it heralded the beginning of a new era of understanding for the ethnic phenomenon. In a very real sense it meant the demise of the melting pot and the rise of cultural pluralism as the model for American unity. ... We are preserving our cultural heritage in an environment which appears to be significantly more amenable to ethno-national

diversity. And we are gaining—slowly in America, more rapidly in Canada—a modest degree of political influence.[1]

It is the intent of this paper to look at the political success of the Ukrainian community in Canada by examining the Ukrainian participants in the eleven legislative bodies.

It has been relatively simple to collect data on participation rates of ethnic groups in political institutions at the federal, provincial or municipal levels.[2] This information is used in time-series analyses conducted to measure and compare the extent to which various ethnic groups are represented in such institutions as legislatures, courts, cabinets and the civil service.

The "Statistical Compendium on the Ukrainians in Canada, 1891–1976" provides this kind of data from over 600 federal and provincial constituencies in which Ukrainian candidates ran for office between the years 1904 to 1975.[3] In Appendix A the names of those Ukrainians appointed, rather than elected, to higher political office are included.[4] The Compendium defines political participation as "running for or seeking election to political office." It claims that

> this definition implies more political participation than may be apparent at first sight. It implies an awareness of local or "grass root" problems and of larger provincial and national issues, the existence of a political philosophy on the part of the candidates and a motivation to stand for election. It also implies that considerable preparatory efforts have been undertaken: running for office in local governments, being active in business or community affairs, joining or being active in political parties, going through the nomination procedures and conducting the campaign itself.[5]

The Compendium found that "886 Ukrainian candidates, 23 being women, contested 645 federal and provincial elections in the period 1904–1975...."[6] This data is summarized in Table 1 below.

Federal Elections

The time-series data of all federal elections from 1904, when the first Ukrainian candidate ran, to 1974, when forty-two Ukrainian candidates ran and eight were elected, show that the number of Ukrainian candidates for federal office increased incrementally. At first the overall success rate was quite modest. The first Ukrainian member of Parlia-

TABLE 1

Summary of Election Results for Ukrainian Candidates in Federal and Provincial Elections, 1904 to 1975

Area	Period Covered	Ukrainian Candidates			Elected Ukrainian Candidates	
		Total	Female	Number of Constituencies	Total	Different[a] Candidate
Federal						
Manitoba	1911–74	77	1	60	15	6
Saskatchewan	1904–74	46	1	41	9	3
Alberta	1926–74	78	5	49	25	10
Ontario	1942–74	52	2	45	12	4
British Columbia	1940–74	9	—	9	—	—
Quebec	1953–65	4	—	4	—	—
Canada	1904–74	266	9	208	61	23
Provincial						
Manitoba	1914–73	233	6	147	69	28
Saskatchewan	1912–75	113	2	91	37	17
Alberta	1913–75	207	4	136	67	32
Ontario	1945–75	51	—	48	14	4
British Columbia	1941–75	16	2	15	1	1
Total Provincial	1912–75	620	14	437	188	82
Federal and Provincial	1904–75	886	23	645	249	105

Source: Darcovich and Yuzyk, "Statistical Compendium," Table 33.2, 321.
Note: [a]Some candidates are elected more than once and this column shows the number of different candidates elected. For example, four different candidates were elected (or re-elected) fourteen different times to the Ontario Legislature.

ment, Michael Luchkovich, was elected from Vegreville, Alberta, in 1926. He was a United Farmers Party (UFA) candidate and the only Ukrainian candidate. Eight Ukrainian MPs were elected in 1968, in 1972 and in 1974. This was the maximum. The number of Ukrainian candidates increased from one candidate in each of the elections from 1904 to 1926 to six in the elections from 1930 to 1940, and rose rapidly from ten in 1945 to forty-two in 1974 (Table 2).

TABLE 2

Ukrainian Candidates and Members of Parliament
in Federal Elections and By-elections

Year of Election	Number of Ukrainian Candidates	Number of Members of Parliament Elected
1904	1	0
1911	1	0
1921	1	0
1926	1	1
1930	6	1
1935	6	0
1940	6	1
1945	10	2
1949	15	1
1953	18	4
1957	19	6
1958	20	7
1962	20	5
1963	21	5
1965	26	4
1968	22	8
1972	34	8
1974	42	8
Total:	266	61

In view of what is known about the prejudice of the Anglo-Celtic and French groups against the other ethnic groups, it is not surprising that the first Ukrainian candidates ran for such non-establishment parties as the UFA and the Co-operative Commonwealth Federation (CCF). Commenting on this phenomenon with respect to the rise of the CCF in Saskatchewan during the 1930s, S. M. Lipset wrote:

Urban middle-class leaders of the CCF differ significantly from farming and working-class leaders in one essential respect—ethnic origins. They belonged, predominantly, to minority ethnic groups; these groups were not part of the urban "upper class," which in Saskatchewan is largely Anglo-Saxon. This is true even in areas where the population of the surrounding countryside is composed overwhelmingly of members of minority ethnic groups. The non-Anglo-Saxon businessmen are often newcomers to the business life of the towns, being former farmers or children of farmers. They tend to retain their ties with the minority ethnic group of the surrounding countryside, and remain socially marginal to the business community. This was clearly brought out in a study of a small, predominantly Anglo-Saxon town in a Ukrainian farming district. According to one young Ukrainian merchant, "The Anglo-Saxons made it plain that they were better than the Ukrainians and didn't want us, so the Ukrainians said 'To hell with you, we can get along by ourselves.'" The two CCF Ukrainian members of the Saskatchewan legislature in 1944 were small town merchants who came from farm families. Both reported close ties with the Ukrainian rural community.[7]

The first Ukrainian Liberal candidate was not elected until 1949, while the first Ukrainian elected as a Progressive Conservative (PC) did not win until the 1953 federal election. In 1957 one CCF, two Social Credit and three PC Ukrainians were elected MPs. From 1958 to 1965 every Ukrainian elected federally was a PC. This underlined John Diefenbaker's ability to attract strong support among Ukrainian Canadians, because he supported the civil rights of non-establishment groups and championed the causes of the "little man" long before he became leader of the PC party. It also reflects increasing conservatism of western Canadian voters.

Pierre E. Trudeau was able to break the PC stronghold in Ukrainian communities when four Ukrainian MPs were elected as Liberals in 1968. However, the pattern established under Diefenbaker was strongly re-asserted in 1972 and 1974, when Ukrainians won thirteen seats for the PCs, one for the NDP and two for the Liberals. It would appear that Ukrainian Canadians are now indistinguishable from others in Manitoba, Saskatchewan and Albera in their united support for the Progressive Conservative Party.

Provincial Elections

The political experience of Ukrainians in the provincial area has been extensive. Political participation has been heaviest in Manitoba where there have been 245 Ukrainian candidates and 66 seats won. The second greatest activity has been in Alberta where 206 candidates won 66 seats, followed by 111 candidates in Saskatchewan and 35 seats won; 51 candidates in Ontario and 14 seats won; and 16 in British Columbia with one seat.

TABLE 3

Ukrainian Candidacies and Seats Won in Provincial Elections
by Political Party

Candidates and Elected Members	LIB	PC	CCF/ NDP	SC	IND	F	LP^a	Other	Total
Manitoba 1914–73 candidates	44	31	53	5	56	3	31	23^b	246
Elected as MLAs	9	3	21	1	4	3	20		61
Alberta 1913–75 candidates	39	43	39	55	8	7		16^c	207
Elected as MLAs	5	21	3	33	0	4			66
Saskatchewan 1912–75 candidates	30	20	40	10	7	0	0	4^d	111
Elected as MLAs	8	0	27	0	0	0	0		35
Ontario 1945–75 candidates	14	14	11	4	3	0	0	5^e	51
Elected as MPPs	5	7	2	0	0	0	0		14
British Columbia 1941–75 candidates	5	1	3	5	1	0	0	1^f	16
Elected as MPPs	0	0	0	1	0	0	0		1

user id:2176101015688501

title:Ukrainian Canadians, mult
author:Lupul, Manoly R.
item id:31761061361432
　　due:24/10/2007,23:59

title:Ukrainians in Canada ; th
author:Darcovich, William
item id:31761018085886
　　due:24/10/2007,23:59

title:Canada's Ukrainians : neg
author:Hryniuk, Stella M., 1939-
item id:31761021535208
　　due:24/10/2007,23:59

title:Changing realities : soci
author:Petryshyn, Walter Roman,
item id:31761021421367
　　due:24/10/2007,23:59

Total candidates	132	109	146	79	75	10	31	49	631
Total elected	27	31	53	35	4	7	20		177

Notes: a The party affiliation of candidates is given according to the following abbreviations:

Communist Party	(CP)	Labour	(L)
Conservative	(PC)	Labour Progressive Party	(LPP)
Co-operative Commonwealth		Liberal	(LIB)
Federation	(CCF)	Liberal Progressive	(LP)
Farmer	(F)	New Democratic Party	(NDP)
Farmer Labour	(FL)	Other	(O)
Government Coalition	(GC)	Progressives	(P)
Independent	(IND)	Social Credit	(SC)
Independent Liberal			
Progressive	(ILP)		

b Other candidates include: ILP—4; LPP—5; CP—4; O—1; L—1; DK—3; CP—3; GC—2.
c Other candidates include: CP—12; O—4.
d Other candidates include: P—2; FL—1; LP—1.
e Other candidates include: LPP—5.
f Other candidates include: O—1.

For all five provinces the CCF/NDP attracted 146 Ukrainian candidates and won 53 seats; the Liberals had 132 candidates of whom 27 won; the Conservatives had 109 candidates and won 31 seats; Social Credit had 79 candidates and won 35 seats (33 in Alberta); and 75 independent candidates won only 4 seats. The farmers' parties were the most successful, running 10 candidates and scoring 7 victories.

Theoretical Considerations

John Porter, a pioneer in the analysis of political participation and mobility in Canada, defines the admission of ethnic groups to the power structure as "entrance status."[8] He found that the English and French "charter groups" relegated most other ethnic groups to low status occupational roles and subjected them to assimilation. In addition to the concepts of "entrance status" and "charter groups," Porter explored the question of whether a Canadian-style ethnic mosaic is less conducive to social mobility than the American melting pot. "The melting pot," he wrote, "with its radical breakdown of national ties and old forms of stratification, would have endangered the conservative tradition of Canadian life, a tradition which gives ideological support to the continued high status of the British charter group."[9] Porter's assumption is that an ethnic group either assimilates or remains locked into a position of limited social status.

His initial findings were rather pessimistic and implied that non-charter groups would not move rapidly out of a low entrance status into higher income and occupation status. This pessimism was based on his assumption that only a drastic alteration in the North American Anglo-Protestant capitalist system toward a more social-democratic form would open up North American society to increased upward mobility among non-charter groups, such as Ukrainians, Poles and Italians. Nowhere in his extensive research does Porter acknowledge that very rapid upward mobility is possible for non-charter groups within the existent liberal-democratic social and political structures.[10]

Recent studies of occupational mobility among non-charter ethnic groups suggests that the process is more rapid than Porter anticipated.[11] The model of assimilation which lies behind these findings is based on the assumption that "all [ethnic] groups enter a linear and cumulative unitary process of cultural assimilation . . . ," with upward mobility being a slow, multi-generational process.[12] This model envisages that minority ethnic groups begin at the lowest educational, occupational and income levels and slowly filter upwards, all the while shedding their linguistic and cultural baggage as they assimilate into the dominant culture. Thus Ukrainians and other ethnic groups will initially enter dominant group institutions at the local, then provincial and finally federal political levels.

In sharp contrast to these linear and cumulative assumptions, William Newman writes that "the most dramatic cases of minority social mobility in the U.S. appear to have been facilitated through the creation of minority-group-controlled parallel structures, not through structural assimilation."[13] As an example of this process, let us examine briefly the basic unit of American political structures, the precinct, which is a neighbourhood encompassing 100 to 700 voters. Dan Nimmo and Thomas Unger write:

> Party organization begins with the precinct. The principal functionary is the precinct committee person, captain, or leader, who is elected either in the party primary or by the precinct party members assembled in convention; in some areas, he or she may be appointed by party leaders of countrywide organizations. The precinct leader works to increase voter registration and achieve a respectable turn-out of party identifiers on election day. Moreover, he or she preaches party doctrine, passes along information, and performs social and economic services.

The constituency is next above the precinct; it is the lowest level from which a public official is elected. In larger cities, this level is the ward; in rural areas, it is the township; in some sections of the country, it is a state legislative district; and in some states, it is the congressional district. The basic organization is the county committee, usually composed of the precinct leaders. The head of this committee is the county chairperson who is chosen either by the committee or in the party primary. He or she is charged with seeing that precinct leaders mobilize majorities in their precincts and that the party as a whole carries the constituency for local, legislative, congressional, senatorial, gubernatorial, and presidential candidates.

The coordinating level is above the precinct and constituency; it is usually composed of the state central or executive committee and includes representatives from constituency committees.[14]

Since neighbourhoods are usually highly homogeneous, ethnic groups could and did come to control precincts, then wards, counties and even states. Precinct power was the means for ethnic communities to amass political power. However, no such permanent grass roots political organization exists in Canada. Very few Canadian polling divisions have been as strongly organized or decentralized as are their precinct counterparts in the United States. In Canada political power rests in the hands of the small, usually self-selecting constituency executive, which in turn is jealously guarded by the incumbent member of the Legislature or Parliament. Only during elections are ephemeral polling organizations established. Once the election is over, the Canadian poll organization disappears, whereas in the United States the precinct remains intact. One consequence of these fundamentally different approaches to the structuring of politial parties in Canada and the United States is that Canadian ethnic groups have not created permanent bases of political power in areas where they are numerically dominant. Nathan Glazer and Daniel Moynihan see the development of political organization along ethnic lines as the primary mechanism of assimilation and social mobility in the United States and a prelude to political and economic assimilation.[15] Other studies suggest that total assimilation is not inevitable, and that group diversity is a permanent fixture of many modern societies.[16]

The study of ethnic groups in America requires careful reconsideration of the theories that have arisen to account for sociological and historical developments. The experience of the Ukrainian community in Canada suggests that it is possible for an ethnic group to overcome severe restrictions and prejudices against it in a relatively short period. But the political success of Ukrainians in Canada suggests that the success rate of different ethnic communities is quite varied. Ukrainian Canadians have made remarkable progress in achieving political office at the federal and provincial levels in Canada. In doing so, they have avoided the incremental model. Why the Ukrainian community, however, has been able to achieve this high level of political success has still to be explained.

APPENDIX A
Appointees to Higher Political Office
in Federal and Provincial Governments, 1904 to 1975[1]

Federal Government

S. Worobetz	Trudeau	Lieutenant-Governor[2]	1970–6
W. M. Wall (LIB)	St. Laurent	Senator (Manitoba)	1955–62
J. Hnatyshyn (PC)	Diefenbaker	Senator (Saskatchewan)	1959–67
P. Yuzyk (PC)	Diefenbaker	Senator (Manitoba)	1963–
J. Ewasew (LIB)	Trudeau	Senator (Quebec)	1976–8
M. Starr (PC)	Diefenbaker	Minister of Labour	1958–63

Province of Manitoba

N. V. Bachinsky (LP)	Campbell	Deputy Speaker[3]	1950–6
M. N. Hryhorczuk (LP)	Campbell	Attorney General	1955–8
S. Uskiw (NDP)	Schreyer	Agriculture[4]	1969–
P. Burtniak (NDP)	Schreyer	Tourism & Recreation[5]	1969–
B. Hanuschak (NDP)	Schreyer	Speaker[6]	1969–
W. Uruski (NDP)	Schreyer	Motor Vehicle Branch[7]	1973–

Province of Saskatchewan

A. G. Kuziak (CCF)	Douglas	Telephones[8]	1952–64
J. R. Romanow (NDP)	Blakeney	Attorney General	1971–
J. R. Kowalchuk (NDP)	Blakeney	Natural Resources	1974–

Province of Alberta

A. Holowach (SC)	Manning	Provincial Secretary	1959–71
A. Ludwig (SC)	Strom	Public Works	1969–71
A. E. Hohol (PC)	Lougheed	Manpower & Labour[9]	1971–5
W. Diachuk (PC)	Lougheed	Deputy Speaker	1972–5
J. Koziak (PC)	Lougheed	Education	1971–5
G. Topolnisky (PC)	Lougheed	Without Portfolio[10]	1971–5
W. Yurko (PC)	Lougheed	Environment[11]	1971–5

Province of Ontario

J. Yaremko (PC)	Robarts	Without Portfolio[12]	1958–

Notes: [1]Darcovich and Yuzyk, "Statistical Compendium," Table 33.3, 323.
[2]Province of Saskatchewan.
[3]Speaker, 1956-8.
[4]After 1973, also Minister of Co-operative Development.
[5]Cultural Affairs, 1970; Minister of Highways, 1971-
[6]Consumer, Corporate and Internal Services, 1970-3; after 1973, Minister of Education and College and University Affairs.
[7]Public Insurance Corporation, 1974-
[8]Also Minister in charge of Government Finance Office; Minister of Natural Resources and Minister in charge of Northern Crown Corporation, 1956-60; Minister of Mineral Resources, 1960-4.
[9]Advanced Education and Manpower, 1975-
[10]Rural Development, 1975-
[11]Public Works, 1975-
[12]Minister of Transport, 1958-60; Provincial Secretary and Minister of Citizenship, 1960-6; Minister of Public Welfare, 1966-7; Social and Family Services, 1967-71; Provincial Secretary, March 1971-February 1972; Citizenship, March 1971-September 1972; Solicitor General, 1972-4.

APPENDIX B
Identification of Ukrainian Canadians

The procedure used in identifying Ukrainian ethnicity consisted of examining the list of candidates for each constituency and selecting those with Ukrainian surnames. The easiest candidates to identify were those generally known to be Ukrainian by the Ukrainian community at large and these formed a significant portion of the total. Other candidates were identified by reference to biographical materials. Winning candidates had biographical summaries in the Parliamentary Guide. These provided the ethnic origin or birthplace of the candidate or of the parents or gave the Ukrainian surname of the parents if the candidate's name had been Anglicized. *Who's Who* publications provided ethnic background for additional candidates and the *Dictionary of Ukrainian Surnames* provided a check on doubtful surnames. Individuals in provinces familiar with local political affairs were provided with lists of possible Ukrainian candidates and their knowledge was helpful in resolving doubtful cases.

An identification procedure based on surnames is only approximate. The classification may include some non-Ukrainian candidates who are Poles, Russians or Jews as persons of different Slavic origin sometimes have common surnames. On the other hand, Ukrainian candidates may be excluded due to poor transliteration or Anglicization of their surnames. In mixed marriages the practice is to include a candidate if either of the parents is Ukrainian; some omission of candidates can be expected on this account, especially where the one Ukrainian parent is the mother.

Since the classification is based on the ethnicity of either parent, it is broader than that in the census, which is based on male ancestry. In common with the census, however, it is mainly an objective classification. It may therefore classify candidates as Ukrainian who do not feel or identify themselves as such and who may not be sympathetic to such a designation.

NOTES

1. Remarks to the Twenty-Sixth Convention of the Ukrainian National Federation, Toronto, 7 October 1978. The Ukrainian National Association is the largest Ukrainian fraternal insurance company in North America.
2. R. R. March, "Political Mobility of Slavs in the Federal and Provincial Legislatures in Canada," in *Slavs in Canada*, 3 vols. (Toronto: Ukrainian Echo Publishing Co., 1968), 2:16.
3. William Darcovich and Paul Yuzyk, eds., "Statistical Compendium on the Ukrainians in Canada, 1891–1976" (Unpublished typescript, Ottawa, 1977), 316–60. Tables 1 to 3 were compiled in the summer of 1978 from an early version of the "Statistical Compendium." Subsequent research by Darcovich on the 1904–75 period slightly increased total figures. (See Darcovich's article in this collection) Nevertheless, the data presented here to demonstrate an historical development is substantially correct.
4. Ibid., 323.
5. Ibid., 317.
6. Ibid.
7. S. M. Lipset, *Agrarian Socialism: The Cooperative Commonwealth Federation in Saskatchewan: A Study in Politicial Sociology* (Garden City, N.Y.: Anchor Books, 1968), 233–4.
8. John Porter, *The Vertical Mosaic: An Analysis of Social Class and Power in Canada* (Toronto: University of Toronto Press, 1965).
9. Ibid., 71.
10. Elia Zuriek and Robert M. Pike, *Socialization and Values in Canadian Society* (Toronto: McClelland and Stewart, 1975), 51.
11. Merrijoy Kelner, "Ethnic Penetration Into Toronto's Elite Structure," in *Social Stratification in Canada*, eds. J. Curtis and W. Scott (Scarborough, Ontario: Prentice-Hall, 1973), 140; Wsevolod W. Isajiw and Norbert J. Hartman, "Changes in the Occupational Structure of Ukrainians in Canada," in *Canada: A Sociological Profile*, 2 vols., ed. W. E. Mann (Toronto: Copp Clark, 1969), 1:96–112.
12. William Newman, "Theoretical Perspectives for the Analysis of Social Pluralism," in *The Canadian Ethnic Mosaic: A Quest for Identity*, ed. Leo Driedger (Toronto: McClelland and Stewart, 1978), 43.
13. Ibid.
14. Dan Nimmo and Thomas Unger, *Political Patterns in America* (San Francisco: W. H. Freeman, 1979), 236, 258.
15. Nathan Glazer and Daniel P. Moynihan, *Beyond the Melting Pot: The Negroes, Puerto Ricans, Jews, Italians and Irish of New York City* (Cambridge, Mass.: MIT Press, 1963).
16. Driedger, 44.

POSTWAR SOCIAL TRENDS AMONG UKRAINIANS IN QUEBEC

Ivan Myhul and Michael Isaacs

Canada's struggle to preserve its polity and confirm a national identity has focused attention upon cultural heritage. Increasingly, the knowledge of differences, rather than the distinctions themselves, has been the foundation for political action. This has been particularly true in Quebec. To understand the latter, it is necessary to examine the background to recent government actions in that province.[1] What are the differentiating characteristics of those against whom legislation has been directed? Why have dissimilarities provoked forceful political behaviour? This essay will attempt to present a profile of one of the differentiated groups—the Ukrainian community in Quebec. A recent compilation of data has now made that possible.[2]

Not being demographers, we cannot hope to attain the scientific rigour of that discipline. We do believe, however, that our data is an important first step for studies of issues involving minority groups in Quebec.[3] We intend to provide a multi-dimensional image of Quebec's Ukrainians drawing from data on population growth, age structure, geographical dispersion and distribution, religious affiliation, linguistic knowledge, educational attainment, personal income and occupation.

While it is possible to criticize such a portrait as one abstracted from time, fixed in position and removed from a dynamic and developing environment, we will nonetheless attempt to place current characteristics within the framework of the post-Second World War period and then attempt to trace trends over that thirty-year period, recognizing that it is a short interval to examine for social developments. To place the Ukrainians within the total population, wherever possible we will contrast their statistical traits with those of all other Quebecers.

General Characteristics, Age Structure and Geographic Distribution

The small Ukrainian community of Quebec is of relatively recent immigrant origin. Although it has increased twenty-fold since the First World War and doubled in size since the Second World War, it still represents less than 1 per cent of the entire provincial population and accounts for only 3.5 per cent of the Ukrainian-Canadian total.[4]

TABLE 1

Quebec and Montreal, Number and Percentage
of Ukrainian Population, 1921 to 1971

Year	Quebec		Montreal		Montreal Ukrainians as a Percentage of Quebec Ukrainians
1921	1,176	0.05	1,092	0.14	92.85
1931	4,340	0.15	3,850	0.36	88.70
1941	8,006	0.24	6,643	0.56	83.97
1951	12,921	0.32	11,238	0.76	87.97
1961	16,588	0.32	14,519	0.69	87.52
1971	20,325	0.34	18,050	0.66	88.80

Source: Adapted from Darcovich and Yuzyk, "Statistical Compendium," Series 21.1–242, 61; Series 21.243–294, 67.

Unlike recent immigrants, the Ukrainians in Quebec are not characterized by a disproportionately young and male population. The sexes are fairly evenly distributed, with males having a slight edge. This ratio is reversed for those Ukrainian Quebecers born in Canada.[5]

The community is an aging one, as indicated by the recent drop in fertility.[6] Quebec Ukrainians have a disproportionate number of people who were born just before or during the Great Depression. This group remains the largest single age interval. The postwar "baby-boom" generation is the second largest age interval. Excluding the possibility of immigration and migration, this group may be the last significant internal source for the replenishment of the Ukrainian population in Quebec, since there are relatively few Ukrainians in the 0–4 age bracket.[7]

The Ukrainian Quebecers have always been highly urbanized, exceeding 95 per cent for the last two decades.[8] The likely cohesiveness of this community is reinforced by its overwhelming concentration in the Montreal area.[9]

Religion

Members of the Quebec-Ukrainian community remain strongly affiliated with traditional Ukrainian religions in proportions that have virtually remained unchanged since the Second World War.[10] Nearly three-fifths continue to subscribe to the Ukrainian Catholic and Orthodox faiths. However, while the retention of the Ukrainian Catholic religion has risen since 1951, Orthodox affiliation has fallen.[11] During this time Roman Catholic affiliation has fluctuated.[12] There has been a slight increase in the acquisition of Protestant denominations. When this religious transfer occurs, it is primarily in favour of the United Church.[13]

Language

Knowledge of the Ukrainian language and the declaration of it as a mother tongue has fallen drastically over the last two decades.[14] The older portion of the Ukrainian population, those aged thirty-five and over, report the greatest retention and knowledge of Ukrainian.[15] There is no perceptible difference in the retention of the language by sex, though some differences do appear depending on the respondent's place of birth. Ukrainian still accounts for the mother tongue of four-fifths of those born outside Canada and for less than two-fifths of those who are native-born.[16]

Foreign-born Ukrainians also tend to use Ukrainian three times as often at home as do those born here.[17] This apparent loss of the Ukrainian language must be qualified by the fact that most ethnic groups retain their mother tongue to a greater degree in Quebec than in the rest of Canada.[18]

The pattern of language transfer has increased substantially in the postwar period in favour of English with some transference to French.[19] Fully one-third of the Ukrainian community now declares English as its mother tongue, and over one-half consider it the language most often spoken at home.[20] This tendency may continue despite Bill 101 since one-half of the Canadian-born Ukrainians declared English as their mother tongue.[21]

Knowledge of one or both of Canada's official languages has grown in the postwar era.[22] But it is the development of bilingualism that is significant, as nine-tenths of those knowing French now also know English.[23] However, more than one-half of the Ukrainian community in Quebec knows only English.[24] It is conceivable that the lack of

TABLE 2
Ukrainian Mother Tongue Speakers in Quebec, by Age, 1951 to 1971

AGE	Total	0-4	0-4 as % of Total	5-9	5-9 as % of Total	10-14	10-14 as % of Total	15-19	15-19 as % of Total	20-24	20-24 as % of Total
1951	11,743	743	6.33	609	5.19	544	4.63	657	5.59	958	8.16
1961	13,424	676	5.04	929	6.92	870	6.48	656	4.89	516	3.84
1971	11,740	270	2.30	395	3.36	660	5.62	755	6.43	750	6.39

knowledge of the French language alone may contribute toward a future dwindling of the Ukrainian population in Quebec.

Education

Postwar trends in education indicate that Ukrainians have resolutely pursued academic training. In 1951 more than 28 per cent of Quebec's Ukrainians reported having attended school for less than five years. Slightly more than one-quarter had attended for more than eight years.[25] By 1971, less than one-fifth had not reached grade five. Nearly one-half had attained at least the grade nine level.[26]

Comparable figures for all Quebecers show about one-sixth of the population had not attended for more than five years in 1951 and more than one-third had been in the educational system for at least eight years.[27] By 1971, about one-fifth had not reached grade five and about 46 per cent had followed courses at the grade nine level or higher.[28]

The Ukrainian community made rapid advances during the period and in terms of educational attainment overtook the Quebec population as a whole. This phenomenon is even more striking in university education. In 1971, one out of seven Quebec Ukrainians had attended university while the proportion of all Quebecers was only one in thirteen.[29]

Occupation and Income

An examination of the 1951 and 1971 reports on occupations held by Quebec Ukrainians and Quebecers of all origins reveals a startling contrast.[30]

In 1951, the proportion of Ukrainians found in any given category

TABLE 2—*Continued*

5-34	25-34 as % of Total	35-44	35-44 as % of Total	45-54	45-54 as % of Total	55-64	55-64 as % of Total	65-69	65-69 as % of Total	70+	70+ as % of Total
,654	22.60	1,865	15.88	2,026	17.25	1,207	10.28	300	2.55	180	1.53
,700	12.66	3,173	23.64	1,981	14.76	1,754	13.07	604	4.50	565	4.21
955	8.11	1,405	11.97	2,750	23.42	1,780	15.16	915	7.79	1,095	9.33

ource: Adapted from Darcovich and Yuzyk, "Statistical Compendium," Series 31.137–148, 246–7.

differed widely from the proportion of all Quebecers found in the same group. The largest responses among Ukrainians in that year were jobs in manufacturing with 31.47 per cent of the total; services with 15.21 per cent; labourers with 11.79 per cent; clerical with 11.01 per cent; and agricultural, fishing, logging and mining jobs, with 5.42 per cent. Among all Quebecers, the largest single category was manufacturing with 19.17 per cent of the total; followed by agricultural, fishing, logging and mining jobs with 16.77 per cent; clerical with 10.09 per cent; services with 9.16 per cent; professional with 7.63 per cent; proprietors and managers with 7.32 per cent; and labourers with 7.32 per cent.[31]

By 1971, the picture had changed considerably. Where the earlier census could be characterized by wide differences among particular occupations between the Ukrainians and the rest of Quebec, the 1971 report is striking for the closeness in occupational patterns. The five major categories of employment were not only the same for both Ukrainians and all other Quebecers, but the proportions of the two groups found in each category were remarkably similar. Ukrainian responses were clerical, 17.59 per cent; professional-technical, 13.71 per cent; service, 12.65 per cent; product fabrication, 11.04 per cent; and sales, 8.16 per cent. For all Quebecers the figures were clerical, 15.97 per cent; professional-technical, 13.06 per cent; service, 10.43 per cent; product fabrication, 8.99 per cent; and sales, 9.09 per cent.[32] Although prevented by incomparabilities in the data from drawing clear conclusions about trends in the Ukrainian community itself, it is apparent that the occupational mix for the two groups has become significantly more alike during the postwar period.

The average earned income reported by Ukrainian Quebecers during 1970 was $5,315 or 6.96 per cent higher than the average income reported by Quebecers of all origins in the same period.[33] The same proportion of each group was found in the highest bracket of $20,000

230

TABLE 3

Canada, Quebec and Montreal: Mother Tongue of Population of Ukrainian Origin by Place of Birth and Sex, 1971

	English	English as % of TBIC[1]	French	French as % of TBIC	Ukrainian	Ukrainian as % of TBIC	Other	Other as % of TBIC	Total Born in Canada
				BORN IN CANADA					
Canada									
Total	271,515	57.25	2,800	0.59	193,685	40.84	6,250	1.32	474,250
Male	136,050	57.20	1,420	0.60	97,350	40.93	3,030	1.27	237,850
Female	135,465	57.30	1,380	0.58	96,340	40.75	3,220	1.36	236,405
Quebec									
Male	3,250	48.15	730	10.81	2,610	38.67	155	2.30	6,750
Female	2,975	48.41	720	11.72	2,300	37.43	150	2.44	6,145
Montreal									
Male	2,785	47.53	570	9.73	2,360	40.27	145	2.47	5,860
Female	2,540	47.21	555	10.32	2,145	39.87	145	2.70	5,380

NOT BORN IN CANADA

Canada									
Total	10,145	9.53	470	0.44	89,980	84.56	5,820	5.47	106,410
Male	5,435	9.39	255	0.44	49,135	84.91	3,050	5.27	57,870
Female	4,715	9.72	210	0.43	40,805	84.16	2,765	5.70	48,530
Quebec									
Male	340	8.52	130	3.26	3,215	80.58	310	7.77	3,990
Female	325	9.42	120	3.48	2,770	80.29	240	6.96	3,450
Montreal									
Male	285	7.80	105	2.87	2,985	81.67	275	7.52	3,650
Female	285	9.05	80	2.54	2,580	81.90	205	6.51	3,150

Source: Adapted from Darcovich and Yuzyk, "Statistical Compendium," Series 31.40-49 and 31.50-59, 235-6.
Notes: [1]TBIC—Total Born in Canada.
       [2]TNBIC—Total Not Born in Canada.

TABLE 4

Canada, Quebec and Montreal: Language Most Often Spoken at Home, Population of Ukrainian Origin by Place of Birth and Sex, 1971

	English	%	French	%	Ukrainian	%	Other	%	Total
				BORN IN CANADA					
Canada									
Total	408,450	86.13	2,255	0.48	62,485	13.18	1,060	0.22	474,250
Male	205,115	86.24	1,180	0.50	31,025	13.04	530	0.22	237,850
Female	203,330	86.01	1,075	0.45	31,460	13.31	535	0.23	236,405
Quebec									
Male	4,490	66.52	935	13.85	1,290	19.11	30	0.44	6,750
Female	4,180	68.02	800	13.02	1,100	17.90	55	0.90	6,145
Montreal									
Male	3,865	65.96	730	12.46	1,235	21.08	30	0.51	5,680
Female	3,650	67.84	610	11.34	1,070	19.89	60	1.12	5,380

BORN OUTSIDE CANADA

Canada									
Total	33,490	31.47	450	0.42	70,050	65.83	2,415	2.27	106,410
Male	19,440	33.59	235	0.41	36,950	63.85	1,250	2.16	57,870
Female	14,045	28.94	215	0.44	33,105	68.22	1,170	2.41	48,530
Quebec									
Male	905	22.68	180	4.51	2,780	69.67	125	3.13	3,990
Female	705	20.43	160	4.64	2,445	70.87	135	3.91	3,450
Montreal									
Male	785	21.48	155	4.24	2,605	71.27	115	3.15	3,655
Female	610	19.37	115	3.65	2,315	73.49	110	3.49	3,150

TOTAL

Canada									
Total	441,940	76.11	2,705	0.47	132,535	22.82	3,475	0.60	580,660
Male	224,555	75.94	1,415	0.48	67,975	22.99	1,780	0.60	295,720
Female	217,375	76.29	1,290	0.45	64,565	22.66	1,705	0.60	284,935
Quebec									
Male	5,395	50.23	1,115	10.38	4,070	37.90	155	1.44	10,740
Female	4,885	50.91	960	10.01	3,545	36.95	190	1.98	9,595
Montreal									
Male	4,650	48.84	885	9.30	3,840	40.34	145	1.52	9,520
Female	4,260	49.88	725	8.49	3,385	39.64	170	1.99	8,540

Source: Darcovich and Yuzyk, "Statistical Compendium," Series 31.163–167 and 31.168–177, 254-5.

and over. Ukrainians were proportionately more likely to be found in the range from $6,000-19,999. Only in the two lowest classes (under $3,000 and between $3,000-5,999) were Quebecers of all origins relatively more heavily represented.

Conclusion

This descriptive inventory of the Ukrainian community in Quebec indicates that it is highly urbanized, concentrated in Montreal, aging and foreign-born. To a significant extent, members of the community have retained their traditional religions and mother tongue.

In 1951 Ukrainians were not well-known since they lived in different locations, held dissimilar types of jobs and maintained a traditional culture unlike that of the large Quebecois majority. By 1971, however, Quebec had passed through a conscious effort of change. Its Quiet Revolution had brought a new awareness of culture and heritage, urbanization and the need for educational improvement.

In that year Ukrainians still retained their culture, but they had become better known. The majority population could now see them as rivals for jobs, education and income, and as members of an *allogène* community which continued to learn English when it acquired one of the two official languages. This cumulative "otherness" may now be the basis for suspicion and antagonism on the part of the Quebecois.

NOTES

1. Bill 101 can be characterized as a form of ethnic social engineering. It was designed to preserve and enhance French-Quebecer cultural and linguistic identity and to diminish the real or perceived threat posed by the English Quebecers and the *allogènes*. The *allogènes* are Quebecers of any origin other than British or French.
2. William Darcovich and Paul Yuzyk, eds., "Statistical Compendium on the Ukrainians in Canada, 1891-1976," (Unpublished typescript, Ottawa, 1977).
3. Those of British origin account for 10.6 per cent of the provincial population while the *allogènes* constitute 10.4 per cent of the Quebec population according to the 1971 census.
4. From 1,176 Ukrainians in Quebec in 1921, the population increased to 12,921 in 1951 and 20,325 in 1971. If in 1921 the Ukrainian Quebecers were but 0.05 per cent of the provincial population, by 1951 the percentage had increased to 0.32 and in 1971 it was 0.34 per cent. Darcovich and Yuzyk, Series 21.1-242, 63; Series 21.243-294, 67.
5. Of the 10,740 Ukrainian males in Quebec in 1971, 37.15 per cent were not born in Canada; of the 9,595 females, 35.96 per cent were foreign-born. This contrasts radically with the Canadian Ukrainian figures. Of the 295,720 males only 19.57 per cent were foreign-born, as were 17.03 per cent of the 284,935 females. Ibid., Series 31.11-20, 230.

6. There are more Ukrainian Quebecers aged 35-54 (31.17 per cent of all Ukrainians resident in Quebec) than aged 15-34 (27.52 per cent). For the sake of comparisons, it should be pointed out that 26.58 per cent of the Canadian-Ukrainian population is in the 35-54 age interval while 22.33 percent of the Canadian population and 21.70 per cent of Quebec's total population fall in this range. The disproportionate nature of the Quebec Ukrainian age pyramid appears greater if we note that the 45-54 age interval in the total Quebec population constituted 10.31 per cent of the 1971 total. The aging of the Ukrainian community in Quebec is especially apparent when one considers that 10.88 per cent of the population is over 65, while only 6.85 per cent of the Quebec total is found in the same category. Ibid., Series 22.17-56, 149-151.

7. The 0-4 age bracket fell from 9.45 per cent in 1951 to 4.59 per cent in 1971. During the same time period the Quebec total, in the same age interval, diminished from 13.35 to 7.97 per cent. The drop in fertility and the aging of the population becomes even more evident when the 0-14 age categories are compared. In 1971 the 0-14 age interval accounted for only 19.58 per cent of Ukrainian Quebecers, while it was 29.62 per cent for all Quebecers. It should be noted for the sake of comparison that the 0-4 age bracket accounts for 6.88 per cent of Ukrainian Canadians in 1971 and 8.42 per cent of all Canadians. Ibid.

8. In 1951, 95.73 per cent of the Ukrainian community was already urbanized. By 1971, 95.84 per cent of the Ukrainian community was urbanized, constituting 0.40 per cent of the Quebec total. The drop in the Ukrainian farm population in Quebec from 1.93 per cent of the Quebec Ukrainian total to 0.62 per cent was compensated by the rise of the Ukrainian non-farm rural population from 2.35 per cent to 3.54 per cent of Quebec Ukrainians. It should nevertheless be pointed out that the 1971 non-urban Quebec Ukrainian total consisted of only 845 persons. Ibid., Series 20.41-64, 31-4. This high degree of urbanization of the Ukrainian community in Quebec stands in marked contrast to the Quebec-Canadian, and especially the Ukrainian-Canadian, situation. In 1971, 80.79 per cent of the Quebec population, 76.21 per cent of the Canadian population and only 74.97 per cent of the Ukrainian-Canadian population was urbanized. Ibid. Series 20.1-29, 26-9. Further details are available in a paper by Bohdan Tymyc, "A Study of Spatial Change of Ukrainian Settlement in Metropolitan Montreal and Its Immediate Fringe in the Two Decades Between 1951 and 1971" (Paper written at Concordia University, Department of Geography, 1977). Available in the fugitive file, Canadian Institute of Ukrainian Studies, University of Alberta.

9. The Ukrainian population of Montreal has witnessed an increase in absolute figures from 11,238 in 1951 to 18,050 in 1971. But due to the population growth of the Montreal region the Ukrainians now constitute 0.66 per cent of the population. In 1951 they accounted for 0.76 per cent. Ibid., Series 21.243-294, 67.

10. Ukrainian Quebecers have retained the Ukrainian Catholic faith to a degree second only to one other provincial grouping of Ukrainians. Nearly 39 per cent declared this religious denomination in 1971, a proportion exceeded only by Manitoba's 45.4 per cent. When we add to these figures the percentage of Ukrainians declaring Orthodox affiliation, we find that well over one-half of Quebec's Ukrainians (56.8 per cent) retained the two religions. This is virtually identical to the 58.4 per cent of prairie Ukrainians affiliated with these denominations. Ibid., Series 30.1-12, 183-4; Series 30.13-26, 184, 189.

11. The Ukrainian Catholics have followed an interesting pattern since 1951. In that year 32.34 per cent of the Ukrainian community declared itself Ukrainian Catholic, but by 1961 the figure had dropped to 27.91 per cent. Yet in 1971, there was a spectacular rise to 38.78 per cent. It is conceivable that the explanation for this fluctuation lies in the lack of ethnic affimation in 1961 and a reversal of the process by 1971. Ukrainian Catholics probably declared themselves Roman Catholic in 1961 and reverted to the Ukrainian Catholic denomination in 1971. The Ukrainian Catholic community is heavily concentrated in the Montreal region. Ukrainian Catholics accounted for 35.52 per cent of the Montreal Ukrainians in 1951 and for 41.43 per

cent in 1971. The Ukrainian Orthodox church affiliation has dropped steadily since 1951. It accounted for 26.29 per cent of the Ukrainian-Quebec total in that year but for only 17.97 per cent in 1971. The decline in the Montreal region has been from 25.59 per cent in 1951 to 18.55 per cent in 1971. Ibid.

12. The percentage of Ukrainians declaring Roman Catholicism was 28.64 in 1951, 33.13 in 1961 and 22.65 in 1971. Roman Catholics have always accounted for a disproportionate number of rural Ukrainians—45.83 per cent in 1951, 43.28 per cent in 1961 and 36.31 per cent in 1971. In the Montreal region Roman Catholics accounted for 27.24 per cent of the Ukrainian population in 1951, 31.77 per cent in 1961 and 20.41 per cent in 1971. Ibid.

13. The United Church affiliation increased from 7.14 per cent of the Ukrainian provincial total in 1951 to 13.91 per cent in 1971. The Anglicans, Presbyterians, Lutherans, Baptists, Pentecostals and Mennonites constitute a very small, unchanging percentage of the Ukrainian community. Ibid.

14. In 1951, 79.99 per cent of those of Ukrainian origin in Quebec declared Ukrainian as their mother tongue. In 1961 the figure was 70.32 per cent and only 53.62 per cent in 1971. Ukrainian was also declared to be the mother tongue of 11.99 per cent of Quebecers of non-Ukrainian origin in 1951, 13.10 per cent in 1961 and only 4.26 per cent in 1971. Even though there has been a drastic drop of Ukrainian as a mother tongue in Quebec, Ukrainian Quebecers have lost their language to a relatively smaller degree than have Ukrainian Canadians. In 1951, 79.65 per cent of Ukrainian Canadians declared Ukrainian as their mother tongue. By 1961, it was 64.38 per cent and down to 48.85 per cent in 1971. Furthermore, Quebec's very small and urbanized Ukrainian community maintained its traditional language in 1971 to the same extent as did those living in the Prairie provinces. This was in marked contrast to the situation in 1951 when prairie Ukrainians were nearly 7 per cent more likely to know Ukrainian. Ibid., Series 20.1-29, 26-7; Series 20.41-64, 31-2; Series 31.21-39, 231-2; Series 31.60-5, 237-8.

15. The 35-54 age bracket accounted for the highest degree of Ukrainian language retention in 1971. Of persons in this age interval, 35.39 per cent declared Ukrainian as their mother tongue. Only 20.95 per cent of the 15-34 age group declared Ukrainian as their mother tongue. In this respect the Ukrainian Quebecers are similar to Ukrainian Canadians. In 1971, 35.61 per cent in the 35-54 age bracket and only 21.31 per cent of the 15-34 age group declared Ukrainian as their mother tongue.

16. Ukrainian was the mother tongue of 80.44 per cent of Ukrainian Quebecers who were foreign-born and only 38.5 per cent of those who were native-born. Ibid.

17. The foreign-born Ukrainian Quebecers account for 70.27 per cent of those speaking Ukrainian at home. Only 18.51 per cent of the native-born use Ukrainian at home. Ukrainian is the language spoken at home for 39.99 per cent of the Montreal Ukrainian community, if one disregards place of birth. Ukrainian is the language spoken at home by 37.43 per cent of Ukrainian Quebecers and by only 22.82 per cent of Ukrainian Canadians. Ibid., Series 31.163-167 and Series 31.168-177, 254-5.

18. It appears that ethnic cohesiveness is much stronger in Quebec than in the rest of Canada since the rate of mother tongue retention is substantially higher in Quebec. Only those of British origin assimilate linguistically to a higher degree in Quebec than in the rest of Canada. Language retention for all selected origins in Quebec, minus the British and French, was 60.1 per cent in 1951 and 51.1 per cent in 1971. In Canada the retention of the mother tongue for the same ethnic groups was 52.5 per cent in 1951, and 42.9 per cent in 1971. Ibid., Series 20.1-29, 26-7; Series 20.41-64, 31-2; Series 31.60-7, 237-8.

19. English was declared to be the mother tongue of only 13.88 per cent of Ukrainian Quebecers in 1951. By 1971, 33.87 per cent of Quebec Ukrainians considered it as their mother tongue. French, as a mother tongue, rose from 3.29 per cent in 1951 to 8.34 per cent in 1971. Ibid., Series 31.40-9, 235 and Series 31.50-59, 236.

20. In 1971 English was the declared mother tongue of 33.87 per cent of Ukrainian Quebecers and the language spoken at home by 50.57 per cent of the Quebec-Ukrain-

ian community. French accounts for only 10.20 per cent of the language spoken at home. Across Canada 48.51 per cent of Ukrainians declared English as their mother tongue in 1971, a proportion identical to that of Ukrainian as a mother tongue. English also accounted for 76.11 per cent of the language spoken at home by Ukrainian Canadians. Ibid.

21. Currently 48.28 per cent of the native-born Ukrainian Quebecers declare English as their mother tongue. This sector of the population will not be affected by the language of schooling provisions found in Bill 101. Only 8.97 per cent of the foreign-born members of the Quebec-Ukrainian community consider English as their mother tongue. English as the language most often spoken at home was declared by 67.27 per cent of the native-born and 21.56 foreign-born members of the community. Across Canada, English is the mother tongue of 57.25 per cent of the native-born Ukrainian Canadians and of 9.55 per cent of the foreign-born. Ibid.

22. In 1951, 90.06 per cent of Ukrainian Quebecers knew one or both of Canada's official languages. By 1971, 97 per cent of the Ukrainian-Quebec community was in this category. Ibid., Series 31.11–20, 230; Series 31.1–10, 225–6.

23. While French and English bilingualism of the Ukrainian community increased from 28.58 per cent in 1951 to 43.08 per cent in 1971, the knowledge of official languages by those of all origins remained fairly constant. It was 25.60 per cent in 1951 and 27.60 per cent in 1971. Ibid.

24. Ibid.

25. Ibid., Series 32.93–106, 286, 288. Due to differences in the questions asked in different censuses, information is not completely comparable. Nevertheless, recognizing that failures and accelerated advancement are exceptions rather than the rule, years attended is a reasonably close measure of levels attained.

26. Ibid., Series 32.121–136, 293.

27. Ibid., Series 32.93–106, 286, 288.

28. Ibid., Series 32.121–136, 293.

29. Ibid.

30. Definitions used to classify occupations have varied significantly between censuses. Consequently, we have been under particular obligation to make our comparisons between Ukrainians and all Quebecers within the context of given census years.

31. Ibid., Series 40.87–102, 385. The categories followed in descending order for Ukrainians: construction, 5.31 per cent; proprietors and managers, 4.54 per cent; professional, 4.34 per cent; transportation, 4.19 per cent; commercial, 3.09 per cent; not stated, 1.69 per cent; electric light, 1.05 per cent; communication, 0.77 per cent; financial, 0.12 per cent. For all Quebecers the remaining categories were: transportation, 6.32 per cent; construction, 6.19 per cent; commercial, 5.53 per cent; not stated, 1.75 per cent; communication, 1.18 per cent; electric light, 1.04 per cent; financial, 0.53 per cent.

32. Ibid., Series 40.43–58, 380. The remaining categories followed for Ukrainians: not stated, 10.38 per cent; processing, 5.05 per cent; managerial-administrative, 4.66 per cent; machining, 3.55 per cent; construction, 2.94 per cent; materials handling 2.66 per cent; transportation equipment operating, 2.38 per cent; farming, fishing, forestry and mining, 1.44 per cent; other crafts, 1.17 per cent. For all Quebecers, the figures are: not stated, 10.22 per cent; construction, 5.83 per cent; farming, fishing, forestry and mining, 5.15 per cent; managerial-administrative, 4.75 per cent; processing, 4.47 per cent; transportation equipment handling, 3.96 per cent; machining, 2.68 per cent; n.e.s., 2.30 per cent; materials handling, 1.81 per cent; other crafts, 1.30 per cent.

33. Ibid., Series 42.34–43, 454. Average income for all Quebecers was $4,969.

SUMMARY

COMMENTS ON THE CONFERENCE

Charles Keely

The letter from the Canadian Institute of Ukrainian Studies asked me to speak on three subjects. The first was the usefulness and limits of the Compendium as a resource tool. Secondly, I was asked to comment on the various papers given at the conference and, finally, the letter asked me to discuss the importance of social statistics to the conduct of ethnic politics in the United States in contrast to the Canadian experience.

I want to be fairly short about the Compendium. First, the editors and compilers ought to be thanked for the monumental work they have done. Its usefulness is clear from the experience of the last two days. This information and its sources shed tremendous light on the Ukrainian-Canadian experience. The enlightened groups that supported this work, including private foundations and the Government of Canada, should also be thanked.

Quite frankly, what we have heard in the last two days is of immediate importance. It is not just the past we are interested in (although it is of interest), but the present and the future. I might put it this way: the most important part of this conference was not yesterday or even today but tomorrow. That is what you are really interested in; otherwise you would not be here. This is not some esoteric study or an interest to be pursued as a hobby on Saturday afternoons. You would not be here unless you had an interest in it for your children and for your children's children. In fact, some of you are even young enough for this to be of interest to your own future. I would like to discuss a few issues in the papers with fairly broad strokes with this future in mind.

A problem that came up time and again was what social scientists call the unit of analysis. What exactly are we studying? We have heard discussion about changes among Ukrainians from 1891 to 1971. Obviously, the Ukrainians of 1921 are not the same people as those of 1971. When talking about the development of Ukrainians in Canadian history, I think it is absolutely necessary to keep this in mind. One must not fall into the trap of using shorthand to talk about the changes Ukrainians experienced from 1921 to 1971. The Ukrainians of 1971 are only a partial remnant of those of 1921.

Further, Ukrainians are not a monolithic group. They are a group with political, social and religious differences, some of which are deep. Some of these differences are newly discovered. For example, Ukrainians, like everybody else, have discovered that there are two sexes. Certain aspects of gender relations are known, but there are others that have been ignored. Other differences are old and well-known: the experiences of various religious groups, the differences between the immigrant and the Canadian-born, particularly the younger members of the community, whose total experience is Canadian. I think all of these differences have to be kept in mind to prevent falling into the trap of talking about Ukrainians as if they are homogeneous. The politics of numbers requires you to talk to the outsider about Ukrainians as a single group. Inside, you know that that is not the case and you must remember the politics of internal group relationships.

In addition to the unit of analysis, we have in social science what is known as the convergence hypothesis. It arises not only regarding ethnic groups, but also, for example, in urban sociology in regard to the growth and structure of cities. Basically, the convergence hypothesis asserts that, over time, there is a reduction in the difference between group A and group B on some dimension. In other words, this verbal model of social reality suggests that groups tend to converge or become indistinguishable over time on certain dimensions.

Models are very alluring because they seem to be able to explain a lot of things. The convergence hypothesis is even more alluring because certain kinds of value judgments are built into it. We all pat ourselves on the back because Ukrainians between 1921 and 1971 got closer to, or maybe even crossed over, the median income mark. Ukrainians increased their proportions in certain professions. Illiteracy is down and so on. But there are some bad occurrences that come with this convergence. Language retention is down. An increasing proportion of Ukrainians are becoming more like Canadians in that they do not know the Ukrainian language. Then there are some other things which may be positive or negative, depending on one's point of view. For example, a drop in fertility may be good because it opens up opportunities for women, but it may be bad because the Ukrainian group is breeding itself out of existence.

Built into all this is the assumption that the target is stationary. Yet the Canadian standard toward which everything is measured does not remain the same. Canadians have urbanized. Canadians have increased their income. Canadians have reduced their fertility. If there is convergence, that means that whatever caused Ukrainians to change made them change faster than all Canadians on these dimensions. Whatever caused Ukrainians to change may not be the same thing that caused the Canadians to change. Or it may have been the same thing, but had greater impact for certain reasons. Just because there is convergence does not mean that we understand why there is convergence. If two things have changed at unequal rates, we cannot assume that the causes of the change in both groups are the same. I did not hear this said today or yesterday. I heard about convergence and I heard a number of possibilities to explain differences, but all the differences explained were Ukrainian differences over time. Nobody said anything about the changes of income, fertility or urbanization of all Canadians. Are Ukrainians so different from Canadians that the factors making them change are unique? If you are interested in the Ukrainian group not only for today but also tomorrow, you should find out the causes of the changes not only among Ukrainians but also in Canadian society as a whole.

The third item I would like to talk about after having discussed the unit of analysis and the convergence hypothesis is a little bit more controversial. Let me suggest an idea. There are three kinds of ethnics. First, there is the "professional ethnic," who makes his or her living because of ethnic identity, and I do not mean that in a pejorative way. I refer to the religious professions, teachers of language, academics who study a particular group and heads of organizations who get status and prestige, if not actually some power and perhaps economic gain, by heading an ethnic organization. There is a second kind of ethnic whom we can call an "ethnic whose consciousness has been raised." This kind of person will respond to a call by the ethnic group to help build a cultural hall or convince people to put down "Ukrainian" on a census. This might be the kind of individual who has a commitment to political problems in the homeland. It may be somebody who likes to take an active part in cultural performances or support groups of youngsters who do that sort of thing. This is the individual who has his ethnic identity very near the surface and who can be called upon fairly quickly. The third group is the "dormant ethnic." These are individuals who are not responsive. These are individuals who may even change their name in order to avoid an ethnic identity. People can move from one to another of these identities. We could get another set of tables in the

Compendium about the distribution of Ukrainians as professional, consciousness-raised and dormant ethnics. At various times in history the dormant ethnics may be a small group; at other times, they may become a larger group or be reactivated under certain circumstances.

The issue of kinds of ethnics brings us to the question of content: "What is Ukrainian ethnicity?" You are at a turning point. What are you going to do within the Canadian experience with its multicultural concept? This is very important to the future of the group. What is it to be Ukrainian in the Canadian context? What are you and what do you want to become?

What you want to become is controlled to a very large extent by the professional ethnics. They have the power to define your future, and I think that it is fair to say that there are severe differences among yourselves about what Ukrainians should be in the future. Is it possible to be a Ukrainian in Canada today or tomorrow without being a nationalist? Is it possible to maintain a Ukrainian identity in Canada without maintaining the language? Is it enough to have an identity without using the Ukrainian language and without making Ukrainian-ness an integral part of your everyday lives? I do not think you have answered these questions. Probably everyone here would say that at least language and the culture must be present.

However, it seems you are split on another dimension. Just what is a Ukrainian in Canadian society? There are those who seem to say that the fate and impact of the Ukrainian nation are part of the essence of Ukrainian-Canadian experience and must continually be so. Then there are those who say that the Ukrainian experience in Canada is in itself the important thing that must be emphasized and retained, because there is a kind of quasi-national experience for Ukrainian language and life in Canada. This latter view was emphasized in the paper concerning the excess of Ukrainian speakers over Ukrainian ethnics in 1931. It suggested that you have influenced the life of the nation to such an extent in certain regions that there ought to be at least a regional recognition of Ukrainian culture and identity. I cannot resolve that division of opinion; you have to.

That brings me to the question of comparing Canada with the United States. To a certain extent, the politics of data may become more and more irrelevant because Canada and the U.S. are facing difficult economic times ahead. Nevertheless, the power and response a group gets is defined by how many of them there are. Make no mistake about it. If the question on ethnic identity which counts Ukrainians is dropped, you are going to be worse off politically in 1981 than you are now. Numbers talk. If you use them wisely, you can make them talk even louder.

We face exactly the same situation in the United States on the question of the census. The most powerful and vocal group on this question of numbers are people of Spanish origin. The U.S. census has now proposed that the following question go to every household: "Is this person's origin or descent: Mexican, Puerto Rican, Cuban, other Spanish, non-Spanish?" Although 85 to 90 per cent of the population will be in the "non-Spanish" category, the question will be asked of all households. That's political power! There will be more Spanish in 1980 than were counted in 1970, even taking immigration into account.

We have also planned to drop the question on the place of birth of parents in the U.S. census of 1980 and to substitute: "Is this person's ethnic ancestry _____ ?" The respondent decides how he or she will fill in the blank. When the computer scientists talk about the information fed into a computer and what comes out, they often say: "Garbage in, garbage out." If you put garbage in, you are going to get garbage out. In the United States we will get garbage out because we do not know what that question means. The census is no place for collecting ethnic self-identity information because we do not know what it means. We do not know what leads certain groups to make the organizational efforts to get the vote out, as it were, and to make sure their ethnics write in an answer. I would much rather see the U.S. retain the question on place of birth of parents and follow the Canadian lead, which conceptualizes "roots" or ethnic background by trying to find out where people came from. I fully expect the United States to be treated to a number of studies during the 1980s comparing the ethnic fertility, income and education of various groups on the basis of this inadequate information.

Here are some examples of the problem. A third-generation Polish person in Chicago who knows no Polish except his name but is caught up in the new ethnicity in the U.S. writes in "Polish." Yet the person who is a recent immigrant from Poland may proudly put down "American" because of his or her pride in the new country and because he thinks he is making a new beginning. Or take the case of the third- or fourth-generation Italian caught up in the new ethnicity who proudly puts down "Italian." Yet his teen-aged son says: "I'm not an Italian. I'm an American." My point is that, when you add up all of this, you will get a number, but that number is garbage. Yet we will use that number to get average income, fertility levels and so on to compare groups to one another. The Canadian case avoids that. You have a long and distinguished literature about ethnic identity in your census and the problems of the data. Use it! Tell the people who are supposed to know about those things to use it. Get counted by the "roots" question as much as possible so that you will be in a solid position to say who you are at least in terms of numbers.

To a certain extent, this may not be as important as what happens to Canadian society in the next few years. A lot of that convergence, particularly on the socio-economic levels, may come to an abrupt halt because the Canadian trends may change and not because the Ukrainians change. North American societies may be in for some very difficult times. Ethnicity may be one of the focal points, one of the flash points of readjustment of economic relationships. This is clearer in the U.S. with the Spanish origin groups. When jobs become scarce, and they will become scarce, when cutbacks come and they will come, the first ones to be hurt will not be the Irish or the Italians, but the Spanish. Economic problems will be fought out in ethnic terms. You may face that in Canada. Ukrainians will not face the equivalent of the Spanish in the U.S. since, comparatively speaking, Ukrainians are top-dogs. You are not, relatively speaking, far from the top.

Finally, I would like to summarize. Who are you in terms of the unit of analysis? What exactly has been changing? What does convergence mean? Is it good or is it bad? What does it portend for the future? The core question that you face is whether you are Ukrainian in Canada or whether you are Ukrainians who happen to be in Canada. Some of you think that the answer to that question is so obvious that it is not really worth discussing. You may say you know the answer because you are on one side. Others know that the answer is obvious because you are on the other side. The answer is not obvious. You and the Ukrainian youth throughout this country have the task of deciding what it means to be a Ukrainian in Canada. Maybe I should put it another way. You need an agenda, but there are deep differences among you about the agenda. If you have an agenda, you have power. You have the numbers; you have the resources. You may not be able to use or co-ordinate those resources, but you have the possibility. Without an agenda, I fully expect to come back in the future not to a symposium where one can seriously discuss ethnic identity in a multicultural society. Without an agenda, without an answer to what it is to be Ukrainian in Canada, the future will be cultural fairs where one can have some pyrogies, see a couple of dances, and maybe even put on a little button which says: "Kiss me, I'm Ukrainian."

CONTRIBUTORS

William Darcovich — Economist, Canada Department of Agriculture, Ottawa. Born 1921. Ph.D. (Iowa State University). Author of *Historical Monthly Statistics* (1964), *Ukrainians in Canada: The Struggle to Retain Their Identity* (1967) and *Rapeseed Potential in Western Canada* (1973).

Leo Driedger — Professor, Department of Sociology, University of Manitoba. Born 1928. Ph.D. (Michigan State University). Editor of *The Canadian Ethnic Mosaic: A Quest for Identity* (1978) and author of articles in many books and academic journals.

Michael Isaacs — Lecturer, Department of Economics, Bishop's University. Born 1953. M.A. (McGill University).

Wsevolod W. Isajiw — Professor, Department of Sociology, University of Toronto. Born 1933. Ph.D. (The Catholic University of America). Author of *Causation and Functionalism in Sociology* (1968). Editor of *Ukrainians in American and Canadian Society* (1976) and *Identities: The Impact of Ethnicity on Canadian Society* (1977).

Warren E. Kalbach — Professor, Department of Sociology, University of Toronto. Born 1922. Ph.D. (University of Washington). Author of *The Effect of Immigration on Population* (1974) and *The Impact of Immigration on Canada's Population* (1961). Co-author of *Demographic Bases of Canadian Society* (1971).

Charles B. Keely — Research Associate, Center for Policy Studies, The Population Council, New York. Born 1942. Ph.D. (Fordham University). Author of *U.S. Immigration: A Policy Analysis* (1979) and co-author of *Whom Have We Welcomed? The Adequacy and Quality of United States Immigration Data for Policy Analysis and Evaluation* (1975).

John M. Kralt — Characteristics Officer, Census and Household Surveys, Statistics Canada. Born 1945. M.A. (University of Western Ontario). Author of *Ethnic Origins of Canadians* (1977), *Language in Canada* (1976) and *The Urban and Rural Composition of Canada's Population* (1976).

Olga Kuplowska — Research Officer, Office of Project Research at the Ontario Educational Communications Authority. Born 1949. M.A. (University of Toronto). Co-author of *Non-Official Languages: A Study in Canadian Multiculturalism* (1976) and *The Junior Kindergarten Study* (1975).

Roman R. March — Associate Professor, Department of Political Science, McMaster University. Born 1935. Ph.D. (Indiana University). Author of *Wspołczesna Kanada* (1978) and *The Myth of Parliament* (1974).

Ivan Myhul — Associate Professor, Department of Political Science, Bishop's University. Born 1940. Ph.D. (Columbia University).

Marusia K. Petryshyn — Law student, University of Alberta. Born 1949. M.Soc.Sci. (University of Birmingham, England).

Madeline A. Richard — Sociology student, University of Toronto. Born 1941. Graduate of Lakeshore Teachers' College.

Jean E. Wolowyna — Assistant Professor, Department of Epidemiology and Preventive Medicine, University of Western Ontario. Born 1945. Ph.D. (Brown University).

Oleh Wolowyna — Research Assistant Professor, Population Laboratories, Department of Biostatistics, University of North Carolina at Chapel Hill. Born 1939. Ph.D. (Brown University).

032380034